D0675142

What is the Worst That Could Happen?

What is the Worst That Could Happen?

The Politics and Policy of Crisis Management

Edited by
HUGH LIEBERT, THOMAS SHERLOCK, & JACK MORROW

2016
Sloan Publishing
CORNWALL-ON-HUDSON, NY 12520

The views expressed in this volume do not necessarily reflect those of the United States Military Academy, the United States Army, or the Department of Defense.

Library of Congress Control Number: 2016017438

Cover design by K&M Design

Sloan Publishing, LLC
220 Maple Road
Cornwall-on-Hudson, NY 12520

Printed in the United States of America

10 9 8 7 6 5 4 3 2 1

ISBN-10: 1-59738-058-X
ISBN-13: 978-1-59738-058-4

Contents

Contributors

EDITORS

Hugh Liebert is Associate Professor of American Politics in the Department of Social Sciences at the U.S. Military Academy.

Thomas Sherlock is Professor of Political Science in the Department of Social Sciences at the U.S. Military Academy.

Jack Morrow is Assistant Professor of American Politics in the Department of Social Sciences at the U.S. Military Academy.

CONTRIBUTING AUTHORS

Aaron Brantly is an Assistant Professor, Cyber Policy Fellow at the Army Cyber Institute, and Cyber Policy Fellow a the Combatting Terrorism Center at the U.S. Military Academy.

Louis L. Bono is an advisor to the U.S. Deputy Secretary of State.

Sean Case is a recent Instructor of English at the U.S. Military Academy and is now a Ph.D. candidate in Boston University's American & New England Studies Program.

Robert Chamberlain is a recent Assistant Professor of International Relations in the Department of Social Sciences at the U.S. Military Academy and now serves as an operations research/systems analysis specialist.

Brian Forester is Assistant Professor of American Politics in the Department of Social Sciences at the U.S. Military Academy.

David Frey is Associate Professor of History and the Director of the Center for Holocaust and Genocide Studies at the U.S. Military Academy.

David Grossman is a graduate of the U.S. Military Academy at West Point, where he majored in economics.

Seth A. Johnston is a recent Assistant Professor of International Relations in the Department of Social Sciences at the U.S. Military Academy and now serves at the North Atlantic Treaty Organization's Supreme Headquarters Allied Powers Europe.

Adam J. Kalkstein is Associate Professor of Geography at the U.S. Military Academy.

John Kendall is a recent Assistant Professor of American Politics at the U.S. Military Academy and is now a Latin American Foreign Area Officer.

Bonnie Kovatch is Assistant Professor of International Relations in the Department of Social Sciences at the U.S. Military Academy.

Charlie Lewis, a recent Assistant Professor of American Politics and Executive Officer in the Department of Social Sciences at the U.S. Military Academy, is now Chief of the Cyber Leader College at Fort Gordon, GA.

Jon Malinowski is Professor of Geography and Director of the Human Geography program at the U.S. Military Academy.

Tony McGowan is Associate Professor of English at the U.S. Military Academy.

John Melkon is Director of the Center for the Study of Civil-Military Operations at the U.S. Military Academy.

Aaron Miller is Assistant Professor of International Relations in the Department of Social Sciences at the U.S. Military Academy.

Robert Person is Assistant Professor of International Relations in the Department of Social Sciences at the U.S. Military Academy.

Cynthia Roberts is Associate Professor of Political Science at Hunter College, CUNY and Adjunct Associate Professor at Columbia University.

Aaron Spikol is a graduate of the U.S. Military Academy at West Point, where he majored in International Relations and Philosophy.

Charles G. Thomas, a recent Assistant Professor in the Department of History at the U.S. Military Academy, is now Assistant Professor of Comparative Military Studies at the Air Command and Staff College.

Wiley C. Thompson is Academy Professor and Head of the Department of Geography and Environmental Engineering at the U.S. Military Academy.

Foreword

MAX BROOKS
AUTHOR, *WORLD WAR Z*

Ask a group of people how they'd survive a bioterror attack. Chances are you'll clear the room. Ask those same people how they'd survive a zombie attack and you might actually get a lively discussion about real life disaster preparedness. That's why the Center for Disease Control developed a zombie protection plan. And it's one of the reasons I've written extensively about the living dead. It's not that I or any member of the CDC actually believe in zombies (at least I hope they don't), but so far we've yet to find a better way to interest the American people in the systems that protect them. At this point, we need all the interest we can get. It doesn't matter what the threat is as long as we're ready for it. And what's a hell of a lot scarier than zombies is that we, as a country, aren't really ready for anything.

Call it the "Home Front" or the "War Effort," but we used to have an understanding in this country that the only way we could effectively respond to threats was by being united. Over half a century ago, during World War II, every American citizen had a job to do. From buying war bonds, to planting victory gardens, from rationing to recycling, everyone did their part.

Not anymore. Militarily, economically, even culturally, there has never been a greater chasm between the American people and those tasked with defending them. Forget serving and sacrificing—most Americans don't have an understanding of what it takes to keep us all safe and comfortable. Many of us have heard the saying, "America is not at war. The American Military is at war. America is at the mall."

That phrase is the end of a long walk back from our once indivisible home front. We took our first step during the Korean "Police Action" when our government decided not to issue war bonds for its citizens. Another leap came after Vietnam as the military morphed from the drafted citizen-soldier model into a professional, all-volunteer force. A very public step came with President Reagan's declaration that, "Government is not the answer to our problems, government IS the problem." Numerous crucial (and largely unreported) steps were taken by the post-Cold War administrations as they quietly dismantled or privatized our civil defense network. The final step off the cliff came with President George W. Bush's famous September 12th 2001 call for the American people to "Pray, hug your children, and participate in our economy." That speech marked the end of the road for America's Home Front, and the consequences are becoming all too apparent.

The loss of the draft has not only created an insulated Warrior Class, but now threatens to spawn a multi-generational Warrior Caste. The more insular the military becomes, the less likely military personnel will be to mix with civilians. And the less civilians know members of the military, the more likely civilians are to use these unknown quantities to fight their wars. When soldiers return from the nation's wars and we don't take care of them as well as we would our own families, what message will that send to Americans considering service? Who wants to end up like the Vietnam veterans who populated the streets of my childhood? Who's going to fight for a country that won't fight for them?

The loss of Home Front programs such as rationing and recycling have robbed everyday Americans of much more than the psychological and physical connections to national defense. It has also killed the education programs that explained why those connections were necessary. The result is a populace that now feels confused, even burdened by the systems that keep them safe. Small wonder that so many elected leaders now call for the reduction, privatization, and sometimes outright abolition of those very systems. How are we going to get first responders in and refugees out of a disaster area across crumbling roads and bridges? How can agencies like the CDC operate effectively with significant budget cuts? How can a government of, by, and for the people, protect a people who see their government as "the problem"?

It doesn't matter if the potential threat is a cyberattack, terrorism, a natural disaster, or even, God forbid, zombies. In our currently vulnerable state, every scenario is a worst-case scenario. And this is why asking this volume's question—What is the worst that could happen?—is so important.

Preface

ROBERT L. CASLEN, JR.
SUPERINTENDENT, *UNITED STATES MILITARY ACADEMY*

According to Clausewitz, war is the "realm of uncertainty."[1] Because three-fourths of what one needs to know in any military action is "wrapped in a fog," military leadership demands "a sensitive and discriminating judgment… a skilled intelligence to scent out the truth." Only a leader as intelligent as he or she is brave can hope to pierce the fog and see things clearly.

Part of West Point's mission is to form leaders to Clausewitz's mold. Cadets receive rigorous academic training, which frequently places them on the frontiers of research and scholarship. In the sciences, cadets learn to design computer networks to resist cyber attacks and robotic limbs to improve the lives of wounded veterans. In the humanities and social sciences, cadets study the history, literature, and political regimes of their own and other nations, including those to which they might someday deploy. In these and countless other ways, cadets' judgment becomes more discriminating, their intelligence more skilled.

At the heart of West Point's mission, however, is not intelligence alone, but character. West Point forms "leaders of character." It does so because in war, as in all human endeavors, intelligence is never enough. Even the smartest leader can be caught off guard by some rough beast slouching out of the fog. It is often just when everything seems most clear and certain, when we feel most confident in our judgment and intelligence, that we are most vulnerable to an unforeseen crisis. And it is in these crossroad moments of crisis that character is revealed.

The worst that has happened within recent memory took place on September 11, 2001. I was working at the Pentagon that day, and recall how clear and sunny that morning was. There were no clouds in the sky, no fog on the ground. And there was little reason—or so it seemed—to think the nation's future was anything but bright. American policymakers, thinkers, and military leaders still basked in the glow of the unforeseen "best case scenario" that had unfolded from November of 1989 to December of 1991, when the Soviet Union finally fell. After a decade of dominance, confident that we understood America's place in the post-Cold War world, we were primed for a crisis. And the crisis came.

In the chaos of that terrible day and the now fourteen years of war that followed, we have seen much of the best in Americans' character. I personally witnessed the heroism of my colleagues amidst the Pentagon's wreckage and have been privileged to lead soldiers of great fortitude and ingenuity in the conflicts that followed. This crisis has also disclosed our military's shortcomings, and I contributed to many of them as well. Many of our U.S. government agencies had difficulty coordinating with each other, even when pressed to do so. We Americans acted with haughty pride toward foreign cultures we hardly understood. We have struggled to help build foreign militaries capable of defending their own homes, and we have seen the challenges those on the front lines face in sustaining the interest and resolve of their fellow citizens. We have learned many of these lessons, even if we learned them with difficulty. Many we are still learning today.

Had our collective intelligence been more skilled, perhaps we could have anticipated these challenges. As it stands, however, we require a sort of intelligence more elusive and important than what Clausewitz had in mind. We need now the probing intelligence that allows us to face our faults and improve our own, and others', character. At West Point, instilling this sort of intelligence is one of our core competencies and our passion. We educate, train, and inspire leaders of character—leaders whose character is strong enough to face the unexpected crossroad of compromise, and leaders who inspire character in those they lead.

Every detail of West Point's curriculum, training regimen, and pedagogy is directed ultimately toward molding young men and women into leaders of character. But there are a number of immersive leadership challenges that play an especially prominent role in West Point's educational program. Among these is the Student Conference on U.S. Affairs, known to cadets and undergraduates across the country as "SCUSA" (pronounced scoosa).

SCUSA is the oldest and most prestigious foreign affairs conference for undergraduates in the world. Each November since 1949 it has brought hundreds of American and international college students to West Point. For many of these delegates, SCUSA is their first encounter with the U.S. military. It is a close encounter. SCUSA delegates sleep in cadet barracks and dine in the cadet mess hall. They tour West Point's campus and bear arms at the renowned "weapons display." They engage with their military academy peers and with one another at keynote addresses, panel discussions, and on student roundtables. All of this—from meeting hundreds of guests at the region's airports and train stations, to leading seminar discussions on challenging topics in U.S. foreign policy—is run by cadets. For the delegates who attend SCUSA, the conference is an unforgettable opportunity for personal and intellectual growth; for the cadets who run SCUSA, it is also an exceptional leadership opportunity. Douglas MacArthur, who played baseball as a cadet, once said that the fruits of victory grow from seeds sown on West Point's "fields of friendly strife." In its own way, SCUSA becomes one of these "fields of friendly strife" that will indeed one day, perhaps in the not so distant future, bear the fruits of victory.

Although led by cadets, SCUSA is truly an Academy-wide effort, as the papers collected in this volume attest. Each of these chapters originated at SCUSA, where they served to inform and stimulate discussion on the conference's policy roundtables. Written by West Point faculty and other scholars, these chapters demonstrate the scholarly excellence that contributes not only to cadet education, but to ongoing debates in a wide range of academic disciplines. The question that unites them—What is the worst that can happen?—could not be more timely.

This question, at bottom, joins together intelligence and character. For the challenge it raises is not only to see clearly into the future, but to react appropriately when things fall apart, as they sometimes do. Perhaps Clausewitz himself would appreciate the utility of a volume like this one. It is by reflecting on the worst that we prepare ourselves, as best we can, to maintain the wit, spirit, resilience, tenacity, and character we need to succeed in a "realm of uncertainty."

NOTES

[1]Clausewitz, *On War*, ed. and trans. M. Howard and P. Paret (Princeton, NJ: Princeton University Press, 1976), 101.

1

What is the Worst?

HUGH LIEBERT

> The worst is not
> So long as we can say "This is the worst."
>
> SHAKESPEARE, *KING LEAR*

Cassandra. Chicken Little. The Boy Who Cried Wolf. We have ways of talking about those who talk too much about the worst that can happen. And who could say now that the sky is falling? By virtually every quantitative measure of prosperity, humanity has never had it better. The world's wealth has increased more than five-fold in the last fifty years, and more than fifteen-fold in the last century.[1] Life expectancy at birth has never been higher; the chances of dying a violent death have never been lower.[2] Poverty, malnourishment, disease—all threaten humans less now than ever before.[3] Has there ever been a worse time to talk about the worst case?

Cassandras and boys who cry wolf worry most when others worry least. In the stories we tell of them, they are not wrong to do so. Troy falls; the wolf arrives. Their trouble is not excessive fear (or hope), but the difficulty of anticipating and discussing drastic change. Even when we are right to switch from hope to fear, it is hard to get the timing right; even when individuals get the timing right, it is hard for them to persuade others to join them. How would we know whether there has been a worse time to talk about the worst case? Our prosperity alone is not conclusive evidence.

Modernity began with the claim that there is never a bad time to talk about the worst.[4] Before the sixteenth century humans commonly believed that what was outside of their control worked ultimately in their interests. *Hubris* or pride—mistrusting the gods by taking matters into one's own hands—was sin, the source of human misery. But this fundamental claim came into doubt. If there were no force outside of humanity looking out for human happiness, the first modern philosophers argued, better for mankind to look out for itself. As the civilization-wide attempt to decrease human vulnerability has progressed, responsibility for "crisis management" has shifted from the church to the state. Now, not priests but bureaucrats are entrusted with authority to contemplate and prepare for misfortunes. "Emergency management" and "crisis response" are conceived as subjects in which one can acquire expertise and scientific mastery. If things have never been better, perhaps it is thanks to those who have thought—and still think—about nothing but the worst.

All of the big-picture gains in human prosperity notwithstanding, a number of recent crises have called into doubt our capacity to anticipate and respond adequately to worst cases. Some of these disasters have been natural—Hurricane Katrina, the earthquake in Haiti, the Indian Ocean Tsunami. Others, like the recent "Great Recession," have been man-made. Still others, like the meltdown of the Fukushima nuclear plant, arose from nature's interaction with man-made systems. Each was a unique event unto itself, and each had its own consequences—not only humanitarian, but political, economic, and spiritual. What do they share? For an earlier age all would have served as reminders of the limits of human power. For us, they are prods to further planning.

The goal of this volume is to learn what worst cases have to teach. Each of the following chapters will consider what U.S. policy should be in the event of a worst-case scenario. Some of these scenarios are more probable than others. Climate change seems likely; the zombie apocalypse seems less so (as of this writing). Some scenarios are located in the future, raising the question of what policymakers can do now to prepare and prevent. Others are located in the past, forcing policymakers to consider how to repair and restore after the worst has come to pass. All test our normal assumptions about U.S foreign policy and policymaking. This introductory chapter raises the questions to which subsequent chapters will respond.

I. U.S. Foreign Policy and Regional "Worst Cases"

For as long as anyone living today can remember, U.S. foreign policymakers have enjoyed a best-case scenario. With about five percent of the world's population and seven percent of its land, the United States has commanded about twenty percent of the world's wealth and, recently, a considerably greater portion of its military power.[5] The United States also has not had to fear an invasion of its territory and has succeeded in preventing serious security threats from emerging overseas. A position of such strength is an aberration in world-historical terms, and many U.S. strategists fear that it is now waning. Well into the nineteenth century, China and India accounted for more than half of the world's population and its wealth; today, they account for about a third of world population and about a fifth of global wealth.[6] If economic growth in

India, China, and elsewhere restores something like the relation between population and wealth that obtained before the Industrial Revolution, the United States' economic power will decrease significantly in relative terms even if its wealth continues to increase in absolute terms.[7] And U.S. military power seems likely to follow in tow. Against this backdrop, crises that might not have worried a previous generation of U.S. policymakers seem rather more foreboding.

As of this writing, each of the regions traditionally considered vital to U.S. national security interests—Asia, Europe, and the Middle East—has confronted new levels of instability, many of which have already raised real-world worst-case scenarios. In Asia, China's economic growth continues to raise the prospect of a revised regional balance of power, particularly as China translates economic into military might. What should U.S. policy be in the event of a Chinese military effort to overturn the existing Asian order? The European order—a German and French entente at the core of a united continent—has proven more durable than many had anticipated in the immediate wake of the Cold War.[8] But the recent recession and Russia's encroachments into Eastern Europe have caused some to question whether European nations are truly capable of coordinating their economic and military policy. While the United States' stake in maintaining a unified Europe is commonly acknowledged, its support measures might at some future point fall short: How then would U.S. policymakers respond to European disunion, whether driven by market pressures or by separatist movements (such as those active in the UK and Spain)? More pressingly, how should the United States respond to Russian aggression and the very real possibility that a new Cold War is in the offing? Will China and Russia form a new partnership, spreading the model of authoritarian state-led development? By contrast to Asia and Europe, worst-case scenarios in the Middle East require little imagination. The U.S. invasions of Iraq and Afghanistan, the subsequent U.S. withdrawal from Iraq, the aftermath of the Arab Spring, the ongoing civil war in Syria, and a resurgence in violence between Israel and Palestine have all contributed to a moment of profound flux. These recent events have further complicated longstanding policy problems, among them Iran's pursuit of nuclear weapons. What should U.S. policy be amidst the now-unfolding "worst case" of regional instability? In light of this instability, how would U.S. policymakers respond to Iran's acquisition of nuclear weapons?

Latin America and Africa figure in U.S. foreign policy as settings for vexing humanitarian crises more than great-power rivalry (except by proxy).[9] The strength of Latin American drug cartels, however, raises not only humanitarian, but political, economic, and national-security challenges for the United States, in large part owing to the blurry line between domestic and foreign drug policy. U.S. domestic demand for drugs drives international supply, and instability in Latin America frequently drives immigrants to U.S. borders, as well as across, over, and under them. In several regions within Latin America, the line between state and cartel is similarly blurry. Will Latin American regimes decay to the point where democratic institutions lose legitimacy and the coherence of the state itself comes into question? Should an actual narco-state arise—should drug cartels come to possess a monopoly of violence and extractive power within an expansive region—how should the United States respond?

Questions regarding U.S. intervention arise not only during a crisis, but before and after a crisis takes place. 2014 marked the twentieth year since Rwanda's genocide, perhaps the most dramatic recent case of U.S. non-intervention in a humanitarian crisis. Whether and what kind of U.S. intervention could have stopped the killing is still hotly debated. But perhaps the most remarkable aspect of the Rwandan genocide, seen with hindsight, is the success of Rwanda during those twenty years. And this raises a question for U.S. policymakers to consider, in addition to the vital one of how best to prevent future genocides: What role should the United States play after a humanitarian crisis of Rwandan proportions? What lessons can be learned from not only the fearsome events of recent Rwandan history but also the hopeful Rwandan response to them, and what implications do these lessons hold for U.S. policy toward Africa more broadly?

II. Worst Case Studies

When scholars and statesmen refer to the present as an age of "globalization," they invoke a number of related developments. In part, they refer to the integration of markets through trade and, in part, to the integration of nations into a single moral community.[10] The first is credited with increasing global wealth and reducing global poverty; the second, with increasing awareness of—if not always action against—abuses of human rights. Both are generally understood to be positive developments.

But globalization has also raised unfamiliar challenges. As previously discrete entities—nations, sub-national groups, individuals—have become linked to one another, both goods and evils have become more difficult to contain. Crises in seemingly remote parts of the world are, increasingly, global concerns. Also, as critics of market economies have pointed out for centuries, economic integration and its attendant specialization increase dependency as surely as they increase wealth; an advanced nation that must import food to feed its population or oil to power its factories, for instance, can be wealthy and needy at once. As systems increase in complexity, they do not always increase in resiliency. Is globalization, like a house of cards, most impressive immediately prior to its collapse? The answer to this question depends in large part on policymakers' ability to anticipate and overcome a range of unprecedented worst-cases.

Many troubling scenarios arise from the sheer complexity of global systems. The recent economic downturn, for instance, revealed that disruptions in one sector of one nation's economy—in this case, the U.S. housing market—can have a vast impact on the whole. While the fallout from this crisis seems now to have been contained—in 2009 global GDP dipped for the first time since 1946, but rebounded rapidly—the "great recession" is unlikely to be the last worst case to threaten the global economy.[11] What lessons should be learned from the great recession? As globalization has attenuated national borders, the Platonic ideal of a globalized world—the virtually borderless virtual world of the Internet—has emerged as an increasingly vital venue for trade and communication. With all of the benesfits of freely flowing information comes the difficulty of preventing proprietary information (whether personal passwords, trade secrets, or classified intelligence) from falling into the wrong hands. Various forms of private and public cyber crime are already a pressing problem, and yet scholars of cyber security warn that the worst is yet to come. What would a "cyber Pearl Harbor" look like, and how would U.S. policymakers respond to it?

If the economic downturn and the challenge of cyber security suggest the difficulty of controlling complex man-made systems, climate change reveals the difficulty of controlling nature, a system of even greater complexity. Recent reports have stressed that climate change is not only a future prospect but a present reality, the implications of which are understood only imperfectly.[12] It seems, as of this writing, that most states' efforts to improve resiliency are inadequate, that climate change is likely to have profound geostrategic as well as humanitarian effects, and that the global poor will suffer considerably more than the better-off.[13] But what else can we discern about the world that climate change will usher in, and how can confronting this scenario improve policy in the present? Outside of a rather narrow band of the earth's surface, human beings have always had to adapt to a hostile climate by inventing forms of clothing, shelter, and food production. Until quite recently, however, humans have had less success inventing modes of resistance to microorganisms. Since agriculture first allowed urbanization, a series of pandemics have killed millions until the human body developed its own resistance, with little help from human ingenuity. This changed in the late nineteenth century, and since that time rates of infectious disease have plummeted.[14] But there is reason to worry that this happy period is drawing to a close. Increased urbanization across the globe, combined with the intermingling of populations through international migration, tourism, and trade, have created conditions comparable to those that preceded prior plagues.[15] Additionally, antibiotics have come to be used so widely that potent drug-resistant strains of disease have emerged. The institutional infrastructure to combat global pandemic is now well-established—both the Center for Disease Control and the World Health Organization having been founded in the wake of World War II—but has yet to confront a crisis equivalent to historical plagues. What would happen in the event of a truly global pandemic?

In addition to heightening the risks that arise from complex man-made and natural systems, the integration of the post-Cold War world seems to have made the "worst case" of nuclear proliferation more likely while making military coups less so. Counter-proliferation has become more challenging owing to lowered technological barriers for entry, the emergence of supply networks that are difficult to detect due in part to the volume of international trade, and the resulting increase in available nuclear material and know-how. These factors have increased the likelihood of both "nuclear cascade," a scenario in which new nuclear states (such as Iran or North Korea) cause others (such as Saudi Arabia or Japan) to acquire nuclear capabilities, and nuclear terrorism. Nuclear cascade might not be catastrophic, some argue, because historically nuclear weapons have raised the stakes of international competition and served, on the whole, as a stabilizing force.[16] Nuclear terrorism is more troubling, because the stabilizing effects of states' desire to avoid destruction do not necessarily apply to elusive terrorist networks, much less to individual terrorists themselves. What would the "worst case" of nuclear terrorism look like in practice, and how should U.S. policymakers respond? Peaceful uses of nuclear power have their own "worst cases" as well, as the recent disaster in Fukushima, Japan reminds us. If globalization has made nuclear proliferation more troubling and nuclear power disasters more salient, it seems to have made military coups both rarer and less harmful to democratization.[17] While military coups have historically posed a significant threat to democratic regimes, the frequency of military coups has fallen, from just under six per year from 1960 to 1990, to just over three from 1991 to 2004. Many of these post-Cold War coups have occurred within democracies, but relatively few have derailed democratization: In most post-Cold War coups, in fact, competitive elections follow within five years.[18]

These findings have led some political scientists and commentators to call for a revision to the United States' policy of suspending aid to states established by military coups.[19] How, then, should U.S. policymakers respond to the "worst case" known to scholars of civil-military relations, the military coup? In light of ongoing events in Egypt and Thailand, this scenario is far from fictional.

Nevertheless, there is something essentially fictional about the worst case scenario. Cases that accord with our everyday experience of the world are easy to anticipate; they are less likely than outliers, black swans, and unknown unknowns to disrupt our plans and policies.[20] A "worst case," however, is as much a subjective experience as an objective reality; it is constituted in large part by the surprise and fear that one feels when confronted by an unforeseen threat. For the policymaker, learning to respond properly to the emotional experience of the worst case is as important as discovering what novel crises might conceivably arise.

For this reason, poetic and prophetic accounts of the end times are as valuable to the modern "crisis manager" as they were to the pre-modern person of faith, albeit for different reasons. Whereas apocalyptic literature reminded pre-modern man of his subordinate place in the whole and helped to align his hopes and fears accordingly, it reminds modern man of present limits on his mastery—of himself and his surroundings—so that he might better extend his mastery in the future. We train our hearts and minds for the worst reality has to offer by our encounters with the worst we can imagine.

It is for this reason, perhaps, that fictional accounts of zombie apocalypses have captured the attention of so many. The international relations scholar Daniel Drezner, in his timely work *Theories of International Relations and Zombies*, reports that more than one-third of all zombie films have been released within the last decade alone, while scholarly publications on the zombie apocalypse have increased exponentially since the 1990s.[21] The popularity of zombie stories has a number of causes, to be sure, but their place in the education of the "crisis manager" stems from the special properties that fictional worst cases have. They extend our emotional range and our imaginative reach better than real-world cases.

And perhaps these stories serve, still, to suggest the ultimate limits of our power to master the world around us. The gods cursed Cassandra to issue futile warnings, and in doing so revealed the inherent difficulty of persuading others to abandon expectations based on the normal run of events. Chicken Little was wrong to think the sky was falling, but her mistaken belief was based on real evidence that managed to convince not only herself—and who is to say that the sky couldn't fall, or some other worst case couldn't violate our expectations as dramatically?[22] The boy who cried wolf was certainly not the first to covet the attention that comes to those who speak confidently of the worst that can happen, particularly when widespread prosperity coincides with anxiety and uncertainty. The difficulties that attend discussions of the worst case seem intractable—even more so, perhaps, than lost wars, falling skies, or wolves at the gates. So long as we can say what the worst is, we are better off than we could be. But can we ever say the worst that can happen?

NOTES

[1]For data on world GDP, see Angus Maddison, "Historical Statistics of the World Economy: 1–2008 a.d.," http://www.ggdc.net/maddison/Historical_Statistics/horizontal-file_02-2010.xls.

[2]For data on life expectancy, see The United Nations, "World Population Prospects: The 2012 Revision," http://esa.un.org/wpp/. Steven Pinker's *The Better Angels of Our Nature* (New York: Penguin, 2011) details the decline in violence.

[3]The World Bank reports that global rate of extreme poverty fell by half between 1990 and 2010; see The World Bank, "Poverty Overview" (updated April 6, 2015), http://www.worldbank.org/en/topic/poverty/overview#1. For information on malnourishment, see the Food and Agriculture Organization of the United Nations (FAO), et al., *The State of Food Insecurity in the World: The Multiple Dimensions of Food Security* (Rome: FAO, 2013), http://www.fao.org/docrep/018/i3434e/i3434e00.htm, which reports that the total number of undernourished people has fallen 17 percent since 1990–92 (8). For information on disease, see the World Health Organization (WHO), *World Health Statistics 2014* (Geneva: WHO, 2014), http://apps.who.int/iris/bitstream/10665/112738/1/9789240692671_eng.pdf?ua=1, particularly the discussions of progress towards health-related Millennium Development Goals (11–34) and infectious disease (93–103).

[4]The following discussion focuses on modernity and premodernity in the West. For a consideration of the quite different experience of philosophical modernity within Eastern thought, see, for instance, Harold Coward, *The Perfectibility of Human Nature in Eastern and Western Thought* (Albany, NY: SUNY Press, 2012).

[5]For data on the U.S. share of global wealth, see Maddison, "Historical Statistics of the World Economy: 1–2008 A.D." http://www.ggdc.net/maddison/Historical_Statistics/horizontal-file_02-2010.xls. On the U.S. share of global military power, see Anup Shah's summary of the Stockholm International Peace Research Initiative (SIPRI) data: "World Military Spending" (updated June 30, 2013), http://www.globalissues.org/article/75/world-military-spending.

[6]Maddison, "Historical Statistics of the World Economy: 1–2008 A.D.," http://www.ggdc.net/maddison/Historical_Statistics/horizontal-file_02-2010.xls. For discussion and application to China and India, see "More 2,000 Years in a Single Graphic," *The Economist* (June 20, 2012), http://www.economist.com/blogs/graphicdetail/2012/06/mis-charting-economic-history.

[7]Ibid.

[8]For doubts about the stability of the durability of the post-Cold War European order see, for instance, John J. Mearsheimer, "Why We Will Soon Miss the Cold War," *The Atlantic* 266: 35–50 (August 1990), http://mearsheimer.uchicago.edu/pdfs/A0014.pdf.

[9]It is possible that Chinese investment in Africa might someday make this continent an arena for more direct great-power confrontation. For comment, see Howard French, *China's Second Continent: How a Million Migrants Are Building a New Empire in Africa* (New York: Vintage Books, 2014), and Christopher Alessi and Stephanie Hanson, "Expanding China-Africa Oil Ties," *Council on Foreign Relations Backgrounder* (February 8, 2012), http://www.cfr.org/china/china-africa/p9557#.

[10]On globalization as an economic phenomenon, see for instance Thomas Friedman, *The World Is Flat* (New York: Farrar, Strauss, and Giroux, 2005), 8–11, and Martin Wolf, *Why Globalization Works* (New Haven, CT: Yale University Press, 2004), esp. 19 and 40–57. On globalization as a moral phenomenon, see in particular Peter Singer, *One World: The Ethics of Globalization* (New Haven, CT: Yale University Press, 2004), esp. ix, 148, 150–95, as well as the works of cosmopolitan critics of John Rawls' political thought, such as Thomas Pogge, *Realizing Rawls* (Ithaca, NY: Cornell University Press, 1989), *World Poverty and Human Rights* (Cambridge: Polity, 2002), and Martha Nussbaum, "Beyond the Social Contract: Capabilities and Global Justice," in *The Political Philosophy of Cosmopolitanism*, eds. Gillian Brock and Harry Brighouse (Cambridge: Cambridge University Press, 2005).

[11]For economic data, see the Central Intelligence Agency, *The World Factbook 2014*, s.v. "Economy: World," https://www.cia.gov/library/publications/the-world-factbook/geos/xx.html. On the recurrence of financial crises, see especially Carmen Reinhart and Kenneth Rogoff, *This Time is Different: Eight Centuries of Financial Folly* (Princeton, NJ: Princeton University Press, 2009).

[12]Intergovernmental Panel on Climate Change, *Climate Change 2014: Impacts, Adaptation, and Vulnerability* (Cambridge: Cambridge University Press, 2014), http://ipcc-wg2.gov/AR5/report/.

[13]Center for Naval Analyses (CNA) Military Advisory Board, *National Security and the Accelerating Risks of Climate Change* (Alexandria, VA: CNA Corporation, 2014), http://www.cna.org/reports/accelerating-risks.

[14]William H. McNeill, *Plagues and Peoples* (New York: Anchor Books, 1976).

[15]According to U.N. statistics, more than half the world's population lived in cities in 2014, as compared to thirty percent in 1950. See Population Division of the Department of Economic and Social Affairs of the United Nations Secretariat, *World Urbanization Prospects: The 2012 Revision* (New York: United Nations, 2013), http://esa.un.org/unpd/wup/CD-ROM/Default.aspx.

[16]For the argument that nuclear weapons stabilize international relations, see especially Kenneth Waltz's contributions in Scott Douglas Sagan and Kenneth N. Waltz, *The Spread of Nuclear Weapons: An Enduring Debate*, Third Edition (New York: Norton, 2012, and Waltz, "Why Iran Should Get the Bomb: Nuclear Balancing Would Mean Stability," *Foreign Affairs* 91: 2–5 (July/August 2012), http://www.foreignaffairs.com/articles/137731/kenneth-n-waltz/why-iran-should-get-the-bomb.

[17]On the frequency of military coups, see Jonathan M. Powell and Clayton L. Thyne, "Global Instances of Coups from 1950 to 2010: A New Dataset," *Journal of Peace Research* 48: 249–59. On military coups' effect on democratizations, see Nikolay Marinov and Hein Goemans, "Coups and Democracy," *British Journal of Political Science* 44 (October 2014): 799–825, and Thyne and Powell, "Coup d'état or Coup d'Autocracy? How Coups Impact Democratization, 1950–2008," *Foreign Policy Analysis* 12, no. 2 (2016): 192–213.

[18]Marinov and Goemans, "Coups and Democracy."

[19]See, for instance, Joshua Keating, "Should We Always Oppose Military Coups?" *Slate* (June 5, 2014), http://www.slate.com/blogs/the_world_/2014/06/05/should_we_always_oppose_military_coups.html.

[20]On "black swans," see Nassim Nicholas Taleb, *The Black Swan: The Impact of the Highly Improbable* (New York: Random House, 2010). The phrase "unknown unknowns" originated in a February 2002 press conference by then-Secretary of Defense Donald Rumsfeld.

[21]Daniel Drezner, *Theories of International Relations and Zombies* (Princeton, NJ: Princeton University Press, 2011).

[22]The likelihood of a catastrophic asteroid strike is a favorite topic among scholars of worst-case scenarios. See, for instance, Lee Clarke, *Worst Cases: Terror and Catastrophe in the Popular Imagination* (Chicago: The University of Chicago Press, 2006), 175–7, and chap. 2, "The Sky Could Be Falling: Globally Relevant Disasters and the Perils of Probabilism;" also see Richard Posner, *Catastrophe: Risk and Response* (Oxford: Oxford University Press, 2004), especially 24–9 and 173–81.

2

Tiananmen Take Two

Prospects for Democratization in China

ROBERT CHAMBERLAIN AND DAVID GROSSMAN

The American foreign policy community has spent a great deal of time worrying about the rise of China and its portents for the future of American security.[1] Will China act aggressively to establish a dominant position in its region and translate its newfound economic capacity into security, or will it become a status quo power, happy to enjoy its wealth and prestige within the current limits of the international system? American policymakers also worry about whether China will democratize: Will China's expanding middle class result in an irresistible demand for liberalization or will the "Beijing Consensus" model of undemocratic capitalism endure?[2] This essay suggests that these two questions are related. The challenges that China faces from abroad will impact the character of any democratic transition, and Chinese democratization would almost inevitably impact its behavior abroad.[3]

China has a set of extraordinarily capable neighbors. Japan, South Korea, and Taiwan all boast technologically advanced militaries, large populations, and strong economies.[4] Russia has a demonstrated willingness to conduct military operations to protect its interests, thousands of nuclear weapons, and significant oil and gas reserves near Chinese territory.[5] Vietnam and Thailand have burgeoning populations, developing economies, and modernizing militaries. And, of course, the United States maintains robust military capabilities in the region, is an active participant in regional politics, and has a global naval presence capable of interfering with China's maritime supply of oil and other minerals.[6]

China also faces a set of extraordinary challenges along its borders. North Korea is a totalitarian, nuclear state beset by famine. The "golden triangle" in Burma and northern Thailand is notorious for its drug smuggling. Hemorrhagic fever, unexploded ordinance, and human trafficking plague the jungles of Cambodia and Laos. Climate change is melting the Himalayan glaciers that feed the Yangtze River and irrigate China's agricultural heartland.

This mix of external challenges is daunting enough, but China also faces serious domestic problems. China has been governed by a party-army-state nexus since the 1949 revolution, and that arrangement's legitimacy is rooted in the argument that it provides protection, stability, and prosperity to the Chinese people.[7] However, China faces both ideological and material challenges to its governing elite. Ideologically, the party and the state are still in the process of creating and refining the "Beijing Consensus," which is nowhere near as stable as it seems.[8] For example, the very notion of "intellectual property" seems irreconcilable with communism, yet is a necessity for continued growth, advancement, and participation in global commerce. Materially, the ability of the state to offer to trade prosperity for liberalization might wither in coming years. The Chinese population is aging rapidly, thanks to the legacy of the one-child policy, and the proportion of workers to non-workers is declining.[9] The Chinese economy is deeply integrated into global markets, and is vulnerable to shocks elsewhere.[10] Finally, in some parts of China the legitimacy of the state is already threatened. The high Himalayan plateau is home to large non-Han populations, some of which have mounted violent protests. While these areas are sparsely populated and economically marginal, they are strategically vital for the conventional protection of the Chinese industrial and agricultural regions along the coast.[11]

The management of these internal and external dynamics in a coherent fashion is the strategic challenge faced by the Chinese leadership. While one can certainly hope that China navigates these challenges in such a way that its billion inhabitants experience freedom and prosperity, it is nevertheless prudent to consider darker possibilities. How might the challenges facing China interact with each other to cause elites (or counter-elites) to make catastrophic decisions? What are the pathways that lead to a China that is a source of massive regional and global instability?

This chapter considers four such scenarios, which are represented in Figure 2.1 below. In the worst case, China may break apart or implode due to threats from within; alternatively, it may launch wars of aggression due to threats from abroad. To summarize briefly: an unthreatened and non-democratic China may

Figure 2.1 Worst Case Scenarios

	Low External Threat	*High External Threat*
No Democratization	Implosion	Cult of the Offensive
Democratization	Separation	Nationalistic Conflict

collapse in on itself, as it has done in the past;[12] a China that rapidly democratizes with no external threat might be ripped apart by the centrifugal forces of the various nationalisms contained within the Chinese state; a Chinese military establishment that is modernized to meet growing external challenges may develop a predilection towards the offense that drives it toward preemptive attacks; and a China that democratizes might actually be more likely to address foreign threats with force. Obviously, reduced external threats and democratization do not represent panaceas in these scenarios. But before the United States crafts a policy to help mitigate the chance of any of these scenarios coming to pass, it is important to examine each in more detail.

I. Four Worst-Case Scenarios

Scenario 1: Implosion

This scenario assumes that the party elite becomes mired in internecine competition and loses their ability to navigate a changing world. Currently, authority in China originates at the top of the party-state-army national system and is delegated downward to local subordinate agents.[13] However, given the vastness of China, these agents are empowered to exercise autonomy in achieving the objectives set forth by the national authority. Those agents who are able to do so earn favor with patrons higher up in the organization and gain opportunities for future advancement. Thus, power can be understood in China both as a tightly controlled top-down mechanism for social control and as a federated set of overlapping relational networks. Recent reforms have attempted to deemphasize informal, relational considerations in favor of a more meritocratic / technocratic mechanism for advancement.[14]

It is easy to imagine, though, that these reforms might break down and that informal networks within the party might attain pre-eminence. In such a situation, the top-down logic described above might begin to slip. The top requires the resources and stability generated by its subordinates to survive.[15] Eventually, it may strike one or more of the various networks that constitute power in China that they would be better off hoarding resources and capabilities for themselves, rather than yielding them to the national authorities. In such an event, national reforms necessary for China's continued technological, economic, and military advancement would be extremely difficult to achieve—the state-party-army nexus could break apart, with the state at the mercy of the party and army.

This would not be the first time a weakened Chinese state was at the mercy of its elites. As Theda Skocpol discusses in *States and Social Revolutions*, precisely this dynamic led to the collapse of Imperial China and the eventual emergence of Mao and the Chinese Communist Party (CCP). She argues that powerful elites, acting in an individually rational way, atrophied the state to the point of impotence. When the state finally collapsed, it pulled with it the entire system of social and political relationships that it relied upon. China imploded, collapsing into warring fiefdoms, widespread banditry, and enormous human suffering.[16] If the same scenario were to unfold today—that is, if local elites were able to become rulers unto themselves and refuse to support the overall growth and progress of the nation—then the world would face the ultimate "failed state" scenario.

Scenario 2: Cult of the Offensive

In the second scenario, assume that the Chinese elite maintains its coherence but that the expanding military capabilities of Japan and Korea, combined with the United States' shifting its security focus to the Asia-Pacific, continue to force China to modernize and professionalize its military.[17] This would represent a shift in the composition and identity in the People's Liberation Army (PLA) at the same time that Party leadership is no longer drawn from the ranks of military veterans.

President Eisenhower is said to have told his advisors, "God help this country when someone sits in this chair who doesn't know the military as well as I do." Weeks later he gave his famous speech on the military-industrial complex, in which he argued that the maintenance of a large, standing military supplied with expensive modern weapons had the potential to capture American security policy. This same general idea is articulated in a more rigorous form by Jack Snyder's *Ideology of the Offensive*, which argues that European armies prior to World War I became enamored with the offense because doing so gave pride of place to a professional, technocratic military culture over both reserve forces and civilian government. The logic of military necessity was able to constrain policymakers, and as a result regional security policy in early twentieth-century Europe became increasingly belligerent and risk-tolerant.[18]

This logic may come to apply to China as well. Within the Chinese military there are signs that an identity independent of the party is emerging; the party and state object vociferously to this development.[19] As the PLA becomes smaller and more professional, this distinct identity may find expression in a uniquely "military" identity. This identity would come with its own logic of appropriateness, and it would define solutions to regional problems in martial terms. Once primed for the offense, any number of trends might trigger a regional armed conflict: Taiwanese moves towards independence, Japanese maritime challenges, and/or the deployment of U.S. capabilities designed to strike at the Chinese mainland. Such a conflict would involve multiple high-technology militaries, nuclear-armed or -capable states, and the urban infrastructure that supports hundreds of millions of people.

Scenario 3: Nationalistic Conflict

In the third scenario, the outcome is the same—regional war between modern, nuclear-capable militaries—but the mechanism is different. A school of thought in political science argues that because democracies do not attack one another, democratization is a sure path to peace and stability.[20] Scholars find empirical support for this claim in the observation that mature liberal democracies never (or at least almost never) go to war with one another.[21] However, this finding does not extend to new democracies. Prior to the development of robust liberal democratic institutions, states that have recently emerged from authoritarian rule are actually the most conflict-prone of any state type.[22]

Why are new democracies prone to conflicts? Snyder proposes that young democracies are vulnerable to coalitions among nationalist politicians, old elites, and partisan media outlets. Because there are no traditional parties, political entrepreneurs race to find messages that appeal to broad swaths of the population and gain the resources necessary to mount nationwide campaigns. One especially resonant set of messages appeals to national identity and grievances—when pointed abroad, these messages justify preserving some of the privileges of the old elites while facing the greater enemy lurking abroad. Becausee the media in a new democracy is also only beginning to develop its own professionalism and tradition, rather than subjecting the nationalist claims of emerging leaders to sober and critical scrutiny, they tend to have an amplifying effect. Thus, because nationalist leaders supported by old elites tend to whip up popular frenzy against enemies abroad, new democracies have an elevated propensity for international conflict.

Applied to China, the narrative would look like this: to satisfy the demands of an emerging middle class, the Chinese Communist Party agrees to open elections. However, it still has a fearsome media apparatus, wealthy members, and a credible historical claim to have erased the humiliations of the nineteenth century. The elites within the party would prefer to retain the wealth they accrued during the one-party era, and in any event the party needs a message other than "preserve the privileges of our elites." Because this scenario assumes that the international environment is becoming more threatening to

China, one viable message would be: "We will protect the Chinese people from [Japan, Korea, the West] and will protect the rights of the hundreds of thousands of Chinese nationals living abroad." Thus, for purely domestic political purposes, a democratizing China might engage in visible, confrontational policies with its neighbors, who may respond in kind. With the pressures of popular demand stoked by a partisan media, China would be much more likely to escalate in conflict scenarios. Thus the possibility of a massively destructive regional war could become reality.

Scenario 4: Separation

Perhaps, however, China could democratize without an obvious international competitor to help rally popular support. Democratization does not imply that stability and prosperity will automatically welcome the new regime; in fact, the opposite is more likely. In this scenario, the pressures of nationalism do not unify China around an aggressive regional agenda; instead, they splinter China into a Han core along the coast and sparsely populated statelets that happen to occupy strategically important regions in the highlands.

Nationalism is a powerful motivator of human action. It tells people not only who they are, but implies that their group has its own destiny and requires its own independent political institutions.[23] Whether nationalism is a function of a colonial past, print capitalism, the legacy of mass literacy, or governmental strategies for bureaucratically sorting populations is not important for present purposes. Let us simply posit that there are groups of people in China who would prefer to rule themselves rather than continue as members of a larger Chinese state.

In the democratic transition, there seems to be a strong pressure, a function of both state weakness and the logic of democratic arguments, to allow people to choose their own political destiny. However, the reversion to older political communities and boundaries can have dangerous consequences for regional stability. In China today, there are dozens of minority nationalities.[24] For the purposes of this essay, however, consider the Tibetans and the Uighers. Both nationalities live on the Himalayan plateau, and both have engaged in nationalist violence and separatism in the past. It is not unreasonable to imagine that in a future democratic transition, one group would attempt to renew and reinvigorate its struggle for independence.

In the worst case scenario, these struggles could go one of two ways. Either the Chinese state would be forced to put down these movements by force, or the state would accept the fragmentation of China. The former case would bode poorly for China's democratic future. It is difficult to maintain a liberal democracy while retaining possession of a large group of people that would prefer different governing arrangements altogether. However, accepting fragmentation would make China's borders even more difficult to defend than they already are. A Tibet that allied with India, Russia, or the United States could allow the introduction of foreign bases and soldiers onto the "high ground" overlooking China's industrial and population centers. And, of course, there would be large Han populations left in these newly formed states that might prefer to be part of China, much as the collapse of the Soviet Union left many Russians in Ukraine who would prefer to be part of Russia. In either case, the potential for a serious conflict and humanitarian crisis is quite real.

II. The Least-Worst as Best

The purpose of this essay is to present worst case scenarios that will challenge U.S. policy-makers in the years to come. The obvious worst case—an unrestricted nuclear exchange between China and Russia or the United States—is as outlandish as it is horrifying. The scenarios presented here, while not as catastrophic as a global nuclear conflict, are nonetheless logical extensions of current trends that would have massive human and political implications and could be first steps towards a broader conflict that might have unimaginable consequences. A free and prosperous China is a goal the United States ought to continue to pursue, as is the goal of strengthening allies in the region. However, this essay has suggested that an American policy encouraging democracy and developing military capabilities in the region might lead to a less stable China and a less stable world. Then again, ignoring democracy or military preparations seems imprudent as well. How the United States and China manage these seeming contradictions in the years to come will determine if, and how, they can avoid each of these worst case scenarios.

Given the zero-sum nature of these risks, one potential American policy would be to accept an increased risk of separatism as the "least worst" scenario. This would entail a very mild regional presence, a military acquisition strategy that doesn't threaten the Chinese mainland, and support for democratizing elements in the Chinese elite. While America may have an ideological predisposition to support democratic practices as such, America's relevant material interests are concentrated in regions that have not experienced separatist violence like that of the more restive provinces in China's hinterland. While America might be accused of seeming callous when it allows the aspirations of a minority nation to be crushed, this is still an outcome to be preferred over the alternatives. However, the United States has a limited ability to determine which future scenario, whether one of these worst-cases or (one hopes) something better, might unfold.

How, then, should U.S. policymakers prepare for—and ideally prevent—the worst that can happen in China?

RECOMMENDED READINGS

Chong, Ja Ian, and Todd Hall. 2014. "The Lessons of 1914 for East Asia Today: Missing the Trees for the Forest." *International Security* 39, no. 1 (Summer): 7–43.

Christensen, Tom. 2006. "Fostering Stability or Creating a Monster? The Rise of China and U.S. Policy Toward East Asia." *International Security* 31, no. 1 (Summer): 81–126.

Lampton, David. 2014. *Following the Leader: Ruling China from Deng Xiaoping to Xi Jinping.* Berkeley, CA.

Li, Cheng. 2013. "Top-Level Reform or Bottom-Up Revolution? *Journal of Democracy* 24, no. 1 (January): 41–8.

Mansfield, Edward and Jack Snyder. 2007. *Electing to Fight: Why Emerging Democracies Go To War.* Cambridge, MA.

Nathan, Andrew and Andrew Scobell. 2012. *China's Search for Security.* New York.

----. 2012. "How China Sees America: The Sum of Beijing's Fears." *Foreign Affairs* (September/ October): 32–47.

Pei, Minxin. 2006. *China's Trapped Transition: The Limits of Developmental Autocracy.* Cambridge, MA.

Rowe, William T. 2009. *China's Last Empire: The Great Qing.* Cambridge, MA.

Skocpol, Theda. 1979. *States and Social Revolutions.* Cambridge.

NOTES

[1]For two different approaches to U.S. security strategy, see Thomas J. Christensen, "Fostering Stability or Creating a Monster? The Rise of China and U.S. Policy Toward East Asia," *International Security* 31, no. 1 (2006): 81–126. For more on the economic growth of China and its global impact in this century, see Nicholas D. Kristof, "The Rise of China," *Foreign Affairs* 72, no. 5 (1993): 59–74, 59.

[2]Stefan A. Halper, *The Beijing Consensus: How China's Authoritarian Model Will Dominate the Twenty-first Century* (New York: Basic Books, 2010). Also see Cho Young Nam and Jong-Ho Jeong. "China's Soft Power: Discussions, Resources, and Prospects," *Asian Survey* 48, no. 3 (2008): 453–72.

[3]See Shaohua Hu, *Explaining Chinese Democratization* (Westport, CT: Praeger, 2000).

[4]Understanding China's neighbors is paramount to any conversation concerning China's future actions. See Paul W. Kuznets, "An East Asian Model of Economic Development: Japan, Taiwan, and South Korea," *Economic Development and Cultural Change* 36, no. 3 (April 1988): S11–S43. Also see Robert A. Scalapino, "China's Relations with Its Neighbors," *Proceedings of the Academy of Political Science* 38, no. 2 (1991): 63–74.

[5]On Russian economic development, see Fiona Hill, "Russia: The 21st Century's Energy

Superpower?" *The Brookings Review* 20, no. 2 (2002): 28. For more on the Russo-Chinese conflict, see James Clay Moltz, "Regional Tensions in the Russo-Chinese Rapprochement," *Asian Survey* 35, no. 6 (1995): 511–27.

[6]On the U.S. response to Chinese naval presence, see Robert S. Ross, "China's Naval Nationalism: Sources, Prospects, And the U.S. Response," *International Security* 34, no. 2 (2009): 46–81.

[7]Minqi Li, "Socialism, Capitalism, and Class Struggle: The Political Economy of Modern China." *Economic and Political Weekly*, no. 52 (2009): 77–85.

[8]See especially Yuri Pines, "Local Elite," Chap. 4 in *The Everlasting Empire: The Political Culture of Ancient China and Its Imperial Legacy* (Princeton, NJ: Princeton University Press, 2012), 104–33.

[9]See, for instance, S. Irudaya Rajan, "China's One-Child Policy: Implication for Population Aging," *Economic and Political Weekly* (1994): 2502–6. On the comparative advantage of the Chinese labor market, see Cliff Waldman, "The Labor Market in Post-Reform China: History, Evidence, and Implications," *Business Economics* (2004): 50–62.

[10]For an in-depth analysis on the relationship of the Chinese economy to the international market, see R. Bin Wong, "Chinese Political Economy and the International Economy: Linking Global, Regional, and Domestic Possibilities," in C. Calhoun and G. Derlugian, eds., *Aftermath: A New Global Economic Order* (New York and London: New York University Press, 2011). On vulnerabilities in the Chinese economy, see the papers collected in Huw McKay and Ligang Song, eds., *Rebalancing and Sustaining Growth in China* (Canberra, Australia: Australian National University Press, 2012).

[11]Because these areas are so important to Chinese industrial and agricultural regions along the coast, China is hoping for "peaceful development" in the region. See Thierry Mathou. "Tibet and Its Neighbors: Moving Toward a New Chinese Strategy in the Himalayan Region," *Asian Survey 45*, no. 4 (2005): 503–21.

[12]For a historical account of the collapse of imperial China see William T. Rowe, *China's Last Empire: The Great Qing* (Cambridge, MA: Harvard University Press, 2009).

[13]The second- and third-order affects caused by the delegation of Chinese authority go beyond the political realm. See Michel Oksenberg, "China's Political System: Challenges of the Twenty-First Century," *The China Journal* (2001): 21–35.

[14]On the late twentieth-century origins of China's technocratic movement, see L. Cheng and L. T. White, "China's Technocratic Movement and the World Economic Herald," *Modern China* 17, no. 3 (1991): 342–88. Also see Daniel A. Bell. "Toward Meritocratic Rule in China? A Response to Professors Dallmayr, Li, and Tan," *Philosophy East and West* 59, no. 4 (2009): 554–60.

[15]Chinese government officials use the promotion system to gain favor. See Victor Shih, Christopher Adolph, and Mingxing Liu, "Getting Ahead in the Communist Party: Explaining the Advancement of Central Committee Members in China," *American Political Science Review* 106, no. 1 (2012): 166–87.

[16]For a more in-depth analysis of several such implosions, shown through an investigation of a negative correlation between national disorder and national unity, see Hongyi Harry Lai, "The Life Span of Unified Regimes in China," *China Review* (2002): 93–124.

[17]On U.S. strategy, the INF Treaty, and he U.S. response to the modernization of China's military, see David W. Kearn, "The Challenge of China's Military Modernization," chap. 4 in *Facing the Missile Challenge: U.S. Strategy and the Future of the INF Treaty* (Santa Monica, CA: RAND Corporation, 2012), 57–92.

[18]Stephen Van Evera, "The Cult of the Offensive and the Origins of the First World War," *International Security* 9, no. 1 (1984): 58–107.

[19]Andrew J. Nathan and Andrew Scobell, "Haow China Sees America," *Foreign Affairs* 91, no. 5 (2012): 32–47.

[20]On "democratic peace theory," see especially Barbara F. Walter, "Designing Transitions from Civil War: Demobilization, Democratization, and Commitments to Peace," *International Security* 24, no. 1 (1999): 127–55. Additionally, see Michael W. Doyle, "Kant, Liberal Legacies, and Foreign Affairs," *Philosophy & Public Affairs* (1983): 205–35.

[21]Harvey Starr, "Democracy and Integration: Why Democracies Don't Fight Each Other," *Journal of Peace Research* (1997): 153–62; Ale Mintz and Nehemia Geva, "Why Don't Democracies Fight Each Other? An Experimental Study," *Journal of Conflict Resolution* 37, no. 3 (1993): 484–503.

[22]Revolution is often a catalyst for conflict, making states that have just undergone a regime change extremely conflict-prone. For a full theory on the link between revolution and war see Stephen M. Walt, *Revolution and War* (Cornell, NY: Cornell University Press, 1996). Also see Edward D. Mansfield and Jack Snyder, "Democratization and War," *Foreign Affairs* (May/June 1995).

[23]For more on the role that democratization plays on the destabilization of a region, see Joshua Cohen and Charles F. Sabel, "Global Democracy," *NYUJ International Law and Politics* 37 (2004): 763–97.

[24]On Chinese nationalism see especially Peter Hays Gries, *China's New Nationalism: Pride, Politics, and Diplomacy* (Berkeley: University of California Press, 2004). On the role of national minorities in Chinese nationalism, see Dru C. Gladney, "Representing Nationality in China: Refiguring Majority/Minority Identities," *The Journal of Asian Studies* 53, no. 1 (1994): 92–123.

3

Breaking Up Is Hard to Do

Envisioning European Disunion

SETH A. JOHNSTON

The progress of peaceful integration in Europe since the end of World War II is a historic achievement which appears to be in jeopardy. Consider recent electoral victories for anti-European Union parties in Britain, Finland, Greece, Poland, and Spain. Embodying more than mere campaign rhetoric, British Prime Minister David Cameron set a specific promise for a national referendum on withdrawal from the European Union by 2017. In France, the rise of the Eurosceptic National Front challenges that country's celebrated membership in the Union. Separatist movements such as those in Catalonia and Scotland threaten the cohesion even of European countries themselves. Greece has remained on the brink of financial collapse and exit from the Euro for years, while the European Central Bank moves from one crisis to another in its efforts to stem continental economic malaise while preserving the common currency. Migrants die by the thousands trying to reach nearby Europe, while the European Union has struggled to tackle these humanitarian or other foreign policy problems. Russia invaded Ukraine and the European response has hardly been unified. Altogether, as domestic and international pressures mount, distressing news has cast doubt on the efficacy of Europe's political and economic integration. Is a break-up of the Eurozone or even the European Union possible? Would this break-up be the "worst that could happen?"

Either scenario would have far-reaching consequences, but an unraveling of the post-1945 institutions of European integration may not be the only, or even the worst, potential crisis. Consider a longer view. For more than four hundred years following the age of exploration, Europe played an outsized role in international affairs, and it remains one of the most prosperous and influential regions today. The two world wars of the twentieth century hastened the end of Europe's centuries-long dominance, but they also demonstrated two other significant historical lessons: first, the worst things for Europe can be bad for the rest of the world too; second, too narrow a focus on troublesome news about the European Union may obscure more basic risks to peace and stability in Europe. In the long run, Europe's worst case scenario includes not only the break-up of the current institutions but the resurgence of old patterns of conflict.

I. Europe in Historical Perspective: What's the Worst that has Already Happened?

The prospect of *both* EU collapse and a return of conflict are linked ultimately to integration. In an age of autobahns and high-speed rail, Europe's physical geography contains few obstacles to integration; its political geography, however, remains fragmented. Most regions of the world contain a vast country, hegemonic relative to smaller neighbors in one or more aspect of material power (land area, population, economic or military strength, etc.): the United States in North America, Russia in North and Central Asia, China in East Asia, Australia as a continent and country unto itself. Brazil's reach is stopped by the great physical barriers of the Amazon and the Andes. The Sahara and absence of navigable rivers present physical barriers to integration in Africa. But Europe contains few such barriers. Navigation on Europe's rivers and across the relatively flat north European plain is reasonably easy. Modern infrastructure such as the bridges through and tunnels under the English Channel, the Alps, and the Pyrenees mitigate the obstacles that have historically frustrated movement. People and commerce move freely, yet integration of European political life remains hard. There is no vast European mega-state.

But the absence of a unitary pan-European realm is not for lack of attempts to create one. Imperial Rome conquered much of the ancient world, but Germanic tribes thwarted its expansion into northern Europe.[1] Charlemagne briefly united European lands under a single ruler in 800 C.E., though his successors divided them just decades later. The so-called Holy Roman Empire never achieved the unity or power that its name implied. In more modern times, the House of Habsburg battled to establish continental dominance for three hundred years, but was frustrated successively by Ottoman Turks, social transformation in the Reformation and the Enlightenment, the rise of nationalism in Hungary and other minority areas, and the unification of a rival German state outside Austria.[2] In the meantime, Napoleon came closer than anyone since Charlemagne to unifying Europe through conquest, but his successes were short-lived. Hitler's bid for living space in a greater Germany of continental scale was shorter still. All of these efforts to consolidate Europe ultimately failed. But the historical pattern of attempting European integration through military force is longstanding.

Failure to achieve unity through conquest has made war common in European affairs. The dominant pattern, at least since the creation of the European state system following the Thirty Years War in 1648, was of a constellation of

European great powers rising and falling relative to one another in a balance of power. Attempts by one to rise too far above the others often resulted in war and eventual re-equilibration, on the continent if not also among colonial possessions around the world. World Wars I and II (sometimes lumped together as a "second" Thirty Years War) wrought such destruction in Europe that they represented a turning point: for the first time in centuries, European powers declined relative to new global superpowers.

After 1945, the United States and Soviet Union underwrote a postwar European order characterized not by a multipolar balance of power, but a bipolar standoff in the Cold War. With security concerns largely dominated by this external dynamic, the Cold War freed countries in Western Europe to pursue peaceful internal cooperation in liberal international institutions. Beginning with the consolidation of coal and steel industries in the 1950s, countries steadily integrated their economic, political, and social life into what has become the European Union, its twenty-eight member countries now comprising more than five hundred million people, the largest economy in the world, and a historic record of peace and prosperity that has lasted more than seventy years.[3]

Thus, for many, the worst thing that could happen in Europe is a reversal of the post-1945 pattern of integration in the European Union. European "disintegration" could undo all of the positive progress. But there is a negative, more insidious risk that attempts at "integration" in Europe could be worse if it means a return to the old fashioned method of violence and conquest.

II. Envisioning European Disunion

Centrifugal forces of disunion challenge Europe from within. Politically, sub-national regionalism and separatism have grown despite (or perhaps because of) supra-national integration in the European Union. Arguments marshaled in favor of Scottish independence during the 2014 referendum included proposals for the continued use of the British pound sterling and membership in the European Union. Other minority groups and regions have also agitated for greater independence, either within or outside the EU, even as their central governments deny the wisdom or viability of a break-away state. Catalonia has long considered itself distinct from Spain, and its citizens signaled overwhelming support for independence in an informal poll in 2014.[4] Belgium, while home to the headquarters of European institutions, has struggled in recent years to sustain a national government due to rivalries between its Walloon and

Flemish populations. Czechoslovakia split in 1993. Minority tensions remain less than fully resolved in the Balkans, Basque regions of France and Spain, and Northern Ireland.

Forces of political disunity in Europe are not only geographic but also ideological. The rise of right wing nationalist parties in many European countries is a notable sign of this polarization. The success of the *Front National* (FN) and Jean-Marie Le Pen's advance to the run-off round of the French presidential election in 2002 surprised observers, and Le Pen was roundly defeated in the final poll. But the FN has entrenched itself in the mainstream since then, with Le Pen's daughter, Marine, at the head of what is now France's third-largest political party. Right wing parties in other European countries promote similar brands of social, cultural, and economic nationalism with often-overt anti-immigration and anti-EU policies. Hungary's anti-Semitic Jobbik group, the Flemish nationalist Vlaams Belang in Belgium, Greece's far-right Golden Dawn, Austria's Freedom Party, Italy's Lega Nord, and the UK Independence Party—to name just a few—have demonstrated increased prominence in public discourse or success at the polls in recent years. Such parties are active not only at the local and national levels, but also at the EU-level, enjoying particularly notable success in the 2014 European Parliament elections.

Tensions continue to exist among the member-states of the European Union as well. Foreign and defense policy have historically hindered cooperation in the EU. In fact, some of the earliest and more significant setbacks to the entire project of post-1945 European integration involved disagreement in this area, to include the failed proposal in the early 1950s for a European Defense Community, the Empty Chair Crisis about European political cooperation in the 1960s, *Ostpolitik* and détente versus more traditional defense in the 1970s and 80s, post-Cold War growing pains, and high-profile disagreements about the post-9/11 U.S.-led Iraq War.

Difficulties in establishing a common foreign policy remain evident in Europe's response to Russia's 2014 invasion of Ukraine and the ongoing crisis there. Eastern European countries are most concerned about Russia's threat to their own security, while also remaining economically vulnerable owing to their dependence on Russian oil and gas. Western European countries do not approve of Russia's aggressive moves in Ukraine, but their responses to it differed for a long time and for different reasons: France is mostly independent of Russian energy, but initially resisted cancelling lucrative sales of advanced warships to Russia. The United Kingdom stands to lose most in sanctions affecting its London finance and banking industry, and was largely preoccupied with its own domestic politics. Germany maintains greater economic and political links to Russia than France or the United Kingdom, but enjoys a safer position than Eastern European states with respect to security. The resolution of these differences within the structures of European institutions would be an argument in favor of their utility. But national leaders such as German Chancellor Angela Merkel rather than EU officials have played the leading roles.[5]

Just as there is an East/West political or foreign policy cleavage in Europe, so there is a North/South cleavage in economics. "Northern" countries Luxembourg, Denmark, Sweden, and Austria lead the Union in per capita GDP, while "southern" countries Bulgaria, Romania, and Hungary trail it. Unemployment between five and seven percent prevails in Germany, Britain, and the Netherlands; in Italy, Portugal, and Cyprus unemployment is in double digits; in Greece and Spain, overall unemployment has reached twenty-five percent, while youth unemployment has surged past fifty percent. Economic growth is a more mixed story from one country to another, but has been generally feeble throughout Europe since the 2008 financial crisis. The average rate of GDP growth among the eighteen countries that share the Euro currency was just .01 percent in 2013, up from negative 0.4 percent in 2012. The United Kingdom, the largest European economy outside the Eurozone, has fared better with growth of 1.6 percent in 2013 rising to 2.6 percent in 2014.[6] But sustained economic stagnation—a Eurozone average 0.5 percent GDP growth rate over the period from 2005 to 2013—has called into question the efficacy and desirability of the European Union's brand of integration.

The Euro common currency is at the center of these economic concerns. Set in motion by the same 1992 Maastricht Treaty that gave the name "European Union" to the institutions of European integration, the common currency was adopted for reasons both economic and political. Economically, the Euro was intended to be an important step in "ever-closer" economic and monetary union, which would increase efficiency and prosperity by reducing transaction costs within Europe. Politically, the end the Cold War prompted moves toward greater integration to lock in the gains of peaceful inter-state European cooperation. Viewed this way, a common currency would contribute to making another Franco-German or general European war unthinkable. But in the haste to achieve an agreement on the common currency in the politically opportune moment of the Cold War's end and Germany's reunification, the Euro agreement contained important design flaws. The most significant of these is the institutional mismatch between monetary and fiscal policy: the European Central Bank controls Eurozone currency policy, but each country retains its own national budget. Although European countries were committed to limiting deficit spending individually to prevent undue pressure on the common currency, no credible enforcement mechanism existed, and even large countries like France and Germany almost immediately flouted these rules. Unlike the systems that underpin other continental-scale currencies in the United States, Brazil, or India which share the challenges of varying regional economic conditions but are able to address them with the powers of a unitary state, no such genuinely federal European government or tax system exists to sustain the Euro currency.[7]

III. Scenarios for Eurozone or European Union Breakup

The disorderly collapse of the Euro has seemed a real possibility since the 2008 financial crisis, as concerns about public debt and bank solvency put enormous and uneven pressure on Eurozone members. It manifested in Greece, which in 2009 had a public debt that amounted to 113 percent of its GDP (roughly twice the Eurozone limit of 60 percent) and a budget deficit of 13.6 percent of GDP (more than four times the Eurozone limit of 3 percent). Ratings agencies began to downgrade the quality of Greek government and bank debt, leading to concerns by 2011 about default and widespread discussion that Greece would have to leave the Euro. Meanwhile, concern about similar debt problems spread to Portugal, Ireland, Spain, Italy, and even France, threatening both the core and periphery of the European economy. (Probably the worst-affected country, Iceland, saw the collapse of its entire international banking system. Iceland was not a Euro member and suspended its 2009 application to join the EU following these developments although it has since recovered solvency.) Loan and bailout programs, the European Financial Stability Facility and European Stability Mechanism, together with cooperation from the International Monetary Fund, the G7, and G20, abated the worst concerns about catastrophic implosion of these countries' financial sectors for a time. But voters and politicians in some countries ultimately resisted some of these measures, most notably in Greece where elections in 2014 and 2015 favored the Syriza party of Alexis Tsipras and its left-wing platform explicitly to oppose painful, EU-imposed austerity measures. In the summer of 2015, Greece became the first developed country ever to default on loan payments to the International Monetary Fund. Athens ordered bank holidays and imposed capital controls as crisis diplomacy dominated headlines and a major rupture seemed imminent. The possibility of the so-called "Grexit" from the Eurozone remains.

A more general unravelling of the Euro also remains a possibility so long as its basic design flaws endure. In the absence of a radical (and politically inconceivable) transfer of fiscal power away from member-states toward a more genuinely federal European Union, it may be only a matter of time before an urgent crisis again upsets the Euro. Alternatively, some have proposed the "technically feasible, politically difficult" possibility of a deliberate walking back of the Euro, with a reinstitution of more limited forms of monetary cooperation among separate national currencies.[8] These measures could take the form of smaller currency areas, such as a German-led Deutschmark zone in northern Europe. Another obvious and less exclusionary alternative would be to return to the previous forms of monetary cooperation in the European Monetary System, established in 1979 to link independent national currencies with a European Exchange Rate Mechanism and artificial European Currency Unit.

History confirms that chaotic, disorderly currency splits are worse than deliberate, planned ones.[9] But any undoing of the Euro would entail negative consequences for nearly everyone. "Southern" European countries would find their new currencies untrusted and weak, leading to high borrowing costs, low purchasing power, and generally poor economic opportunity for their people. "Northern" countries, especially export-oriented economies like Germany (which regularly vies with China for having the world's largest trade surplus), would also suffer from a Euro collapse, as an increase in the value of their new national currencies would drive up the costs of their exports, reducing their competitiveness in international markets and putting downward pressure on their economic performance. Foreign investors and trading partners of Europe could lose in the currency instability that ensued. The Euro is the second most widely held international reserve currency. Its unraveling could be expected to create a flight toward U.S. dollar assets, which would place upward pressure on the value of the dollar, impairing U.S. exports and threatening higher unemployment as U.S. firms could hire labor abroad more cheaply. All told, the economic consequences of a Euro collapse could easily plunge the world back into recession or worse. As a result, most stakeholders are committed to the Euro's preservation.

Paradoxically, however, clinging to the Euro's survival might increase the risk of broader European Union collapse. Despite the economic logic of preventing the Euro's demise, saving it entails costs and perceptions of fairness that may undermine political support for European integration. As depicted in Figure 1, membership in the EU is already somewhat heterogeneous: some

EU "members" do not participate in the Union's more noteworthy features. The United Kingdom, for example, belongs to the EU but is party to neither the Euro nor the Schengen Agreement, which allows for passport-free travel across borders. Meanwhile, non-members of the EU, such as Norway, Iceland, and Switzerland, are part of the Schengen Area but do not use the Euro. Despite recent efforts to consolidate and clarify the legal standing of the European Union, including the failed Constitutional Treaty of 2004 and the successful but more modest Lisbon Treaty in 2007, the European Union remains a complex institutional patchwork in which states have varying levels of participation and influence.

Although the Euro is the official currency of the European Union, only nineteen of the EU's twenty-eight members use it. Although many newer members are legally bound to adopt the Euro and aspire to do so, the reality for now is that EU member countries outside the Eurozone must live by EU financial decisions though they are not full members of the decision-making process. For countries like the United Kingdom and Denmark that have chosen monetary independence over influence in the Eurogroup, increasing demands for bailouts or other financial and economic measures needed to support the Euro decrease the attractiveness of their entire relationship to the European Union.[10]

British Prime Minister David Cameron's promise to hold a referendum by 2017 on continuing UK membership in the EU helped his Conservative party maintain power after the 2015 parliamentary elections, and gave him a mandate to seek special treatment from other EU leaders. Recent polls indicate the historically Eurosceptic British people are split on EU membership, indicating that a vote to leave is at least plausible. Moreover, the legal process by which members could exit is relatively straightforward: a qualified majority of EU members could vote to approve the measure under Article 50 of the Treaty of European Union. Although Greenland (part of the Danish realm) and Algeria (following its independence from France) exited the EU's forerunner institutions, nothing as large or significant as a potential British withdrawal from the EU has been undertaken before.

IV. Back to the Future: War and European Integration

Just as centrifugal forces threaten the post-1945 European integration from within, an externally unstable regional and global international system threatens Europe from without. As described above, externally-imposed stability was an important condition for the development of the European Union. But developing crises outside the Union, especially in Ukraine, contain important warnings about the durability of the post-war European order.

Many of the same ingredients that have historically destabilized Europe persist today. Unresolved disputes and frozen conflicts persist in Kosovo, Transnistria, and Nagorno-Karabakh, and with Turkey's relations with Armenia, Greece, and the Kurds. Ethno-linguistic differences lingering from Russification policies in the former Soviet Union loom in the Baltic states, Ukraine, the Caucasus, and others. Open conflict on Europe's frontiers in North Africa and the Middle East has, since 2010, embroiled European and/or U.S. forces in Syria, Iraq, Libya, Mali, Niger, the Central African Republic, and elsewhere.

The possibility of a return to conflict among great powers, especially involving Russia, is the most significant danger facing Europe. Russia remains an enormously important country with vital interests in Europe. The largest country in the world by land area, Russia maintains the world's largest arsenal of nuclear weapons and is the second largest global producer of oil and of natural gas. Russia's leading political figure since the Cold War, Vladimir Putin, has sought to reestablish Russian influence via a Eurasian Union, a Collective Security Treaty Organization, and other alternatives to Western institutions.

Russia has also demonstrated a pivotal turn toward military force as an instrument of foreign policy. Russia's annexation of Crimea in 2014 is the first time since World War II that a European country used force to seize the territory of another and thus change international borders. This is not Russia's first use of inter-state military force, to be sure; its 2008 invasion of Georgia is similar. But the Ukraine case is particularly dangerous. Russia's invasion, combined with a sweeping military modernization program that has seen more than fifty percent increase in military spending since 2009, challenges the material balance of power in Europe. Ukraine voluntarily surrendered the world's third-largest nuclear weapons arsenal in exchange for territorial assurances from Russia, the United States, and United Kingdom in the so-called Budapest Memorandum of 1994. Any country contemplating the importance of nuclear weapons as the ultimate guarantor of national sovereignty (e.g. Iran, North Korea, Pakistan) is sure to notice what followed. Moreover, Ukraine is more central to European security than Georgia. The largest country by land area wholly within Europe, Ukraine borders four NATO countries and serves as a major energy corridor for oil and natural gas bound for Europe.

Worst case scenarios of a return to great power conflict invoke analogies from Europe's historical record. If the proper analogy is to pre-World War II appeasement, failure by the West to stand up to Russia might embolden it to further aggression and territorial expansion. If the proper analogy is to the Crimean War of the nineteenth century, on the other hand, it may be folly for the West to try to reverse by force of arms what Russia has clearly established. If one considers the role of alliances in causing World War I, one might expect the Baltic region to be the powder keg that sparks conflict between Russia and NATO. Latvia, Lithuania, and Estonia were once part of the Soviet Union and have large Russian minority populations; but unlike Georgia and Ukraine, they are members of NATO and the EU. Perhaps the most likely possibility is a return to the Cold War's tense deterrence, in which military confrontation is threatened but avoided for fear of mutually assured destruction.

Worst case scenarios are rarely also the most likely ones. None of the challenges to European integration (or dis-integration) are historically unprecedented. Political differences, economic downturn, institutional crisis, and threats to international peace and security have been common, even during the generally successful, prosperous decades of European integration since 1945. This history can be a cause for confidence in the will and capacity of Europeans, as well as their partners and allies, to overcome the most recent iterations of these challenges.

Yet Europe's history also cautions against complacency. One hundred years after the beginning of Europe's second Thirty Years War, the conflict that destroyed, perhaps irrevocably, European primacy in international affairs, a common view of the events leading up to the Great War invokes the notion of "sleepwalking," aimless and ignorant of the dangers ahead.[11] At the very least, contemplating the worst cases can inform our efforts to prevent them.

RECOMMENDED READINGS

Ash, Timothy Garton. 2012. "The Crisis of Europe: How the Union Came Together and Why It's Falling Apart." *Foreign Affairs* 91, no. 5 (September/October): 2–15.

Clark, C. 2013. *The Sleepwalkers: How Europe Went to War in 1914*. New York.

Deighton, Anne. 1998. "The Remaking of Europe, 1945–1990" in Michael Howard and William Roger Louis, *The Oxford History of the Twentieth Century*. Oxford.

Heisbourg, F. 2014. "The EU without the Euro." *Survival* 56, no. 2 (April/May): 27–48.

Judt, Tony. 2006. *Postwar: A History of Europe since 1945*. New York.

Menon, Anand. 2011. "European Defence Policy from Lisbon to Libya." *Survival* 53, no. 3: 75–90.

Moravcsik, Andrew. 2012. "Europe After the Crisis: How to Sustain a Common Currency." *Foreign Affairs* 91, no. 3 (May/June): 54–68.

Rosamund, Ben. 2000. *Theories of European Integration*. New York.

Stirk, Peter. 1996. *A History of European Integration Since 1914*. New York.

Taylor, A.J.P. 1954. *The Struggle for Mastery in Europe, 1848–1918.* Oxford.
Zielonka, J. 2007. *Europe as Empire: The Nature of the Enlarged European Union.* Oxford.

NOTES

[1]Rome's defeat in the Battle of the Teutoburg Forest (9 C.E.) decisively ended its planned conquests past the Rhine River into northern and eastern Europe, even as it enjoyed new heights of power elsewhere during this time. See, for example, Peter S. Wells, *The Battle that Stopped Rome: Emperor Augustus, Arminius, and the Slaughter of the Legions in the Teutoburg Forest* (New York: W. W. Norton, 2003). For an interesting take on the geographical influences of imperial expansion, see Peter Turchin, Jonathan M. Adams, and Thomas D. Hall, "East-West Orientation of Historical Empires and Modern States," *Journal of World-Systems Research* (December 2006).

[2]A.J.P. Taylor, *The Habsburg Monarchy, 1809–1918: A History of the Austrian Empire and Austria-Hungary* (Chicago, IL: University of Chicago Press, 1948), 10.

[3]There have been no major inter-state wars in Europe during this time. This record does not deny the adversity of the Cold War or the violence of intra-state wars such as those in breakup of Yugoslavia during the 1990s.

[4]See Raphael Minder, "Catalonia Overwhelmingly Votes for Independence From Spain in New Straw Poll," *The New York Times* (November 9, 2014), http://www.nytimes.com/2014/11/10/world/europe/catalans-vote-in-straw-poll-on-independence-from-spain.html?_r=0.

[5]Differences in national approaches occur despite recent institutional efforts to enhance the capacity of EU foreign and security policy institutions. The 2007 Lisbon Treaty, the EU's most recent major constitutional document, included the creation of a High Representative of the Union for Foreign Affairs and Security Policy and a European External Action Service (essentially an EU diplomatic corps). Although various sanctions against Russia have been applied at the EU level, many of the most significant European actions have occurred on a national rather than EU-wide basis, as when the leaders of France and Germany (rather than the EU's top foreign policy official) travelled to negotiate cease-fires among the parties in Ukraine.

[6]"Taking Europe's Pulse: European Economy Guide," *The Economist* (May 7, 2015), http://www.econ-omist.com/blogs/graphicdetail/2015/05/european-economy-guide.

[7]Francois Heisbourg, "The EU without the Euro," *Survival* 56, no. 2 (April/May 2014): 27–48, 28.

[8]Ibid., 35.

[9]Consider the unmaking of imperial currencies following World War I (Austro-Hungarian krone, Russian tsarist ruble, Ottoman lira) or the Cold War (Soviet ruble, Yugoslav dinar), all of which entailed high levels of inflation as well as other economic and social disruption. To be sure, they also accompanied the disintegration of political unions and often also war. Currency changes in the breakup of the Scandinavian Monetary Union in 1914, application of the Deutschmark for German reunification in 1990, or Brazil's switch from the cruzeiro to the real in 1994 were a great deal more orderly and less painful. Heisbourg, "The EU Without the Euro," 34–5.

[10]In fact, political opposition to the costs of saving the Euro has developed even in states with a high degree of influence over the currency. In Germany, for instance, thousands of ordinary citizens filed a legal complaint against the European Central Bank's moves to protect

the public debt of imperiled Eurozone members. Despite this policy's centrality in ECB efforts to stabilize European financial markets, the complaint is rooted in a perception that ordinary Germans have unfairly had to bear the costs of rescuing the less fiscally responsible. The German constitutional court's decision to criticize ECB policy while not ruling it illegal walks a careful line: allowing ECB policy to continue, for the moment at least, while also acknowledging growing domestic political dissatisfaction. Erik Jones and R. Daniel Kelemen, "The Euro Goes to Court," *Survival* 56, no. 2 (April-May 2014): 15–23.

[11]Christopher Clark, *The Sleepwalkers: How Europe Went to War in 1914* (New York: Harper, 2013). This is by no means an uncontested view, of course. For an argument that European leaders knew exactly what they were doing, see Jack Snyder, "Better Now than Later: The Paradox of 1914 as Everyone's Favored Year for War," *International Security* (Summer 2014): 74–94.

4

What Hath America Wrought?

Post-Occupation Instabilities in Afghanistan and Iraq

AARON MILLER

On one subject there is little debate: the United States invasions of both Iraq and Afghanistan removed the centralized government of each country. The immediate impact of U.S. intervention in each country was essentially a civil war, that is, the "breakdown of state and cross-group institutions… [with] institutions [becoming] incapable of enforcing agreements between groups…."[1] While the removal of centralized political control in Iraq and Afghanistan certainly contributed to the creation of the Islamic State and the resurgences of the Taliban respectively, it is not obvious that this current state of affairs is permanent. The political order of each country is evolving.

What has the United States wrought in Iraq and Afghanistan? To answer this question, an observer must first understand the political order—that is, "the structure and distribution of authority [among] armed organizations"—of each state prior to U.S. intervention.[2] But political order is not a fixed phenomenon. To understand how U.S. efforts impacted the political order of a country, an observer must answer three separate questions: First, how did U.S. training, military equipment, and other aid impact different groups? Second, did combat with U.S. troops and allies cause different groups to develop new tactics and strategies? Finally, how has the last decade of conflict changed the social terrain of each country? Understanding how the United States altered the relationship among groups in Iraq and Afghanistan by means of aid, direct combat, and ushering in a period of sustained conflict, will allow us to understand what U.S. policy has achieved (or failed to achieve) and to consider which groups are likely to enjoy the most influence as U.S. forces draw down.

This chapter will proceed in three parts. Part One briefly describes the political evolution of Iraq and Afghanistan prior to 2014. Part Two adapts a theory developed by Paul Staniland to establish a framework for understanding changes in political order and then discusses three questions, the answers to which aid in identifying the future political order of—and thus the legacy of U.S. intervention in—Iraq and Afghanistan. Part Three concludes with a discussion aimed at helping policymakers chart a path for U.S. policy in post-2014 Iraq and Afghanistan.

I. Iraq and Afghanistan before 2014

Iraq

The fall of Saddam Hussein's Ba'athist's regime in 2003 unveiled social cleavages that were always present in Iraq. Without central control, the country of Iraq descended into violence. This civil war featured at least three distinct conflicts:[3]

1. A sectarian civil war between Sunni and Shi'ite militias
2. An insurgency by (mostly) Sunni militias against the Iraqi government and Coalition forces
3. A communal conflict between Kurds and Arabs in Kurdistan

The elections in 2005 "solidified ethnic and sectarian fragmentation" amongst Sunni, Shi'ite and Kurd.[4] The historically dominant Sunni tribes boycotted, fearing a permanent loss of political power.[5] A little known Shi'ite candidate, Nuri al-Maliki, was elected Prime Minister.[6] Sunni tribes in western Iraq joined with Al Qaeda (AQI) and AQI unleashed turmoil at every available opportunity. In February of 2006, AQI bombed one of the holiest Shi'ite sites in the world, the Golden Mosque in Samarra. Shi'ite militias flocked to the fiery rhetoric of leaders like Muqtada al-Sadr, targeting Sunni populations. Sunni groups responded. Against this backdrop of violence, Kurdish elements cemented their control over northern Iraq.

But Sunni tribes in the west soon found their ally unpalatable. AQI muscled in on territory, targeted Sunni tribal elders, and used rape to build ties with the local population.[7] Several abortive attempts to break with AQI occurred, but it was not until the 2007 surge of U.S. forces that the Sunni "Awakening" was able to drive back AQI.[8] Violence in Iraq started to ebb in 2008, and the political acumen of al-Maliki soon became evident. Passing legislation on January 12, 2008 that allowed ex-Ba'thists (frequently Sunni) to occupy their former government positions, al-Maliki also moved against his Shi'ite opponents, most notably al-Sadr and his army in Basra.[9] These seemingly non-sectarian moves hid al-Maliki's efforts to cement power. Elections in 2010 kept al-Maliki atop a coalition government.

Three days after the December 18, 2011 withdrawal of U.S. forces, Iraqi political fissures widened. Prime Minister al-Maliki accused his Sunni Vice President and leader of a large Sunni bloc, Tariq al-Hashimi, of running a death squad. Al-Hashimi, denying all charges, fled to Kurdish-held territories in northern Iraq. The fragile political alliance between the Sunni and Shi'ite political groups, taped together through U.S. efforts and the excesses of AQI, started to fall apart; even the election of a new Prime Minister, Haider al-Abadi, has not changed the underlying political splits in Iraq. It is now generally believed that the U.S. withdrawal in 2011 left behind little more than the twenty-first century incarnation of an Iraqi strongman,[10] and it is on this social foundation that today's Islamic State is built. Capitalizing on "widespread disenchantment among [Iraqi] Sunnis," ISI seized an opportunity to control terrain, "leap-frogging" off Sunni militias and into urban centers throughout Iraq.[11]

Afghanistan

The Taliban rose out of the "social circumstances created by the war in the 1980's."[12] Madrassas and refugee camps in Pakistan served as Petri dishes, cultivating links between Taliban leadership and clerics in southern Afghanistan, "[transcending] the fragmentary tendencies of Pashtun society."[13] The factional violence of competing mujahedeen following the Soviet withdrawal offered the Taliban "a unique opportunity to sideline existing factions…, [rising] above ordinary tribal divisions."[14] The Taliban swept into Afghanistan, their rapid spread accomplished not so much through military victory but through defections.[15] By 1998, the Taliban controlled approximately 90 percent of the country with many regionally powerful warlords going into exile.[16] But the opportunity to rise above traditional divisions did not always entail a willingness to do so. The Taliban were "unwilling to transition from a social movement to a government," which alienated much of the population.[17] The 2001 U.S. invasion capitalized on a historical trend in Afghanistan: the ruling body, having failed to provide stability, loses legitimacy. The populace looked elsewhere. But, at the time, policymakers in the United States were not looking to build a state. U.S. forces, partnering with local warlords, focused instead on pursuing Al Qaeda.

The U..N.-sponsored Bonn agreement in 2001 ushered in a provisional government composed of Northern Alliance members, limited Pashtu representatives, and mujahedeen leaders from Peshawar.[18] Later confirmed by a tribal council, the new Afghan government was unable to project influence beyond Kabul. Afghan President Hamid Karzai was sometimes referred to as the "mayor of Kabul."[19]

Afghan government weakness undercut the legitimacy of both the government and intervening forces. Warlords, some returning from exile, activated old social networks. Replacing "Soviet" with "U.S.," groups like Hizb-i-Islam began resistance to the foreign presence anew. Others simply ignored the central government. Facing a complex political environment, the Karzai government reinforced a patrimonial model of government instead of the building of state institutions.[20] Karzai's power stemmed from a "dangerous parallel system" of governance based on patronage and access to international funds.[21] He played powerbrokers off of each other in a "divide and rule manner…, [constantly working] to create counterweights against opposing factions."[22] Today's politics are no less fragmented in Afghanistan: warlords are called upon to battle the Taliban. It is this fractious environment that the Taliban re-entered in the mid-2000's. To make it even more chaotic, the executive branch of the Afghan government is now split between a president and government chief executive, a position created to resolve a political impasse in the 2014 Presidential election.[23]

The ties that aid the Taliban and the Islamic State in certain regions of their respective countries are often lacking in the governments of these states. In Iraq, Prime Minister Al-Abadi is hamstrung by the continued presence of Mr. al-Miliki and his strong vertical and horizontal connections to certain Shia factions.[24] Afghanistan, too, suffers from similar divisions. Instead of serving as places for political discourse, the governments of both countries frequently serve as yet another battleground for political factions inside the state. The façade of government shrouds the political order of the country, a political order made of multiple organizations whose ties, both vertical and horizontal, determine the relative power of each actor.

II. Understanding Political Order

There is "no single form of the modern state," according to Paul Staniland; distributions of power vary across even governments of the same type.[25] Failed or fragile states are no different. To file Afghanistan and Iraq under the same category of "failed states" hides a simple truth: "order is not synonymous with a robust state or monopoly of violence."[26] Regimes may rise and fall, but political order merely changes. To understand this redistribution requires an observer to identify two things: the different actors or groups involved in the "state" and how these groups relate to one another.

Given the fluidity of events in both Iraq and Afghanistan as this chapter is being written, we cannot say with certainty just what the United States has wrought. But this framework allows us to begin answering three questions about the U.S. intervention in both Iraq and Afghanistan. What impact did U.S. resources have on each country? How did combat change the behavior of groups, and how did fighting move populations in Iraq and Afghanistan? Answering these questions allows a policymaker to understand the modern-day political order of each country.

Identifying Influential Groups

Numerous groups may exist in a conflict—Syria alone is thought to have over 1000 different factions.[27] But not all groups are created equal. Some are influential—that is, they consistently overcome problems of collective action and mobilize in the pursuit of common goals; others are not. Group influence derives from two attributes: the strength of vertical connections between social groups and their leaders, and the horizontal connections between the leadership inside of a group.[28] These "vertical and horizontal ties combine to create the social terrain upon which politics is conducted."[29] Groups with strong horizontal and vertical ties create the political order of a state. Because of the absence of strong horizontal and vertical ties within the "governments" of Iraq and Afghanistan, this chapter treats these internationally recognized governments as just another group or actor amongst many.

The strength of vertical or horizontal connections can be determined by the number of social ties that connect actors and groups. A greater density of social ties among a particular group improves the "prospects for collective action."[30] While individual ties are not necessarily equal in strength, a single tie—for example, the religious designation Sunni—might not be sufficient to mobilize a group. But a collection of ties, like the strands of a rope, can form a strong bond that transforms a loose coalition of groups into a single cohesive political actor.

Vertical ties are the connection between a leader and his social base such as a village or another type of community.[31] Weak vertical ties result when an outside element imposes itself onto local communities without any prior contact or based on only a superficial connection. Che Guevara, exporting his Cuban revolution to Bolivia, found an Indian population that was "parochial and suspicious of any outsiders"; he failed to win any cooperation.[32] In contrast, a strong vertical connection may be found in a local religious or business leader who grew up in a community and is tightly *integrated* into numerous local networks. But even the strong vertical connection of a "local" leader implies only parochial interests. The impact of a group at a level above the geographic area of a community or village is limited without horizontal connections to other leaders.

Horizontal connections "link people across space and connect different geographic and social sites. They are formed between mobile individuals drawn from beyond a single social and geographical locale."[33] These ties make possible the "consolidation of shared political visions" that cross geographic areas larger than a village or local community.[34] Strong horizontal connections are frequently found among leaders who share a common bonding experience. It was Afghan refugee camps, created by the Soviet invasion of Afghanistan, that produced a core group of leaders who would go on to form the Taliban—a group that would later sweep through the Pashtun regions of southern and eastern Afghanistan.[35] While the common experience of refugee camps and religious schooling strengthened the horizontal ties between Taliban leaders, the powerful warlords, denied the common bond of a Soviet enemy, failed to unify and were thus overrun by the Taliban.[36] In Iraq, Abu Bakr al-Baghdadi, the leader of the Islamic State (ISI), is thought to have connected to other radicals during his time in U.S./Iraqi prisons during the Iraq War.[37]

Figure 4.1 Group Types

	Strong	*Weak*
Strong	Integrated	Vanguard
Weak	Parochial	Fragmented

The relative strength of vertical and horizontal connections results in four generic group types: integrated, vanguard, parochial, and fragmented. Integrated groups are characterized by strong vertical and horizontal ties and tend to indicate a group that may maintain political viability in the long run. Vanguard groups have strong horizontal ties, but lack the strong vertical connections necessary to build a sustained political presence. Parochial groups suffer from weak horizontal ties between leaders but strong ties between an individual leader and a particular community. A parochial group that spans a large geographic area consists of a loose coalition of leaders who maintain little ability to coordinate activities. Finally, fragmented groups are "unable to draw on any kind of strong social ties"—weak horizontal and vertical ties create fluid coalitions with limited ability to coordinate action or draw on sufficient social resources.

III. What Has the United States Wrought in Iraq and Afghanistan?

The framework described in Part Two looks at what makes groups influential and how different types of interactions between groups create different political orders. One can apply that framework to the history of Iraq and Afghanistan to assess the strength of groups and define the political order of these countries. From the standpoint of the initial framework, the United States plays the role of a *vanguard* group. Strong horizontal ties amongst American commanders helped coordinate U.S. efforts, but the decisive question is how the United States impacted the political order inside of Iraq and Afghanistan. Let us focus here on three ways in which the United States may have altered these political orders: How did the distribution of resources (money, equipment, and training) affect different groups? Did military conflict create learning organizations, and thus strengthen some groups over others?[38, 39] Finally, the effects of U.S. policy in Iraq and Afghanistan transcend the aid and combat with which the United States has been directly involved. U.S. forces, in short, unleashed a long period of conflict beyond what they intended or could hope to control. How has this broad and sustained conflict contributed to a new political order in Iraq and Afghanistan?

The Impact of Resources

As the U.S. War on Terror progressed, both Iraq and Afghanistan became the largest recipients of U.S. foreign aid. In Iraq for example, at least $25 billion was spent on equipping and training the Iraqi Army.[40] Resources alone cannot create a strong or influential group, and resources impact different groups in different ways. Looking at the variable impact of outside resources on group effectiveness, Paul Staniland argues that money follows the flow of social networks; i.e., loose coalitions can fragment, bickering over resources while cohesive groups with strong ties can leverage this support.[41] An example of how external support can influence similar groups in different ways can be found in Afghanistan during the 80's and early 90's. While Pakistani intelligence supported multiple Pashtun groups during this time, it was not until the rise of the Taliban and their "overlapping networks of organizers embedded in local communities" that any Pashtun group was able to exert control in Afghanistan. Thus, resources can reinforce groups with strong vertical and horizontal ties, while the same resources in the hands of a less cohesive group can cause group fragmentation. The question remains, which groups have been affected the most by U.S. resources and how?

The Impact of Military Intervention on the Ability of Organizations to Learn

In the selective anarchy of civil war, groups must learn or face extinction. The Islamic State's 2005–2009 incarnation, AQI, killed Sunni elders and attempted to displace traditionally powerful Sunni tribes.[42] These tribes responded by allying with U.S. forces and the Shi'ite-dominated government. But the current Islamic

State may have learned to better capitalize on the grievances of Sunni tribes. As of this writing, violence perpetrated by the Islamic State seems targeted at non-Sunni populations. Similarly, a resurgent Taliban seems to "avoid the strict rules of behavior they imposed before 2002" on the population of Afghanistan.[43] In a 2013 poll of Afghanistan, only 7 percent of those surveyed indicate the Taliban as a reason for Afghanistan "heading in the wrong direction" as a country.[44] Additionally, when it comes to reporting crimes to "authorities," 51 percent of the population in provinces like Zabul frequently submit issues to the Taliban for resolution.[45] Experiencing defeat at the hands of American forces and their allies has revealed that these organizations can learn.

Not all groups learn, however. Kurdish fighters, sheltered from external pressures since Operation Desert Fox in 1994, never truly faced the selective pressures of combat during the U.S. occupation. In the first real encounter between the Islamic State and Kurdish peshmerga fighters, the Islamic State captured towns, an oilfield, and the major hydroelectric dam in Mosul.[46] It was only the introduction of U.S. airpower that allowed the Kurds to recapture this terrain. Groups are not static organizations—there is potential for previously "defeated" groups to learn. And previously successful groups may fixate on lessons that are no longer applicable in a rapidly changing political environment. Which groups have learned the right lessons for today's modern environment?

The Impact on Social Bases

Social bases shift throughout the course of a conflict, altering the strength of vertical ties and the breadth of a group's geographic control. By mid-2003 in Afghanistan, "as many as three million refugees" returned home.[47] This demographic shift has altered the traditional rural/urban divide to the detriment of the traditional rural elite; by 2009 the population of Kabul rose by almost two million.[48] The violence that slowly subsided in Baghdad throughout 2007 coincided with the redistribution of Sunni/Shi'ite populations along ethnic lines.[49] Many of the Sunnis who left Baghdad moved to the periphery of the Sunni dominated city of Baqubah. In 2009, the United Nations High Commissioner for Refugees estimated the Iraqi refugee population as somewhere between 1.7 and 2.3 million.[50] These shifts in a social base can have a strong impact on the influence of certain groups, increasing the power of unknown elements and undercutting traditional sources of power.

What has the United States wrought in Iraq and Afghanistan? "The building blocks of political order and governance are found in [the] interactions between armed actors."[51] This question requires an observer first to understand the group dynamics inside a country.[52]

The United States affected the groups and political typology in at least three ways: the resources it provided potentially fragmented loose coalitions or strengthened groups with strong mechanisms of internal control; fighting over the last decade afforded some groups the opportunity to learn; and the violence inherent in conflict also altered social bases through death and displacement. While this paper does not provide a simple or direct answer to the question, "What has the United States wrought?," by presenting a framework for identifying and evaluating the key groups in Iraq and Afghanistan, it does lay the foundation for understanding the impact of the U.S. intervention in each country. And this answer is critical to understanding how the United States may influence Iraq and Afghanistan in a post–2014 world.

Answering the question of what the United States has wrought in Iraq and Afghanistan permits the development of better U.S. policy in the region going forward. As U.S. policymakers develop future policy, they must confront three key questions. First, what interest(s) is the United States trying to realize? Second, what means are at the disposal of the policymakers, and what are the constraints on those resources? Third (more of a consideration than a question), what influence does the U.S. actually exert over the different groups and actors in these countries?

In light of the history of U.S. involvement and how we answer the question of what the United States has wrought, policymakers might consider the following: the means or "tools" of policy range from the use of military force to diplomacy to food stuffs. Policy tools must be considered in light of the fact that aid follows social connections, fragmenting some groups while reinforcing others.

Policymakers must also consider constraints. The idea of putting "boots on the ground" in the United States of today is rarely welcomed. Regardless of the tools selected, each must be linked to an interest. Removing weapons of mass destruction from the hands of a dictator initially took U.S. troops into Iraq, while the next decade focused on rebuilding a state. The counterterrorism mission in Afghanistan expanded to involve state-building. Policymakers sought to "build a stable, reasonably functional Afghan state," a state that would not become an Al Qaeda safe haven in the future.[53] What are U.S. interests today?

Our final question is one of influence. The last decade of war in Iraq and Afghanistan has generated outcomes that were frequently not anticipated.[54] Recently, the combination of U.S. airstrikes with an *integrated* group—the Kurds—allowed peshmerga fighters to regain control of important terrain like the Mosul hydroelectric dam. But this limited objective was realized because of a common interest held by Kurds and Americans alike.

The U.S. must also understand that the same horizontal and vertical connections that allow powerful groups to survive inside of a political order do not always receive external guidance well, making the achievement of policy objectives through proxy forces highly problematic.[55] Thus, policymakers must develop policies with a strong sense of humility. It is possible that political orders can be influenced at the margins, but the ability to direct large shifts in political order is questionable.

Avoiding foreign policy failures requires understanding what America has wrought. And better understanding these lessons can help us better assess what it is that we as policymakers can achieve.

RECOMMENDED READINGS

Barfield, T. 2012. *Afghanistan: A Cultural and Political History*. Princeton, NJ.

Filkins, D. 2014. "What We Left Behind." *The New Yorker.*

Lahoud, N., and M. al-Ubaydi. 2014. "The War of Jihadists Against Jihadists in Syria." *CTC Sentinel* 7, no. 3 (March): 1–6.

Marr, P. 2012. *The Modern History of Iraq*. Boulder, CO.

Staniland, P. 2014. *Networks of Rebellion: Explaining Insurgent Cohesion and Collapse.* Ithaca, NY.

-----. 2012. "Organizing Insurgency: Networks, Resources, and Rebellion in South Asia." *International Security* 37, no. 1 (Summer): 142–177.

NOTES

[1]Fontini Christia, *Alliance Formations in Civil Wars* (Cambridge: Cambridge University Press), 33.

[2]Paul Staniland, "States, Insurgents, and Wartime Political Orders," *Perspectives on Politics* 10, no. 2 (June 2012): 243–64, 247.

[3]Jacob N. Shapiro, "Iraq Overview," *Empirical Studies of Conflict*, accessed May 26, 2015, https://esoc.princeton.edu/country/iraq#Geography.

[4]Phebe Marr, *The Modern History of Iraq* (Boulder, CO: Westview Press, 2012), 258.

[5]Kenneth Katzman, "Iraq: Elections, Government, and Constitution," Congressional Research Service, 3, accessed May 26, 2015, http://fpc.state.gov/documents/organization/76838.pdf.

[6]Marr, *The Modern History of Iraq*, 298.

[7]This commentary on the use of rape is based on the authors' experiences in the northern deserts of Iraq in 2007–2008. In order to move personnel from Syria into Iraq, AQ operatives would rape the daughters of rural families. Fathers, to avoid losing face, would marry the daughters to the operatives, creating a familial connection in the village. AQI used these connections as way stations for groups transiting between Syria and the major road systems of Iraq.

[8]See Stephen Biddle, Jeffrey A. Friedman, Jacob N. Shapiro. "Testing the Surge: Why Did

Violence Decline in Iraq in 2007?," *International Security* 37, no. 1 (Summer 2012): 7–40, for background on Sunni efforts to break with AQI. Biddle, Friedman, and Shapiro determine that it was the Sunni tribal uprisings *and* the surge of American forces that reduce violence in 2007–2008.

[9]Marr, *The Modern History of Iraq*, 322.

[10]Dexter Filkins, "What We Left Behind," *The New Yorker* (May 15, 2015), http://www.newyorker.com/magazine/2014/04/28/what-we-left-behind.

[11]Tim Arango, Kareem Fahim, and Ben Hubbard, "Rebels' Fast Strike in Iraq Was Years in the Making," *The New York Times* (June 17, 2014), http://www.nytimes.com/2014/06/15/world/middleeast/rebels-fast-strike-in-iraq-was-years-in-the-making.html?_r=0#.

[12]Paul Staniland, *Networks of Rebellion: Explaining Insurgent Cohesion and Collapse* (Ithaca, NY: Cornell University Press, 2014), 129.

[13]Staniland, *Networks of Rebellion*, 129.

[14]Thomas Barfield, *Afghanistan: A Cultural and Political History* (Princeton, NJ: Princeton University Press, 2012), 263.

[15]Barfield, *Afghanistan: A Cultural and Political History*, 270. This method of conquest—defection instead of military victory—is not isolated to Afghanistan. The Islamic State has benefited greatly from the inclusion of certain local Sunni tribes, allowing IS forces to expand more rapidly than a force dependent solely on military victory.

[16]Christia, *Alliance Formations in Civil Wars*, 101.

[17]Barfield, *Afghanistan: A Cultural and Political History*, 261.

[18]Barfield, *Afghanistan: A Cultural and Political History*, 283.

[19]Mujib Mashal, "After Karzai," *The Atlantic* (June 23, 2014), http://www.theatlantic.com/features/archive/2014/06/after-karzai/372294/.

[20]Barfield, *Afghanistan: A Cultural and Political History*, 304.

[21]Mashal, "After Karzai."

[22]Philipp Munch, "Local Afghan Power Structures and International Military Intervention: A Review of Developments in Badakhshan and Kunduz provinces," *Afghanistan Analysts Network 2*, http://www.afghanistan-analysts.org/wp-content/uploads/2013/11/20131110_PMunch_Kunduz-final.pdf.

[23]Mujib Mashal, Joseph Goldstein, and Jawad Sukhanyar, "Afghans Form Militias and Call on Warlords to Battle Taliban," *New York Times* (May 24, 2015), http://www.nytimes.com/2015/05/25/world/asia/as-taliban-advance-afghanistan-reluctantly-recruits-militias.html?smprod=nytcore-iphone&smid=nytcore-iphone-share#. "Profile: Abdullah Adbullah," *BBC* (September 29, 2014), http://www.bbc.com/news/world-asia-27138728.

[24]Guy Taylor, "Nouri al-Maliki undermines U.S. interests in Iraq, plots return to power," *Washington Times* (June 15, 2015), http://www.washingtontimes.com/news/2015/jun/15/nouri-al-maliki-undermines-us-interests-in-iraq-pl?page=all#!.

[25]Staniland, "States, Insurgents, and Wartime Political Orders," 246.

[26]Ibid., 256.

[27]"Syria Crisis: Guide to armed and political opposition," *BBC* (December 13, 2013), http://www.bbc.com/news/world-middle-east-24403003.

[28]Paul Staniland's social-institutional theory looks at prewar social bases and the strength of both horizontal and vertical ties to derive the different wartime organization types identified in Table 1. This paper moves beyond this framework and assumes that groups with stronger horizontal and vertical ties are more influential. It is these influential groups that create the political order of a country. See Staniland, *Networks of Rebellion*, 9, for a brief description of his

social-institutional theory.

[29]Staniland, *Networks of Rebellion*, 23.

[30]Gerald Marwell, Pamela E. Oliver, and Ralph Prahl, "Social Networks and Collective Action: A Theory of Critical Mass," *American Journal of Sociology* 94, no. 3 (November 1988): 502–34, http://www.jstor.org/stable/2780252.

[31]Staniland, *Networks of Rebellion*, 21.

[32]Robert B. Aspery, *War in the Shadows: The Guerrilla in History* (New York: Doubleday and Company Inc., 1975), 974.

[33]Staniland, *Networks of Rebellion*, 21.

[34]Ibid.

[35]Staniland, *Networks of Rebellion*, 129–30.

[36]See Fontini Christia's *Alliance Formations in Civil Wars* (Cambridge: Cambridge University Press, 2012), for an examination of the shifting alliance structures in Afghanistan both during the Soviet era and the wars of the mujahideen.

[37]Tim Arango and Eric Schmitt, "U.S. Actions in Iraq Fueled Rise of a Rebel," *New York Times* (August 11, 2014), http://www.nytimes.com/2014/08/11/world/middleeast/us-actions-in-iraq-fueled-rise-of-a-rebel.html?_r=0#.

[38]Staniland, *Networks of Rebellion*, 29.

[39]Ibid., 30.

[40]Ibid., 32.

[41]Eric Schmitt and Michael R. Gordon, "The Iraqi Army Was Crumbling Long Before Its Collapse, U.S. Officials Say," *New York Times* (June 12, 2014), http://www.nytimes.com/2014/06/13/world/middleeast/american-intelligence-officials-said-iraqi-military-had-been-in-decline.html?_r=0#.

[42]See Staniland, *Networks of Rebellion*, 228, "Organizing Insurgency: Networks, Resources, and Rebellion in South Asia," *International Security* 37, no. 1 (Summer 2012): 142–77, 143.

[43]To better understand the evolution of AQI into the Islamic State, see Nelly Lahoud and Muhammad al-Ubaydi, "The War of Jihadist Against Jihadist in Syria," *CTC Sentinel* 7, no. 3 (March 2014): 1-6, https://www.ctc.usma.edu/posts/the-war-of-jihadists-against-jihadists-in-syria.

[44]Munch, "Local Afghan Power Structures and International Military Intervention," 35.

[45]Keith Shawe, "Afghanistan in 2013: A Survey of the Afghan People," *The Asia Foundation* 19, http://asiafoundation.org/resources/pdfs/2013AfghanSurvey.pdf.

[46]Ibid., 35. This report identifies this level of crime reporting as being regionally specific. Zabul Province is home to many Pashtuns.

[47]Amhed Rasheed and Rahmeem Salman, "Islamic State grabs Iraqi dam and oilfield in victory over Kurds," *Reuters* (August 3, 2014), http://www.reuters.com/article/2014/08/03/us-iraq-security-idUSKBN0G20FU20140803.

[48]Barfield, *Afghanistan: A Cultural and Political History*, 275.

[49]Ibid., 281–3.

[50]Nils B. Weidmann and Idean Salehyan, "Violence and Ethnic Segregation: A Computational Model Applied to Baghdad," *International Studies Quarterly* 7, no. 1 (March 2013): 52–64, 58.

[51]Marr, *The Modern History of Iraq*, 367.

[52]Merely identifying groups is not sufficient. Media coverage of Iraq focuses on the displacement of minority populations like the Yazidis and Christians, but the unfortunate truth is that the very persecution of these groups reveals how little they matter to the long-term

political order of the country. *Integrated* groups with access to large social bases and a common political vision have a better chance of being permanent members of a state's political order. Only when an observer understands the key groups and political order of a country can the impact of U.S. intervention be analyzed.

[53]Staniland, *Networks of Rebellion*, 223.

[54]Rajiv Chandrasekaran, *Little America: The War Within The War for Afghanistan* (New York: Alfred A. Knopf, 2012), 51.

[55]Erica D. Borghard, "Proxy War Can Have Dangerous Consequences," *The Washington Post: Monkey Cage* (July 25, 2014), http://www.washingtonpost.com/blogs/monkey-cage/wp/2014/07/25/proxy-war-can-have-dangerous-consequences/.

5

The Persian Bomb

Prospects for a Nuclear Middle East

BRIAN FORESTER

Writing during the Cold War, defense scholar Edward Luttwak noted that "we have lived since 1945 without another world war precisely because rational minds... extracted a durable peace from the very terror of nuclear weapons."[1] Current U.S. policy with respect to a nuclear Iran, though, seems to reject this Cold War era assumption. While the United States and international community have aimed their recent efforts at slowing, if not altogether preventing, a nuclear armed Iran, Iranian nuclear ambitions are nothing new. In the 1950s, the Shah of Iran received assistance with nuclear technology through the U.S. Atoms for Peace Program.[2] Despite signing the Non-Proliferation Treaty (NPT) as a non-nuclear weapon state in 1970, Iranian efforts to develop nuclear weapons technology continued until disrupted by the 1979 Iranian revolution and subsequent war with Iraq. Upon the termination of that costly conflict in 1988, Iran renewed its pursuit of nuclear technology, signing nuclear cooperation agreements with both Pakistan and China. Iranian leaders have long claimed that Iran's nuclear program is for peaceful purposes; however, President Barack Obama has noted that "time and again [Iran] has failed to take the opportunity to demonstrate that its nuclear program is peaceful... and that is why the United States will do what we must in order to prevent Iran from obtaining a nuclear weapon."[3]

The President's sentiments represent the culmination of rising tensions between Iran and the United States throughout the first decade of the twenty-first century. In the wake of the September 11th attacks, a heightened sense of urgency arose regarding the proliferation of nuclear weapons. Weapons of mass destruction in the hands of terrorist organizations would result in catastrophe, and the fear was that a nuclear Iran would increase the likelihood of such a possibility. Tensions further escalated in 2009 when Iran disclosed to the International Atomic Energy Agency (IAEA) that it was building an underground uranium enrichment facility. New rounds of U.N. sanctions, continued Iranian equivocation, and heated rhetoric from world leaders—including discussion of "red lines"—punctuated the period between 2009 and 2012. The election of Hassan Rouhani as Iran's new president in June 2013 represented a watershed moment in the relationship between Iran and the United States. The leaders of the two nations spoke over the phone, representing the first direct contact between Iranian and U.S. leaders since 1979. Rouhani's election offered a glimmer of hope as he indicated openness to new negotiations and a willingness to increase the transparency of Iran's nuclear program.[4] In subsequent months, the P5+1 opened negotiations with Iranian leaders that resulted in the crafting of a Joint Plan of Action (JPOA), which lays the roadmap for a more comprehensive agreement with respect to Iran's nuclear future. The framework for a final agreement was reached on April 2, 2015; however, the entire negotiations process was rife with delays and setbacks. While a final agreement was ultimately reached on July 14, 2015, diplomats involved throughout the negotiations noted that Iran "appeared to row back on its previous openness."[5] Moreover, Israel publicly voiced its opposition throughout, criticizing the agreed-upon framework and vowing to act in the best interest of its security irrespective of any final agreement.[6] Finally, as of this writing, the agreement is beset with significant resistance within the U.S. Congress, with elements of both parties claiming that the substance of the deal represents a major defeat for the United States.[7] Though the resistance has failed to pass a resolution against the agreement, the issue remains highly contentious in the domestic political arena. Thus, the prospect of a comprehensive and viable agreement that is satisfactory in the long term for all major domestic, regional, and international actors is still highly uncertain.

In light of these developments, how should U.S. policymakers respond to Iran's acquisition of nuclear weapons? To answer this question, this chapter first offers a possible scenario that could proceed from the current situation. This "worst case" scenario begins from the failure of the current agreement and outlines possible effects in the near and longer term. Second, the chapter then poses a series of questions that U.S. policymakers should consider when planning for the possibility of a nuclear armed Iran. These questions are by no means prescriptive, but rather meant to provoke thoughtful analysis of the issue. Finally, concluding thoughts summarize the chapter.

I. Toward a Nuclear Iran

The failure of the current agreement over the future of Iran's nuclear program sets in motion the "worst case" scenario for U.S. policymakers. There are two possible reasons for a breakdown of the deal. First, while a deal was reached under the JPOA, the agreement may ultimately fail politically because of a change in Iranian leadership, because of a significant change in the regional and geopolitical conditions of the moment, or because of resistance to the terms of the final agreement in the U.S. Congress. Importantly, though, the failure of the agreement could result in a return to the escalating tensions and mistrust between the U.S. and Iran characteristic of the 2009 to 2012 period. Second, if Israel rejects the terms of the current agreement as unacceptable, then the risk increases that Israel will launch preventive military strikes against Iran's nuclear facilities in the near future.[8] Inevitably, Israel's public rejection of the agreement will place the United States in an awkward diplomatic position, and it is likely that there will be many voices within the United States calling for strong support of Israel.[9]

The end result of either scenario described above is that Iran would most likely continue its pursuit of a nuclear "break-out capability," the possession of all of the separate elements of a nuclear weapon that can be quickly assembled and readied for employment. This prospect is especially threatening given that Iran possessed all elements except the necessary fissile material prior to agreeing to the JPOA with the P5+1, and most analyses place Iran within three to five years from actually having the capacity to arm missiles with nuclear weapons.[10]

In the medium term, Iran's continued pursuit of a nuclear break-out capability is likely to result in military strikes by Israel and the United States aimed at destroying and degrading Iran's nuclear capabilities. This is because the United States and, in particular, Israel will have what one scholar terms the "preventive motivation for war."[11] This motive for military action arises when a state perceives its own military power is declining relative to an adversary. Therefore, "the temptation is to fight a war under relatively favorable circumstances now in order to block or retard the further rise of an adversary and to avoid...the risk of war under less favorable circumstances."[12] As Iran gets closer to developing a nuclear weapon, Israel's motivation to conduct preventive strikes will mount, even at the risk of wider war, given the alternative of a potential conflict with a nuclear-armed Iran. Thus, Israel, with U.S. support, would likely conduct precision strikes on Iranian nuclear facilities and missile sites. These actions are consistent with statements from both Israeli and U.S. leaders indicating active planning for military options to counter the Iranian nuclear threat.[13]

The preventive strikes are likely to have several pernicious effects. First, strikes against Iran will invite retaliatory Iranian military action, which will most likely involve conventional missile strikes against Israel or against U.S. bases in places such as Iraq and Afghanistan. While largely symbolic, these attacks will invite a stronger response as the United States spirals into an escalating game of "tit-for-tat" with Iran. A second effect of the preventive strikes against Iranian nuclear facilities will likely be an escalation of Iran's proxy and covert activities in the region. While Israel is already waging a covert war of assassination and sabotage, Iran will step-up its own proxy operations against U.S. and Israeli interests in Lebanon, Iraq, Afghanistan, and Syria.[14] Such Iranian efforts would further complicate U.S. policy in these areas of persistent instability. Finally, U.S. and Israeli preventive strikes may actually stiffen Iranian resolve to obtain and deploy nuclear weapons. A stronger Iranian effort to weaponize will invite further military strikes, thus raising the stakes in an escalating episode of crisis bargaining that risks a regional war.

The end result will be an Iran that achieves nuclear status amidst an escalating arms race with the United States, Israel, and Arab states in the region. This arms race will be highly unstable in its early years as Iran attempts to harden its nuclear facilities and create a "survivable force," thus increasing the risk of a regional war.[15] Of course, the effects of a regional war in the Middle East will be global, as approximately thirty percent of the world's oil supply comes through that region.[16] Finally, a regional war with a nuclear-armed Iran raises the prospect of the unthinkable—a nuclear exchange between Iran and Israel. Whether undertaken covertly through a proxy such as Hezbollah or propagated openly, an Iranian nuclear attack against Israel, no matter how limited, would likely be met with an unrestrained Israeli response. Such an eventuality would be a humanitarian catastrophe of epic proportions.

II. Questions to Consider

The preceding paragraphs have painted a dire picture of what may transpire should the current agreement fail and Iran continues its pursuit of a nuclear weapon. While this "worst case" description may seem inflated, it is instructive to consider how policy may help us avoid even broaching this nightmarish scenario. In what follows, a series of questions help frame the key issues for consideration in managing or altogether preventing this crisis from unfolding.

What Impact Would a Nuclear Iran Actually Have on Regional Stability?

While U.S. policy has historically been clear in its opposition to an Iranian weapon's program, some scholars have argued that a nuclear Iran would actually improve overall stability in the region. Political scientist Kenneth Waltz, for instance, contends that it is "Israel's regional nuclear monopoly… [that] has contributed most to the current crisis."[17] Waltz's assertion is grounded in his theory of international politics which conceptualizes security as the primary motivator of state behavior in the international system.[18] Thus, Iran's nuclear efforts are the natural byproduct of security-seeking behavior of a state attempting to balance against its primary regional adversary. "Power, after all, begs to be balanced," and the current crisis between Iran and Israel "will end only when a balance of military power is restored."[19] Adopting such a position would represent a dramatic shift in U.S. policy. Given the increasing instability in the region, however, a shift in U.S. policy may be appropriate. Embracing the nuclear balancing hypothesis would radically change the questions facing U.S. policymakers. Instead of struggling to stop Iran's nuclear progress, U.S. policymakers would consider how to facilitate the peaceful nuclearization of Iran. Could the United States mitigate the fears of Israel as Iran acquires nuclear weapons? How would U.S. leaders sell this change in strategy to skeptical elements of Congress and the electorate?

The opposing view envisions a nuclear Iran as the impetus behind a "nuclear cascade" throughout the region as other states attempt to acquire nuclear capability. Specifically, Saudi Arabia, a regional Iranian rival, seems likely to pursue nuclear capability should Iran successfully develop a weapon.[20] Proliferation of nuclear weapons throughout the region raises the prospect of a high-risk arms race in an already unstable Middle East. Additionally, the spread of nuclear weapons in this volatile region increases the likelihood of a weapon falling into the hands of a terrorist organization bent on mass destruction. This hypothetical—a nuclear-armed terrorist group—is arguably an even worse case than a nuclear Iran. Regardless of U.S. policy toward Iran, preventing nuclear terrorism is in the U.S. national interest. Is it possible for U.S. policy to acquiesce to Iranian nuclear weapons without increasing the risk of nuclear terrorism?

What Is Motivating Iran's Nuclear Ambition?

Beyond the broad question of nuclear weapons' effect on international stability, it is useful to consider the motives behind states' pursuit of nuclear arsenals. After all, Iran's motives may have some bearing on how the United States could best achieve its own policy objectives. In "Why Do States Build Nuclear Weapons?" Scott Sagan reviews the three primary theoretical models that attempt to explain nuclear armament. The widely accepted "security model" suggests that the anarchy of the international system induces states to pursue nuclear weapons when rival states pursue such weapons. As former Secretary of State George Shultz once noted: "proliferation begets proliferation."[21] The "domestic politics model" holds that while international threats certainly play a role in the process, these threats are likely to be molded to suit the parochial or bureaucratic interests of domestic actors. Thus, political interests, not security, are the primary cause of weapons decisions. Finally, the "norms model" posits that nuclear armament serves a symbolic function that both shapes and reflects a state's identity.[22]

Each of Sagan's models bears different implications for U.S. policy. The security model implies that U.S. policy should be aimed at providing security assurances to Iranian leaders. This will require a brokered agreement that includes Israel. Otherwise, Iran's regional security concerns—and thus its nuclear pursuits—will continue unabated. The domestic politics model suggests that U.S. diplomatic efforts will have to become more personal, with direct engagement between U.S. and Iranian officials. Understanding the domestic constraints of Iranian leaders will aid in crafting a coherent and realistic U.S. policy. Finally, the norms model insinuates a menu of policy choices that reinforces existing norms of nuclear weapon policy favorable to U.S. interests. Beyond the norm of nonproliferation as outlined in the NPT, the United States may find it challenging to explain its own nuclear "first-use doctrine," given the imperative to dissuade a nuclear Iran from adopting a similar first-use policy.[23] Taken together, the various models suggest that no one policy prescription will do. U.S. policymakers will need to account for multiple Iranian motivations while also avoiding the pitfall of creating contradictory policy initiatives. What are some of the primary motivations of Iranian nuclear ambitions? How should U.S. policy address and account for these motivations?

How Does Iran Perceive the United States?

A large body of international relations literature posits that perceptions play a prominent role in the strategic interaction of states. In a world of imperfect information, how states perceive each other in terms of power, capabilities, or threat can have significant bearing on how states behave.[24] In the realm of international politics, reality is truly in the eyes of the perceiver.

If perception is so significant, how do states learn about each other? The most direct method by which states may learn about one another is conflict. Through combat, states gain new information, learning about the other's destructive capacity (military strength) and political will (resolve).[25] However, states attempt to assess their opponents' strength and resolve even before the fighting begins. In the case of asymmetric conflicts, scholars have noted the important role that resolve may play in shaping the course of conflict. Because of the significant military power asymmetries, weaker states are much more sensitive to changes in the strong state's political will (resolve) than in its military strength.[26] This is because weaker states recognize that, in a crisis with a much more powerful opponent, they "can only achieve their ends if their opponent's political capability to wage war is destroyed."[27] Political will is thus a significant variable in the formation of states' perceptions of one another.

When weighing policy options with respect to the Iran nuclear crisis, U.S. policymakers should consider Iran's perception of the United States. In particular, how does Iran perceive U.S. resolve to prevent the regime from acquiring and deploying nuclear weapons? If Iranian leaders view U.S. leaders as having the political will to risk the costs associated with military action, then Iran is more likely to be responsive to the diplomatic efforts of the United States and international community. Conversely, if Iran sees diminishing American resolve to maintain the nuclear status quo in the Middle East, then economic sanctions and other diplomatic efforts will have minimal effect on Iranian behavior, and military force may be necessary to compel Iran's compliance. Iran's perception of U.S. resolve will necessarily be informed by its assessment of U.S. domestic politics, public opinion, and observation of recent U.S. experience in Iraq and Afghanistan. How does Iran view U.S. resolve in the Middle East? How will Iran's assessment in turn influence its behavior with respect to its nuclear program?

Iran's nuclear ambitions represent a vexing problem for U.S. policymakers. On one hand, the United States, and in particular Israel, have an interest in preventing Iran from acquiring nuclear weapons. President Obama has reiterated this as a critical national interest, suggesting the United States will take a hard stance against Iranian nuclear efforts. On the other hand, failure to achieve a comprehensive agreement acceptable to Israel will re-escalate tensions and significantly increase the likelihood of military conflict in a region already at a boiling point of instability. Thus, a softer U.S. stance on the nuclear issue may be appropriate. Regardless of the approach, U.S. policy must account for Iranian motivations, perceptions, and the regional effect of another nuclear power.

RECOMMENDED READING

Cordesman, Anthony and Bryan Gold. 2014. *The Nuclear and Missile Dimension*. Vol. 2 of *The Gulf Military Balance*. New York: Center for Strategic and International Studies (January).

Gerson, Michael S. 2010. "No First Use: The Next Step for U.S. Nuclear Policy." *International Security* 35, no. 2 (Fall): 7–47.

Sagan, Scott D. 1996/1997. "Why Do States Build Nuclear Weapons? Three Models in Search of a Bomb." *International Security* 21, no. 3 (Winter): 54–86.

Sagan, Scott D. and Kenneth Waltz. 2012. *The Spread of Nuclear Weapons: An Enduring Debate*. Third ed. New York.

Waltz, Kenneth N. 2012. "Why Iran Should Get the Bomb: Nuclear Balancing Would Mean Stability." *Foreign Affairs* 91 (July/August): 2–5.
Zarif, Mohammad Javad. 2014. "What Iran Really Wants." *Foreign Affairs* 93 (May/June): 49–50.

NOTES

[1]Edward Luttwak, "Of Bombs and Men," *Commentary* (August 1983): 82.
[2]"Iran," *Nuclear Threat Initiative*, http://www.nti.org/country-profiles/iran/nuclear/.
[3]Barack Obama, "Remarks to the U.N. General Assembly," September 25, 2012, http://www.whitehouse.gov/the-press-office/2012/09/25/remarks-president-un-general-assembly.
[4]Thomas Erdbrink, "Iran's President puts New Focus on the Economy," *New York Times* (August 3, 2013), http://www.nytimes.com/2013/08/04/world/middleeast/irans-president-puts-new-focus-on-the-economy.html?pagewanted=all&_r=0.
[5]Justyna Pawlak and Fredrik Dahl, "Exclusive: Iran's Reactor Fuel Demand Emerges as Sticking Point in Nuclear Talks," *Reuters* (June 3, 2014), http://www.reuters.com/article/2014/06/03/us-iran-nuclear-idUSKBN0EE20G20140603.
[6]Anthony H. Cordesman and Bryan Gold, *The Nuclear and Missile Dimension*, vol. 2 of *The Gulf Military Balance* (New York: Center for Strategic and International Studies, January 2014), 10.
[7]Krishnadev Calamur, "Why Senator Chuck Schumer is Opposing the Iran Deal," *The Atlantic* (August 7, 2015), http://www.theatlantic.com/politics/archive/2015/08/why-senator-chuck-schumer-is-opposing-the-iran-deal/400736/.
[8]Cordesman and Gold, *The Nuclear and Missile Dimension*, 10.
[9]For a discussion of the power of the Israeli lobby in U.S. domestic politics, see John J. Mearsheimer and Stephen M. Walt, "The Israel Lobby and U.S. Foreign Policy," *Middle East Policy* 13, no. 3 (Fall 2006): 29–87.
[10]Cordesman and Gold, *The Nuclear Missile Dimension*, 9–13.
[11]Jack S. Levy, "Declining Power and the Preventive Motivation for War," *World Politics* 40, no. 1 (October 1987): 82–107.
[12]Ibid., 87.
[13]For a U.S. assertion that "all options are at the table," see Barack Obama, "Remarks with President Benjamin Netanyahu," March 5, 2012, http://www.whitehouse.gov/the-press-office/2012/03/05/remarks-president-obama-and-prime-minister-netanyahu-israel. For Israeli threats of military action, see Rebecca Shabad, "Netanyahu Says Israel Will 'Make Sure' Iran Not a Nuclear Threat," *The Hill* (March 4, 2014), http://thehill.com/video/in-the-news/199874-netanyahu-says-israel-will-make-sure-iran-not-a-nuclear-threat.
[14]Cordesman and Gold, *The Nuclear Missile Dimension*, 11.
[15]Ibid., 12.
[16]International Energy Agency, "Key World Energy Statistics 2012," 10, http://www.iea.org/publications/freepublications/publication/KeyWorld2014.pdf.
[17]Kenneth N. Waltz, "Why Iran Should Get the Bomb: Nuclear Balancing Would Mean Stability," *Foreign Affairs* 91 (July/August 2012): 3.
[18]For his theory, see Kenneth N. Waltz, *Theory of International Politics*, (Long Grove, IL: Waveland Press, 2010).
[19]Waltz, "Why Iran Should Get the Bomb," 3.
[20]Gawdat Bahgat, "Nuclear Proliferation: the Case of Saudi Arabia," *The Middle East Journal* 60, no. 3 (Summer 2006): 421–43.

[21]Scott D. Sagan, "Why Do States Build Nuclear Weapons? Three Models in Search of a Bomb," *International Security* 21, no. 3 (Winter 1996–1997): 54–86, 57.

[22]Ibid., 73.

[23]For a discussion of recent changes in U.S. nuclear policy, see Michael S. Gerson, "No First Use: The Next step for U.S. Nuclear Policy," *International Security* 35, no. 2 (Fall 2010): 7–47.

[24]For an example, see Stephen M. Walt, "Alliance Formation and the Balance of World Power," *International Security* 9, no. 4, (Spring 1985): 3–43.

[25]Patricia L. Sullivan, "At What Price Victory? The Effects of Uncertainty on Military Intervention Duration and Outcome," *Conflict Management and Peace Science* 25, no. 1, (Spring 2008): 49–66.

[26]Cochran, K.M.N., "Strong Horse or Paper Tiger? Assessing the Reputational Effects of War Fighting" (PhD diss., Duke University, 2012).

[27]Andrew Mack, "Why Big Nations Lose Small Wars: The Politics of Asymmetric Conflict," *World Politics* 27, no. 2, (January 1975): 175–200, 179.

6

Russia Gone Rogue

The Fate of Ukraine and the Limits of Global Integration

ROBERT PERSON

Throughout its difficult history, Russia has frequently come face to face with worst-case scenarios, producing an austerity that has left a deep mark on the Russian psyche. Whether bearing the weighty Tatar-Mongol Yoke of the thirteenth through fifteenth centuries, toiling under a feudal system of serfdom that lasted well into the nineteenth century, watching Moscow burn under the occupation of Napoleon's troops, or starving through Hitler's 900-day blockade of Leningrad, the masses scattered across its vast expanse have rarely known times of abundance. For much of its history, austerity in Russia has undermined accountability of the ruling elites to the people. The deprivations the First World War and the pressures of Russia's late industrialization brought down the autocratic Tsarist regime but replaced it with a brutal Soviet dictatorship that, contrary to the claims of its ideology, was neither accountable to nor representative of the people. The austerity of the late Soviet period, product of a decades-long economic decay, eventually brought down the Soviet regime as Soviet citizens demanded a better quality of life and the freedom to live as they wished. However, the openness and accountability borne of the Soviet collapse was short lived, as Russia's new government struggled to meet the high expectations of the people for the new political and economic system. In the famous words of Viktor Chernomyrdin, prime minister of Russia from 1992–1998, "we hoped for the best, but what we got was the usual." And so the traumatic, painful, and deep austerity of the post-Soviet economic collapse once again eventually ushered in a new regime as the people demanded order and stability at nearly any cost. The government of Vladimir Putin offered a tempting bargain to the country: order and stability in exchange for freedom and liberty. To avoid the worst, accept something short of the best. It was a bargain accepted by many, one which allowed Putin to build the authoritarian system he rules today.

Yet cracks have recently appeared in the system, and some (but certainly not all) Russians have begun to question the terms of the bargain. As memories of the austerity of the 1990s recede into history, is a restrictive regime that bears little accountability to its subjects really the best form of government for

Russia? The protests following the elections of 2011–12 showed that support for—or at least passive acceptance of—Putin and his regime is not as iron-clad as once was.[1] Though the fissures in the foundations of the regime may still be small, under the right conditions—perhaps another wave of austerity as the world continues to grapple with economic turmoil—these weaknesses could develop into major cracks that threaten the stability of the Russian polity, economy, and society.

It is informative to view Russia's involvement in the Ukrainian crisis of 2013–14 through the lens of domestic political stability and control as well. While Russia's intervention in Ukraine can be understood as the result of long-standing Russian perceptions of Western encirclement at the expense of Moscow's security interests, it has also provided an injection of popular support and legitimacy for Putin's rule that had been flagging since the 2011–12 protests. Putin's approval ratings reached an all-time high of 87 percent in August 2014, up from a low of 61 percent in June 2013.[2] This robust "rally around the flag" reaction to Russia's intervention in Ukraine has been fueled by increasingly nationalistic rhetoric from the government and has been broadcast by a pliant state-controlled media. Yet some warn that such boosts to popular support are always short-lived, and recent survey evidence suggests that Russians' support for deeper direct involvement in Ukraine is waning.[3] If Putin's support begins to slide, particularly in conjunction with a sanctions-induced recession, there may be good reason to worry about who will get mauled by the wounded bear lashing out in desperation. There is little doubt that the victims of such a scenario could be Russia's neighbors as well as her own citizens.

To the degree that Russia's leaders may be increasingly focused on maintaining domestic stability as the fallout of the Ukrainian crisis continues, the ability for U.S. policy makers to engage with Russia on issues of national and international security will be greatly constrained. Despite some successes associated with the Obama administration's "reset" of relations with Russia early in the Obama presidency, domestic developments in Russia in recent years, as well as Russia's involvement in Ukraine have erected immense roadblocks in the bilateral relationship.[4] With U.S.-Russian relations at their worst since the Soviet invasion of Afghanistan in 1979, there is little opportunity today to engage Russia on issues of central importance to U.S. security. This crisis comes at a time when the United States faces its most difficult global strategic environment since the end of the Cold War, and many of the greatest threats the United States faces require Russian cooperation if they are to be resolved. Bilateral engagement with Russia has always been a challenge, and that challenge that will only get steeper if the regime's grip on power is threatened. But to fully appreciate the domestic constraints faced by those who rule with little accountability from behind the Kremlin walls, and to appreciate how these domestic constraints have led to Russia's recent adventures abroad, it is necessary first to explore the process that brought the country and its rulers to their current position.

I. The Autocrat's Tightrope

When Boris Yeltsin resigned the Russian presidency on December 31, 1999, the country issued a collective sigh of relief. The announcement brought to a close a decade of chaos, disorder, and social, economic, and political trauma, most of which had been presided over by Yeltsin and his government. In the first several years following Russia's independence from the defunct Soviet Union, economic output experienced a precipitous decline on a scale far more severe than had been seen in modern history, including the Great Depression.[5] Ordinary Russians suffered this economic dislocation while a new class of elites, to become known simply as "the Oligarchs," became increasingly powerful and prosperous by taking control (often through dubious means) of the privatized remnants of the Soviet economy. The state, confounded by political gridlock between Yeltsin and the Communist-dominated parliament, struggled to fulfill many of its basic functions. Not surprisingly, it was the Russian citizenry that suffered most from the brutal economic and political collapse that took place in the first several years of Russia's post-Soviet existence.

It thus comes as no surprise that after a decade of such trauma under Yeltsin—not to mention the tumultuous Gorbachev years that brought the Soviet state to its knees—the citizens of Russia welcomed, even demanded, a leader who could restore some semblance of order and stability to the chaotic reality that had characterized their lives for so many years. Their savior was none other than Vladimir Putin. Following a career as a midlevel KGB officer, Putin led a relatively unremarkable post-Soviet bureaucratic career in St. Petersburg, before being brought to Moscow as part of Yeltsin's presidential administration. Plucked from the Russian National Security Council to become Yeltsin's prime minister in August 1999, Putin quickly cemented a reputation as a strong, stable leader through a forceful execution of the second Chechen War. In short, Putin emerged as the anti-Yeltsin. With Yeltsin's surprise resignation in December, his antitype succeeded to the presidency according to constitutional procedures.

An implicit bargain seemed to be struck between Putin and the Russian populace: the regime would provide the order and stability that the country so badly desired, while Russia's citizenry would allow the regime to take the necessary measures to do so, even if it meant a reduction in the regime's accountability to the people and a ratcheting back of many of the liberties gained in the Yeltsin period. After all, Russians reasoned, freedom of speech is of limited use when one cannot put food on the table. And so, as Putin consolidated his power and brought order and stability to the country, Russians willingly witnessed the "creeping authoritarianism" that characterized the first Putin presidency. Russia's nationwide independent media outlets were brought under state control, Oligarchs who resisted Putin's warning to stay out of politics—men like Boris Berezovsky, Vladimir Gusinsky, and Mikhail Khodorkovsky—were de-facto exiled or imprisoned, and Russia's once-autonomous and influential regional governors were reined in after presidential appointments took the place of direct gubernatorial elections.[6] Kremlin loyalists in these gubernatorial positions quickly became key players in the electoral fraud that produced favorable results for the Kremlin and its "party of power," United Russia.[7] As United Russia gained a "supermajority" in the Duma with the ability to pass any legislation and amend the constitution, reforms in Russia's electoral institutions made it more difficult for small opposition parties and independent candidates to gain representation. Soon the Duma became more or less a rubber stamp for the Kremlin, as United Russia's raison d'être was support of President Putin. Any of these measures taken individually might not have been undemocratic or necessarily illiberal, but when considered as a whole, there was by 2008 little doubt among Russia experts that, during his eight years as President, Putin had succeeded in significantly rolling back democracy and liberal freedoms.

Russia's regime from 2000–2008 bore the hallmarks of a competitive authoritarian regime "in which formal democratic institutions exist and are widely viewed as the primary means of gaining power, but in which incumbents' abuse of the state places them at a significant advantage vis-a-vis their opponents."[8] Extensive public opinion research[9] suggests that the Russian population accepted and even supported this trend away from liberalism and democracy during Putin's first presidency because they believed in what McFaul and Stoner-Weiss have described as the "myth of the authoritarian model."[10] Though the authors argue that Russia's impressive economic performance in the 2000s came despite—and not because of—Putin's semi-authoritarian model, the fact remains that much of Russia's population in the 2000s credited Putin and his strong style of rule with the stabilization of Russia.[11] As such, they believed that Putin had fulfilled his end of the bargain quite admirably and were less concerned about the authoritarian and illiberal direction the country had taken during his presidency.

II. Cracks in the System

Such was Putin's popularity in 2008 when his second presidential term came to an end that he was able to engineer a seamless handover of power to his chosen successor, then-Prime Minister Dmitri Medvedev. The Duma elections of 2007 and the presidential elections of 2008 represent perhaps the apex of "high Putinism," as the political machine built to support the "power vertical" (the central line of political authority flowing down directly from the Kremlin) executed its mission nearly flawlessly, thereby ensuring an electoral result favorable to the Kremlin.[12] In fact, Putin had drawn important conclusions from Georgia's Rose Revolution in 2003 and Ukraine's Orange Revolution of 2004–5, wherein semi-autocratic incumbents or their chosen successors were swept from office following sloppily-executed fraudulent elections that allowed an opening for opposition candidates to take power. Instead, Putin would leave nothing to chance, maintaining tight control over a campaign and election that lived up to Levitsky and Way's archetypical competitive authoritarian regime.[13] Rumors among followers of Russian politics both inside and outside the country suggested that the Kremlin had set an explicit target of approximately seventy percent of the vote total going to Putin's pick, Medvedev. Such a result would imply a landslide endorsement of what was then referred to as "Putin's plan" for the transition of power while avoiding the absurdly fraudulent appearances of electoral results common in authoritarian regimes, where the leader receives upwards of ninety percent of the vote. Dmitri Medvedev won approximately seventy-one percent of the vote total, a picture-perfect outcome for Medvedev and Putin alike.[14] The machinery of electoral fraud "stuck the landing."

Putin maintained a strong stake in the outcome of the 2008 presidential election despite the fact that he was not allowed to run for reelection. Thanks to a peculiarity of Russia's constitution, while greater than two successive presidential terms was prohibited, a president could run for office for additional terms having sat out for one term. In other words, Putin would be eligible to run for president again in 2012. Thus, as many believed at the time, Medvedev was chosen as an obedient and relatively weak seat-warmer in the Kremlin who would voluntarily step aside to make way for a second Putin presidency in 2012. In the meantime the immensely popular Putin would maintain his public profile as prime minister while holding what many believed were the real reins on power. The fact that Putin engineered and executed such a plan (for indeed, this is precisely the plan that was implemented in 2012) demonstrated his confidence in his hold over the political system. Rather than amend the constitution, which could have easily been achieved with United Russia's constitutional majority, Putin remained confident that he could formally vacate the Kremlin for four years, only to return again in 2012.

While public support in the Putin-Medvedev tandem remained high, undercurrents of dissatisfaction were building under the frozen surface of the Russian political sphere. Research shows that support for greater democracy in Russia had been building throughout Putin's second term (2004–8).[15] As the painful memory of the traumatic Yeltsin era receded and the Russian economy took off, increased prosperity led to greater aspirations among Russia's growing urban middle class, particularly among younger generations who were less scarred by the chaos of the late-Soviet and early post-Soviet periods. As a result, some began to question the terms of the original exchange of stability for freedoms that was the foundation of Putin's early popularity. The validity of the bargain was further called into question by the financial crisis that began in 2008, which hit Russians particularly hard. After nearly a decade of continuous economic growth, the crisis ushered in the chill of economic austerity that had not been felt on a macro level since the chaotic final years of Yeltsin's rule. If the regime and its stage-managed "democracy" could no longer deliver prosperity, had it outlived its purpose? Was it time to reconsider "Putin's plan" and his illiberal competitive-authoritarian model of governance?

Perhaps the first serious cracks in the façade of regime support appeared in September 2011 when Putin and Medvedev answered the question that had held Russians captivated for months: who would stand for election for president in 2012? Would the long-suspected but never confirmed plan be enacted wherein Medvedev dutifully stepped aside, allowing Putin to run uncontested by anyone than the usual communist and nationalist token candidates? Or would the increasing friction within the tandem lead Medvedev to contest the election himself, with or without Putin as an opponent? The mystery was resolved when it was announced that Medvedev would step aside in favor of Putin's return to the presidency in 2012. In what was perhaps a serious misstep Putin noted to the delegates of the United Russia party convention, that the decision between he and Medvedev had in fact been reached "several years ago," and had not been revealed for reasons of "political expediency." This unashamed admission that the 2008 and 2012 elections were all part of the same predestined stage-managed political theater in which the will of the Russian people mattered little touched a nerve in some spheres of society. The Putin-Medvedev tandem, however, did not fully appreciate the gravity of their situation at the time.

The Duma elections of December 2011 tapped into this simmering but growing dissent, touching off a wave of popular protest that took the Russian leadership (and indeed many Russians) by surprise. Rather than the convincing (or at least convincingly manipulated) display of popular support for United Russia in 2007, wherein the party of power won 64.3 percent of the vote, in 2011 the party won only 49.3 percent of the vote amidst widespread allegations of electoral fraud.[16]

In the Duma elections and the resulting mass protests that soon took place in Moscow and other large cities, two features stood out: first, it is important to keep in mind that the Kremlin's mechanisms for committing relatively sophisticated electoral fraud were quite developed and had performed admirably in 2007. The fact that Russia's leaders were caught off guard and failed to falsify enough votes to ensure a more comfortable showing suggests that they had systematically overestimated their own popularity in the run-up to the 2011 elections. The troubling conclusion to draw from this fact is that the Putin-Medvedev regime had become significantly out of touch with the country, a phenomenon that is often characteristic of authoritarian regimes where the absence of political competition prevents leaders from accurately gauging popular support.

The second surprising feature of the post-election protests was the fact that there were protests at all. Russians had been willing to look the other way when electoral fraud was committed in the 1999–2000, 2004–5, and 2007–8 electoral cycles. Explaining this puzzling reversal is beyond the scope of this chapter, though the answer is likely that the stability-for-freedom bargain had been undermined by the economic crisis that lasted throughout Medvedev's entire presidential term.

In any case, by December 2011, many in Russia were no longer willing to give Putin or his protégé the benefit of the doubt. A series of opposition rallies in Moscow in late 2011 and early 2012 represented the most significant incidents of mass protest in Russia since the troubled Yeltsin years in the 1990s, shattering the illusion of a Russian public content with its path of political and economic development under the strong control of the Kremlin.[17] To be sure, many have noted that these protests did not extend beyond Russia's largest cities and that the percentage of the population that participated was relatively small and largely limited to younger, better educated members of Russia's still-small middle class. Yet the boy who declared that the emperor was wearing no clothes had spoken: popular support for Putin's version of the social contract had been shown to be far from universal.

III. Maintaining Control

These cracks in the system only increased calls for greater accountability from opponents of Russia's increasingly authoritarian political system. In an attempt to quell the protests, President Medvedev offered some concessions in early 2012 that built upon other liberalizing measures he had introduced, often with public criticism from Prime Minister Putin. One such concession was the restoration of gubernatorial elections in Russia, a measure slated to go into effect in late 2012. Just as Putin had drawn lessons from the revolutions in Georgia and Ukraine that toppled undemocratic incumbents, so too did he and Medvedev draw lessons from the uprisings that swept across Middle East in what has become known as the "Arab Spring."[18] Recognizing that harsh crackdowns on protesters could easily generate a backlash that only fueled the fires of opposition, in the lead-up to the presidential election in March 2012, the regime took a cautious approach, calculating that allowing the still-limited protests to proceed was less risky than the alternative. The gamble, characteristic of a pragmatism that has appeared at various points throughout Putin's decade of dominance, seemed to pay off: On March 4, 2012, Putin was elected as president with 63.3 percent of the vote. While such a result would be considered a landslide in most western democracies, it fell noticeably short of the 71.2 percent received by Medvedev in 2008 and the 71.9 percent received by Putin in 2004. Putin would maintain his perch above Russia's political apparatus but without the Teflon-like invincibility he once possessed.[19]

Despite winning the presidency (this time for a six-year term thanks to a constitutional amendment passed during Medvedev's tenure), Putin's election was characterized by continued protests and calls for greater accountability before and after his election.[20] Major protests were held in Moscow shortly after the election, and another series of protests occurred before his inauguration. Yet these protests did not unleash the kind of country-wide cascades of protest that would be required to bring down the regime as they did in the Arab Spring countries or the Soviet Union in its dying days.[21] While some initially thought that Putin's pragmatic streak would lead to a grudging acceptance that a greater degree of political opposition would have to be tolerated, subsequent events revealed that Putin had not abandoned his authoritarian instincts. Besides reversing many of the liberal reforms introduced during the Medvedev presidency, Putin has overseen a new reining in of opposition and protest activity, including the introduction of far harsher penalties for participation in unauthorized demonstrations. Additional restrictions on independent media and opposition Internet outlets have led many analysts to drop the "competitive" modifier in describing Putin's brand of authoritarianism: Russia in 2014 is correctly understood as a case of consolidated authoritarianism.

IV. The Threat from Without: The Ukrainian Crisis of 2014

In November 2013, Viktor Yanukovych, the president of Ukraine, took a decision that—unbeknownst to anyone—would fundamentally alter the political geography of Eurasia and plunge U.S.-Russian relations to their lowest point since the depths of the Cold War. It was in that month that Yanukovych, under immense pressure from Moscow, announced that Ukraine would not pursue an association agreement for a free trade area with the European Union.[22] This unexpected decision to reorient Ukraine eastward toward Russia and its own Eurasian customs union—away from Europe and the West—came as a shock to many Ukrainians, particularly those in the western portion of the country who have always considered them culturally closer to Europe than to Russia.

Mass protests in Kyev and other Ukrainian cities built throughout late 2013 and early 2014, punctuated with violence as Yanukovych and his riot police struggled to bring the demonstrations under control. Despite agreeing to an E.U.-moderated compromise with opposition leaders in February 2014, Yanukovych fled to Russia on February 22 when it became clear that his personal safety was under imminent threat.[23] The protestors on the streets of Kyev—nearly a million-strong at times—celebrated a stunning victory.

So did Western governments. But the conflict was about to take a drastic turn for the worse. Fearing that Ukraine was on the verge of passing once and for all from Russia's orbit, Putin seized an opportunity to take drastic action to restore Russia's interests in Ukraine. On February 27–28, well-armed pro-Russian militants in Crimea began seizing key government facilities across the region. Over the next several days, regular Russian military troops executed the invasion and occupation of Crimea. On March 16, Russian troops watched over an independence referendum in Crimea that produced a dubiously high 97 percent in favor of secession from Ukraine in favor of union with Russia.[24] Russia accepted Crimea with a stroke of Putin's pen on March 18. In doing so, Russia achieved several important objectives: 1) it guaranteed a permanent home for the Russian Black Sea fleet in the Crimean city of Sevastapol; 2) it rectified the historical "mistake" made by Nikita Khrushchev in 1954 when he transferred Crimea from the Russian republic to the Ukrainian republic; and 3) it signaled that Russia was prepared to use military force and even violate sovereign borders to defend its sphere of influence in former Soviet states.[25]

However, the conflict between Russia, Ukraine, and the West was not settled by this bold land-grab in Crimea. Inspired by the "success" of the Russian-backed separatist movement in Crimea, pro-Russia separatist movements arose in other regions and cities in eastern Ukraine, including Donetsk, Luhansk, Kharkiv, Odessa. As the conflict dragged on, some of these protest movements evolved into armed insurgencies, of which the Luhansk and Donetsk rebellions have been the most violent. Throughout this period the Ukrainian military's ability to score military successes against the separatists varied, a consequence partly of the poor training and supplies of Kyev's forces and partly of significant Russian military aid for the rebels. It was Russian weaponry provided to separatists that was thought to have been responsible for the tragic downing of Malaysian Airlines flight MY17 on July 17, 2014 in the Donetsk region of Ukraine.

Throughout the summer and fall of 2014, there emerged a significant body of evidence that called into question Russia's denial of a direct role in the conflict. Beyond supplying military and nonmilitary aid to rebels, evidence has shown that Russian troops have been active participants in the fight against the Ukrainian military in rebel-held areas. Moscow has seemingly increased its not-so-secret military activities in Ukraine whenever the advantage appears to be shifting in favor of the Ukrainian military, making it impossible for the government in Kyev under newly-elected president Petro Poroshenko to reassert state control over Ukrainian territory. Of particular concern is Russia's apparent use of "hybrid warfare" in Eastern Ukraine, whereby Russian military personnel in unmarked uniforms use a variety of tactics and weaponry alongside native insurgents under a thin veil of plausible deniability.[26] To be sure, the former Soviet republics of Estonia, Latvia, and Lithuania—now full NATO members with significant Russian populations—have been left to wonder how (or whether) NATO would respond under Article 5 in the event of Russian hybrid attack on their countries.[27]

Though ceasefire agreements were signed in Minsk, Belarus in September 2014 and February 2015, these shaky agreements have been frequently violated, resulting in new waves of fighting. Throughout 2015, the fighting in Eastern

Ukraine has flared up violently at times as the Kyev government, the rebel fighters, or both seek to consolidate their territorial gains. A new urgency was injected into the conflict in February 2015 when it was revealed that the U.S. Government was considering sending lethal defensive weapons to Ukraine in its fight against the insurgents.[28] Though advocates of such a policy argued that such measures would raise Russia's costs of continued interference and thus serve as an effective deterrent,[29] others were skeptical that such weaponry would deter Moscow and many feared that such measures would exacerbate and escalate the conflict.[30] Though the Obama administration has refrained from sending weapons to Ukraine thus far, one can expect the debate to resurface in the event that large scale fighting breaks out again, as many expect it will.

As of this writing, Moscow seems to be little fazed by the increasingly restrictive sanctions levied by the United States[31] and the European Union[32] against Russian governmental officials and state-owned businesses in the financial and natural resource sectors. Indeed, Russia's response to the sanctions—an import ban on food from Europe and the United States —is likely to have a greater negative effect on the lives of average Russians than the West's own measures.

This is not to say that sanctions have not had a significant negative effect on the Russian economy. A combination of western sanctions, plummeting oil prices, and a weak ruble put the brakes on the Russian economy in 2014 and sent it into contraction in 2015, with the World Bank estimating that Russia's economy would shrink by 3.8 percent in 2015 and 0.3 percent in 2016.[33] Particularly challenging will be Russia's inability to access crucial foreign capital and investment as a result of restrictions emplaced by the sanctions regime. Though this may eventually bring serious long-term pain to the Russian economy, in the short term sanctions have so far failed to have the desired coercive effect intended to alter Russia's actions in the Ukrainian conflict.

Even if sanctions—whether the West's or Russia's own—produced public backlash against the Kremlin's policies in Ukraine, Putin's autocratic regime would likely be unresponsive to such pressure. These facts highlight the limited coercive leverage the West has over Putin's Russia at this time, while any inclination for a cooperative resolution to the broader conflict seems to have evaporated.

V. Challenges to the United States

Today, U.S.-Russian relations are bad, but they could be worse. Contrary to what some commentators have argued, the current situation is not currently, and is not likely to become, a "new Cold War." Neither the West nor (especially) Russia have the resources to engage in the kind global competition for influence and arms race that characterized the ideologically-driven Cold War. Nor do they have the desire to do so. Because the current conflict over Ukraine is less ideological than the Cold War, it is more likely that the conflict's trajectory will be shaped by the competition for interests rather than ideas. There can be little question that Ukraine's fate affects Russia's perceived security interests far more directly and deeply than it affects American interests. Put another way, Russia is likely to go much farther for much longer in defending its interests in Ukraine than the United States or European Union. Thus, we can expect for the foreseeable future constant and deliberate Russian pressure—whether overt or covert—against the Kyev government. Only when there is again a pro-Russian government in Kyev, as well as significant autonomy (if not de facto independence) for Ukraine's eastern regions will Putin have a status quo to his liking in Ukraine. Until then, the friction between the United States and Russia will be immense, with little chance of meaningful cooperation on other key issues. Specifically, U.S. policy makers will have to wrestle with the following issues:

- Is there any evidence that sanctions are achieving their purpose of changing Russian state behavior? If not, will additional sanctions make a difference? Are the United States and European Union willing to bear additional costs to their own economies for the sake of punishing Russia?
- Should NATO consider membership for Ukraine or other post-Soviet states that seek the alliance's support? What are the implications of the Ukrainian crisis for the future of NATO?
- What does Russia's use of "hybrid warfare" mean for NATO in the twenty-first century? How would NATO respond to similar Russian tactics carried out in & against a NATO member given Article 5 obligations?
- Should the United States provide direct military assistance to the Ukrainian government in addition to the monetary assistance it has provided? What are the likely immediate and long-term consequences of such assistance?
- How should the United States seek to engage Russia on other areas of mutual and global concern, including nonproliferation, counterterrorism, drug trafficking, and crime? Specifically, how can we engage Russia in opposing Iran's nuclear program, resolving the Syrian conflict, and countering ISIS?

- Opposing Russian actions in Ukraine potentially comes at the expense of the U.S. interests noted above and others. In the grand scheme of U.S. interests and strategy, is Ukraine worth that cost?
- In using force to redraw borders in Europe, some have argued that Russia has upset the entire post-WWII order based on the inviolability of sovereign borders. Is this true, and if so, what are the implications of this change?
- To what degree have U.S. policies (missile defense, NATO expansion) throughout the 1990s and 2000s contributed to the Ukrainian crisis and Russia's perceived erosion of security?[34]
- What are the implications of an increasingly nationalistic Russia governed by an increasingly autocratic Vladimir Putin? Should the United States actively undermine his authority and seek to develop opposition forces in Russia?
- Russian public opinion opposes direct Russian military action in Ukraine, and signs of dissent have arisen as the bodies of the first Russian soldiers killed in Ukraine return for burial.[35] What are the implications for U.S. security if public opinion turns against Putin?

To be sure, the challenges facing U.S.-Russian relations are immense. Cultivating a cooperative, constructive relationship between Moscow and Washington has always been a difficult business, even during the high points of the bilateral relationship. When the Soviet Union collapsed in 1991, many heralded a new era of mutually-beneficial relations as Russia would join an international society based on liberal economics and politics. Today, that dream is farther from reality than it has ever been in the last thirty years. Though the situation is unlikely to get better any time soon, actions taken in Moscow, Washington, and Kyev may very well make it worse.

RECOMMENDED READINGS

Darden, Keith. 2014. "How to Save Ukraine: Why Russia is Not the Real Problem." *Foreign Affairs* (April 14).

Dmitriev, Mikhail, and Daniel Treisman. 2012. "The Other Russia." *Foreign Affairs* 91, no. 5: 59–72.

Koesel, Karrie J, and Valerie J Bunce. 2012. "Putin, Popular Protests, and Political Trajectories in Russia: A Comparative Perspective." *Post-Soviet Affairs* 28, no 4: 403–23.

Kramer, Mark. 2014. "Why Russia Intervenes." *Perspectives on Peace & Security* (August).

McFaul, Michael, and Kathryn Stoner-Weiss. 2008. "The Myth of the Authoritarian Model-

How Putin's Crackdown Holds Russia Back." *Foreign Affairs* 87, no. 1: 68.
Mearsheimer, John. 2014. "Why the Ukraine Crisis is the West's Fault." *Foreign Affairs* 93, no. 5: 77–89.
Puddington, Arch, et al., eds. 2012. *Contending with Putin's Russia.* New York.
Sherlock, Thomas. 2014. "Putin's Public Opinion Challenge." *The National Interest* (August 21).
Shleifer, A., and D. Treisman. 2011. "Why Moscow Says No—A Question of Russian Interests, Not Psychology." *Foreign Affairs* 90, no. 1: 122–38.

ADDITIONAL READINGS

Colton, T.J., and H.E. Hale. 2009. "The Putin Vote: Presidential Electorates in a Hybrid Regime." *Slavic Review* 86, no. 3: 473–503.
Ekman, J. 2009. "Political Participation and Regime Stability: A Framework for Analyzing Hybrid Regimes." *International Political Science Review* 30, no. 1: 7–31.
Gel'man, V. 2008. "Party Politics in Russia: From Competition to Hierarchy." *Europe-Asia Studies* 60, no. 6: 913–30.
Kramer, D.J. 2010. "Resetting U.S.–Russian Relations: It Takes Two." *The Washington Quarterly* 33, no. 1: 61–79.
Levitsky, Steven, and Lucan Way. 2010. *Competitive Authoritarianism: Hybrid Regimes After the Cold War.* Cambridge.
-----. 2002. "The Rise of Competitive Authoritarianism." *Journal of Democracy* 13, no. 2: 51–65.
Mankoff, J. 2009. *Russian Foreign Policy: The Return of Great Power Politics.* New York.
-----. 2008. "Russian Foreign Policy and the United States after Putin." *Problems of Post-Communism* 55, no. 4: 42–51.
McFaul, Michael. 2010. *Advancing Democracy Abroad: Why We Should and How We Can.* New York.
-----. 1999. "Authoritarian and Democratic Responses to the Financial Meltdown in Russia." *Problems of Post-Communism* 46, no. 4: 22–32.
-----. 2002. "The Fourth Wave of Democracy and Dictatorship." *World Politics* 54, no. 1: 212–44.
Remington, T.F. 2011. *The Politics of Inequality in Russia.* Cambridge.
Reuter, O.J., and T.F. Remington. 2009. "Dominant Party Regimes and the Commitment Problem: The Case of United Russia." *Comparative Political Studies* 42, no. 4: 501–26.
Robertson, G.B. 2010. *The Politics of Protest in Hybrid Regimes: Managing Dissent in Post-communist Russia.* Cambridge.
Rose, Richard, William Mishler, and Neil Munro. 2006. *Russia Transformed : Developing Popular Support for a New Regime.* Cambridge.
Schedler, A. 2010. "Authoritarianism's Last Line of Defense." *Journal of Democracy* 21, no. 1: 69–80.
Shevtsova, L. 2012. "Russia under Putin: Titanic Looking for its Iceberg?" *Communist and Post-Communist Studies* 45, no. 3: 209–16.
Trenin, D. 2009. "Russia Reborn—Reimagining Moscow's Foreign Policy." *Foreign Affairs* 88, no. 6: 64–78.
Tucker, J.A. 2007. "Enough! Electoral Fraud, Collective Action Problems, and Post-Communist Colored Revolutions." *Perspectives on Politics* 5, no. 3: 535–51.
Way, L. 2005. "Authoritarian State Building and the Sources of Regime Competitiveness in the Fourth Wave: The Cases of Belarus, Moldova, Russia, and Ukraine." *World Politics* 57, no. 2.
-----. 2008. "The Real Causes of the Color Revolutions." *Journal of Democracy* 19, no. 3: 55–68.

NOTES

[1]Dennis Volkov, "The Protesters and the Public," *Journal of Democracy* 23, no. 3 (2012): 55–62.

[2]Thomas Sherlock, "Putin's Public Opinion Challenge," *The National Interest* (August 21, 2014), http://nationalinterest.org/feature/putins-public-opinion-challenge-11113. See also data from the "Russia Votes" project, a joint endeavor between the Levada Center Moscow and the Centre for the Study of Public Policy at the University of Strathclyde: http://www.russiavotes.org/.

[3]Sherlock, "Putin's Public Opinion Challenge."

[4]Andrew Kuchins, "The End of the Reset: Why Putin's Reelection Means Turbulence Ahead," *Foreign Affairs* (March 1, 2012), https://www.foreignaffairs.org/articles/russia-fsu/2012-03-01/end-reset.

[5]*Regiony Rossii, Sotsial'No-Ekonomicheskie Pokazateli; Statisticheskii Sbornik*. 2008. (Moskva: Federal'naia sluzhba gosudarstvennoi' statistic).

[6]Robert Person, "Pensions, Potholes, and Public Opinion: The Politics of Blame in Putin's Power Vertical," *Post-Soviet Affairs* 31, no. 5 (2015): 420–47.

[7]Mikhain Myagkov, Peter Ordeshook, and Dimitri Shakin, *The Forensics of Election Fraud: Russia and Ukraine* (Cambridge: Cambridge University Press, 2009).

[8]Steven Levitsky and Lucan Way, *Competitive Authoritarianism: Hybrid Regimes After the Cold War*. (Cambridge: Cambridge University Press, 2008), 5.

[9]Robert Person, "Nothing to Gain but Your Chains: Popular Support for Democracy and Authoritarianism in the Former Soviet Union" (PhD diss., Yale University, 2009), http://gradworks.umi.com/34/40/3440584.html.

[10]Michael McFaul and Kathryn Stoner-Weiss, "The Myth of the Authoritarian Model—How Putin's Crackdown Holds Russia Back," *Foreign Affairs* 87, no. 1 (2008): 68–84, 68.

[11]T.J. Colton and H.E. Hale, "The Putin Vote: Presidential Electorates in a Hybrid Regime." *Slavic Review* (2009): 473–503.

[12]Myagkov, Ordeshook, and Shakin, *The Forensics of Electoral Fraud.*

[13]Levitsky and Way, *Competitive Authoritarianism.*

[14]William A. Clark, "The Presidential Transition in Russia, March 2008," *Electoral Studies* 28, no. 2 (2009): 342–5.

[15]Person, "Nothing to Gain But Your Chains."

[16]Jim Nichol, *Russia's December 2011 Legislative Election: Outcome and Implications*, Congressional Research Service, 2011. See also Ora John Reuter, "United Russia and the 2011 Elections," *Russian Analytical Digest 102* (2011): 2–6.

[17]Volkov, "The Protesters and the Public."

[18]Pavel Baev, "Russia's Counter-Revolutionary Stance toward the Arab Spring," *Insight Turkey* 13, no. 3 (2009): 11–19. See also Mark Katz, "Russia and the Arab Spring," *Russian Analytical Digest* 98 (2011).

[19]Gel'man, Vladimir, "Cracks in the Wall: Challenges to Electoral Authoritarianism in Russia," *Problems of Post-Communism* 60, no. 2 (2013): 3–10.

[20]Karrie J. Koesel and Valerie J. Bunce, "Putin, Popular Protests, and Political Trajectories in Russia: A Comparative Perspective," *Post-Soviet Affairs* 28, no. 4 (2012): 403–23.

[21]Mark R. Beissinger, *Nationalist Mobilization and the Collapse of the Soviet State* (Cambridge University Press, 2002).

[22]For a political economic analysis of the European Union's "Deep and Comprehensive Free Trade Agreements," including that which was rejected by Yanukovych, see Panagiota Manoli,

"Political Economy Aspects of Deep and Comprehensive Free Trade Agreements," *Eastern Journal of European Studies* 4, no. 2 (2013): 51–73.

[23]Serhiy Kudelia, "The House That Yanukovych Built," *Journal of Democracy* 25, no. 3 (2014): 19–34.

[24]Carol Morello, Pamela Constable, and Anthony Faiola, "Crimeans Vote to Break Away From Ukraine, Join Russia," *The Washington Post* (March 16, 2014), http://www.washingtonpost.com/world/2014/03/16/ccec2132-acd4-11e3-a06a-e3230a43d6cb_story.html.

[25]Jeffrey Mankoff, "Russia's Latest Land Grab: How Putin Won Crimea and Lost Ukraine," *Foreign Affairs* 93 (2014): 60–8, 60.

[26]Lawrence Freedman, "Ukraine and the Art of Limited War," *Survival* 56, no. 6 (2014): 7–38.

[27]North Atlantic Treaty (1949), http://www.nato.int/cps/en/natohq/official_texts_17120.htm.

[28]Peter Baker, "Obama Said to Resist Growing Pressure From All Sides to Arm Ukraine," *The New York Times* (March 10, 2015), http://www.nytimes.com/2015/03/11/us/politics/obama-said-to-resist-growing-pressure-from-all-sides-to-arm-ukraine.html.

[29]Ivo Daalder, et al., "Preserving Ukraine's Independence, Resisting Russian Aggression: What the United States and NATO Must Do," Joint Report of the Brookings Institution, the Atlantic Council, and the Chicago Council on Foreign Relations, 2015, http://www.brookings.edu/~/media/Research/Files/Reports/2015/02/ukraine-independence-russian-aggression/UkraineReport_February2015_FINAL.pdf?la=en.

[30]John J. Mearsheimer, "Don't Arm Ukraine," *The New York Times* (February 8, 2015), http://www.nytimes.com/2015/02/09/opinion/dont-arm-ukraine.html. Stephen Walt, "Why Arming Kiev is a Really, Really Bad Idea," *Foreign Policy* (February 9, 2015), http://foreignpolicy.com/2015/02/09/how-not-to-save-ukraine-arming-kiev-is-a-bad-idea. Robert Person, "Arming Ukraine is First Step on Slippery Slope," *The Moscow Times* (February 11, 2015), http://www.themoscowtimes.com/opinion/article/arming-ukraine-is-first-step-on-slippery-slope/515772.html.

[31]"Ukraine and Russia Sanctions," U.S. Department of State, http://www.state.gov/e/eb/tfs/spi/ukrainerussia/.

[32]"EU Restrictive Measures In Response To the Crisis In Ukraine," The European Council and the Council of the European Union, http://www.consilium.europa.eu/en/policies/sanctions/ukraine-crisis/.

[33]The World Bank, "The Dawn of a New Economic Era?" Russia Economic Report No. 33 (April 1, 2015), http://www.worldbank.org/content/dam/Worldbank/document/eca/russia/rer33-eng.pdf.

[34]John J. Mearsheimer, "Why the Ukraine Crisis is the West's Fault," *Foreign Affairs* 93, no. 5 (2014): 77–89.

[35]Sherlock, "Putin's Public Opinion Challenge."

7

The Soldier and the Narco-State

Cartels, Federales, *and the Future of Latin America*

JOHN KENDALL

On December 3, 1823, President James Monroe used his seventh State of the Union address to outline what would become the Monroe Doctrine: a foreign policy designed to stake out U.S. interests in Latin America. The doctrine warned that the European powers, particularly those led by monarchs, were henceforth prohibited from attempting to recapture their newly independent colonies. When Theodore Roosevelt reemphasized the Monroe Doctrine by adding his Corollary, he quoted the subtle African proverb, "Speak softly and carry a big stick, and you will go far." Knowing that the threat of force alone could intimidate an opponent into submission, Roosevelt proposed a form of deterrence in Latin America. The Monroe Doctrine was a resource intense strategy that would be tapped as justification for U.S. intervention in the Western Hemisphere throughout the twentieth century. President John F. Kennedy would utilize the doctrine during the Cuban Missile Crisis of 1961. President George H. W. Bush would cite it as impetus for Operation Just Cause in 1989, which resulted in the overthrow of Panamanian President Manuel Noriega. In all of these instances, overwhelming military power was either threatened or utilized to maintain U.S. hegemony in Latin America.

Today, the use of overwhelming unilateral military force in Latin America is not a politically acceptable foreign policy option given recent overseas campaigns in Iraq and Afghanistan. Moreover, domestic budget constraints do not support the means to implement such a strategy over a long time period. Despite these constraints, new external and internal threats have emerged to challenge U.S. hegemony in Latin America. China and Iran are active through their use of economic and diplomatic power in the region. Several Latin American leaders such as the late Hugo Chavez of Venezuela and the Castros of Cuba continue to thwart U.S. interests by supporting other leftist governments while forming alternate international political-economic institutions. Finally, non-state actors have emerged to endanger those democratic governments that have traditionally been strong U.S. allies. These three threats vary in their severity from country to country with some combining to produce significant obstacles to U.S. foreign policy.

Over the past decade, the United States has attempted to address these threats by using diplomacy to strengthen traditional economic organizations while building new military partnerships to bolster U.S. power. The key difference from previous eras of U.S. foreign policy is that the United States is currently facing budget austerity measures that might cripple its already streamlined regional policy. Under the Obama administration, therefore, partnership and burden sharing have become integral parts of a strategy that seeks to maintain, if not expand, U.S. power through old and new alliances.

The central question facing current U.S. policymakers in Latin America is in many ways the same question that faced Monroe in 1823: Given the plethora of threats in this region, where should the United States focus its limited resources? This question is more daunting now than it was when the untamed North American continent seemed to promise U.S. policymakers near-limitless prosperity. This chapter suggests that contemporary U.S. policymakers look on Latin America as a problem to be addressed not with a big stick, but with a range of multilateral "arrows," alliances and agreements that can act in concert to disrupt threats asymmetrically and through the comparative advantages unique to the United States.

I. The Eagle, the Dragon and the Persian Leopard

U.S. presidents have often invoked the Monroe Doctrine to protect U.S. hegemony in Latin America. President Theodore Roosevelt used naval deterrence when dealing with external European powers intent on conducting gunboat diplomacy against debt-ridden countries. During the second half of the twentieth century, the external and internal threat originated from a Soviet Russia bent on spreading Communist ideology and nuclear capabilities. Over the last two decades, China has emphasized its soft power through cheap loans in exchange for natural resources while Iran has flamboyantly paraded its desire for allies. In both cases, the United States has chosen to follow a policy of partnership and burden sharing by appealing to trade while strengthening democratic institutions through both State and Defense Department initiatives.

China's strategy has been simple yet effective: it seeks natural resources for its rapidly growing economy. Unlike the Soviets, the Chinese do not attempt to impose their political ideology of state capitalism, nor do they push their trading partners to adhere to the rule of law. Instead, the Chinese focus on providing Chinese-funded development projects built by their own workers in exchange for resource rights. For example, in 2012 China's Premier Wen

Jiabao pledged $15 billion in loans toward Latin American infrastructure while promising to double bilateral trade by 2017 through additional free trade agreements.[1]

The United States is countering this Chinese economic offensive by reinforcing old and building new international economic institutions that emphasize free trade principles. The United States believes that the convergence of two powerful trends in Latin America—the consolidation of successful market democracies and growing global integration—will create incentives for the hemisphere to embrace free trade regimes and thus remain competitive in the global economy. Reinforcing inter-American partnerships allows the United States to utilize an economic comparative advantage at a time when the United States faces a constrained budget.

The United States dominates global trade, exporting goods and services worth $2.3 trillion in 2013.[2] The extent of trade in the Western Hemisphere is telling, with the region absorbing forty-five percent of U.S. exports.[3] In 2013 thirty-four percent of U.S. imports came from this region.[4]

Key to continuing U.S. trade dominance is the utilization of free trade agreements. The United States has free trade agreements in effect with twenty countries internationally; eleven of these are Latin American nations. The North America Free Trade Agreement (NAFTA) alone represents the largest free trade area in the world, accounting for $1.1 billion in U.S. trade in 2012.[5] Since the passage of NAFTA, total merchandise trade among the United States, Canada, and Mexico has increased by 218 percent.[6] The two most recent free trade agreements with Latin American countries—Columbia (signed November 2006, enforced starting May 2012) and Panama (signed June 2007 and enforced on October 2012)—demonstrate the expansion of the U.S. trade regime. In addition, the United States continues to be the largest investor in the region, supplying approximately one-third of all the foreign direct investment to Latin America.[7] Remittances have also become a critical dimension of the economic relationship between the United States and our Latin neighbors. While the flow of U.S. remittances to Latin America and the Caribbean declined about eleven percent following the 2008 financial crisis, the overall figure of $62 billion the following year underscored the strong family ties with the region.[8] These examples point to the economic and political benefits of expanding hemispheric trade.

The United States wishes to maintain its trading advantage both locally and globally. In November 2009, President Obama announced that the United States would participate in the Trans-Pacific Partnership negotiations to conclude an ambitious, next-generation Asia-Pacific trade agreement that reflects U.S. priorities and values. The proposed Partnership's attempt to link the Latin American and Asian economies is important due to the global economic significance of the Asia-Pacific region. Asia is home to forty percent of the world's population, produces over fifty percent of global GDP, and includes some of the fastest growing economies in the world. While current Trans-Pacific Partnership negotiating partners make up about five percent of U.S. trade, Asia-Pacific economies as a whole make up over sixty percent of U.S. global exports.[9] The successful conclusion of this trade agreement will put the United States in the center of both Asian and Latin America trade flows and act as a major economic deterrent against Chinese expansion in the region. (Note: as of this writing, the pact has yet to be ratified by Congress.)

While China entered almost imperceptibly into the region, Iran's search for allies has been more visible. Whereas China's priority is to seek trade partners, Iran is concerned with resolving its diplomatic and economic isolation by developing diplomatic ties with foreign leaders who also oppose U.S. hegemony. Chief among these are Argentina's Cristina Kirchner and Cuba's Raul Castro; Venezuela's Hugo Chavez was a key member of this group prior to his death in 2013 while his successor Nicolas Maduro attempts to hold on to power despite an increasingly deteriorating economy coupled with the opposition's supermajority victory in the National Assembly. Iran has also seen to it that its proxy Hezbollah, a State Department-designated Foreign Terrorist Organization, is well established in the region. Radical cleric Moshen Rabbani, who is linked to the 1994 terrorist bombings of a Jewish cultural center in Buenos Aires, is known to run multiple Iranian cultural centers.[10] Hezbollah is also known to be active on the island of Margarita, Venezuela, and within the Tri-Border region of Argentina, Brazil, and Paraguay.[11] These areas of interest are suspected to be utilized primarily for fundraising; as a result, the United States has targeted specific individuals by freezing personal assets and imposing sanctions on those companies providing support to Hezbollah.[12]

The United States has countered these two external threats primarily through diplomatic and economic means. On the diplomatic front, the United States has promoted programs such as the Pathways to Prosperity Initiative, which provides a forum for an exchange of participants' experiences and best practices. Economically, the United States continues to expand its free trade regime either through bilateral foreign trade agreements or by enlisting the participation of countries into new initiatives such as the Trans-Pacific Partnership. On the military side, United States Southern Command has demonstrated its commitment to Latin American security through security assistance, training, and multinational exercises that have strengthened the military capabilities of states confronted by complex security environments. All of these modes of power projection rely on innate U.S. advantages: diplomatic leverage, economic incentives, and military expertise, all combined to counter external influence in the region.

External threats are not the only concern, however. Mexicican and Central American drug-related violence, Venezuela's anti-American rhetoric, and Colombia's Fuerzas Armadas Revolucionarias de Columbia (FARC) continue to threaten regional stability.* Which of these threats should be the United States' short- and long-term priority? Do they require radically different strategic approaches, or is it possible that in this case one size fits all?

II. Democratic Socialism or Dictatorial Populism?

The beginning of the Cold War triggered a rash of leftist governments in Latin America. The United States maintained its hegemony through unilateral covert and conventional interventions. The United States backed the overthrow of Guatemalan President Jacob Arbenz-Guzman in 1954, despite a lack of evidence connecting him to a Soviet agenda. Fidel Castro's successful overthrow of the Batista regime in 1959 sparked a failed CIA-sponsored counter-coup that ended with the Bay of Pigs fiasco in 1961. Chile's socialist President Allende would also fall in 1973 to right-wing military forces indirectly sponsored by the CIA.[13] As seen in Grenada in 1983 and Panama in 1989, the United States was also not above conducting unilateral conventional intervention if it felt that its strategic interests were threatened.[14]

Lately, there has been a resurgence of leftist governments as a result of globalization's destabilizing social and economic effects. Populist leftist leaders have tapped the poor's frustration with democratic regimes typically controlled by aristocratic elements.[15] In the international arena, the shift to the left is primarily represented by the establishment of the Bolivarian Alliance for the Americas. Venezuelan President Hugo Chavez and Cuban President Fidel Castro initiated this alliance in December, 2004, to oppose the United States-supported Free Trade Agreement of the Americas. The first Bolivar-

---

*The FARC is a 50-year-old communist insurgency that threatened to overthrow the democratically- elected government of Columbia. The movement shifted to growing and moving drugs but is weakened after 15 years of warfare with the Columbian security forces and U.S. support. Ongoing peace negotiations in Havana, Cuba may result in the end of the conflict in its current form.

ian Alliance trade consisted of Venezuelan oil for Cuban healthcare.[16] Soon the Alliance included Ecuador's President Correa, Bolivia's President Morales, Nicaragua's President Ortega, and a large swath of the Caribbean. Together, these leaders pushed their countries to block U.S. economic influence through initiatives such as the Community of Latin American and Caribbean States. Chavez's control of Venezuela was of particular concern given that eleven percent of U.S. oil imports originate from Venezuela. Chavez's antagonistic rhetoric notwithstanding, it is doubtful that Venezuela will end oil exports to the United States anytime soon, as they account for sixty percent of all Venezuelan exports. This economic interdependence of the United States and Venezuela has not prevented Venezuela from forging close ties with America's enemies, Iran foremost among them. This alliance has yet to produce significant economic ties; however, the United States is concerned that Iran is using Venezuela as a staging area for Hezbollah's drug trafficking and Iranian al-Quds operations. These concerns must also take into account Venezuela's public security situation, which has become increasingly dire as crime has risen to unacceptable levels. Conservative estimates place the crime rate at forty per one hundred thousand in 2010 while a more recent estimate places the estimate at sixty-seven per one hundred thousand. To put these figures in perspective, Venezuela has a murder rate four times that of Mexico; indeed, Venezuela has one of the highest murder rates in South America, having quadrupled since Chavez assumed power. Chavez's reelection in 2012 further cemented his power; after his death, the election of his Vice President, Nicolás Maduro Moros, suggested that Venezuela would not reverse course in the near term despite an economic meltdown.

The United States continues to utilize its economic power to promote its ideology of economic liberalism and to counter the rise of leftist populist governments. International institutions such as the Organization of American States serve as a strong institutional defense as they execute programs like the Inter-American Social Protection Network, which aids in the exchange of information on policies and programs that have proven to reduce economic inequality and extreme poverty. Unilateral covert or conventional action against the members of the Bolivarian Alliance has not been considered a serious option. It seems that the United States is remaining patient and observing whether some of these leftist populist regimes, i.e., Venezuela, implode of their own accord. Yet if these regimes should collapse under the weight of their own inefficiency, it could also create future failed states susceptible to the influence of drug trafficking organizations. Drug cartels prosper in conditions of inequality and extreme poverty, and Latin America has plenty of both. The region has already become a fertile field for these organizations to breed and then extend their tentacles of corruption. Should the United States maintain its wait-and-see strategy, or should it take more active measures against the Bolivarian Alliance?

III. Drugs: Immediate and Future Threats

Like any other market, the drug trade is a function of demand and supply. Significant U.S. drug consumption began with the introduction of marijuana in the early 1940s, which initiated the smuggling routes and networks that later allowed for the introduction of hard drugs such as cocaine and heroin. With its "War on Drugs," the United States responded not only domestically, which witnessed increased law enforcement, but internationally as well. Starting in the 1970s, the United States developed strategies for attacking the source of the sophisticated supply system run by various drug traffickers—and that source was located in Latin America.

Drugs became an official threat once President Nixon launched Operation Intercept along the Mexican border in 1969 to stop the inflow of marijuana. Larger scale operations, such as Plan Colombia and the Merida Initiative, have attempted to retard the supply of drugs entering the United States by attacking both the source and the lines of communication that support the narcotics network. In 1998, Colombian President Andres Pastrana's administration proposed a six-year, $7.5 billion plan that sought to reduce the flow of narcotics and associated violence through two main avenues. First, the plan advocated improving the state's security apparatus so that it could effectively target narco-terorrists while securing the population. Second, the plan sought to rebuild social and economic justice systems that could promote the rule of law and prosecute narco-terrorists. Although a final peace agreement between the government of Colombia and the FARC has not materialized, significant progress has been made towards reaching that goal. Violence levels have dropped dramatically in the last decade while a weakened and fracturing FARC negotiates with an increasingly impatient Colombian government.[17]

Since 2000, the United States has contributed over $7 billion to both security and economic efforts in Colombia, resulting in clear gains in the major cities and certain provinces.[18] These contributions are just 7 percent of all Colombian defense expenditures but represent the development of force multiplying capabilities. As of 2008, Colombia experienced a fifty percent drop in heroin production; coca cultivation, however, increased by fifteen percent due to coca farmers' resistance to drug eradication efforts. Overall, Plan Colombia has contributed to bringing Colombia back from the brink of state failure by degrading key drug traffickers, reducing the influence of the FARC, and rebuilding state institutions damaged by the conflict. Key to the success of the plan was the utilization of U.S. Army Special Forces, who formed enduring partnerships with the Colombian military.[19] Operating in small teams, U.S. Special Forces have a disproportionate impact by increasing foreign military capabilities to the point that they are self-sustaining.

Critics argue that while this type of military-military engagement can produce results, there also exist certain dangers. Partner nation forces can either turn against the very government they are supposed to serve, create blowback by committing human rights abuses or by defecting to the drug traffickers. Others maintain that the strategy has simply pushed coca production into neighboring Peru, Venezuela, Ecuador, and Bolivia.[20] It is estimated that in 2010, Peru alone produced 325 metric tons of cocaine, or roughly seventeen percent more than Colombia. In Bolivia, President Morales has practically legalized the production of cocoa as drug traffickers have overrun government institutions at all levels.[21] This "balloon" or "whack-a-mole" effect is a continual problem as the United States lacks the resources or the allies to fully eliminate the coca supply chain. At most, the United States can hope only to disrupt the flow of drugs.

Despite the strategic drawbacks associated with Plan Colombia, the United States now supports a similar plan for Mexico, Central America, and the Caribbean, under the aegis of the Merida Initiative. For fiscal years 2008 and 2009, the plan called for Mexico to receive $1.3 billion in conjunction with an increased Mexican security budget of $9.3 billion in 2009.[22] Central America would receive $248 million under the Central America Regional Security Initiative and the Caribbean region would gain $42 million under the Caribbean Basin Security Initiative. These new institutions are disrupting organized crime, institutionalizing the rule of law, building a more secure border, and increasing the resiliency of communities.[23] The Merida Initiative's broad spectrum is also intended to address the "balloon" effect as the targeting of drug kingpins in Mexico has shifted drug trafficking into states such as Guatemala, El Salvador, Honduras, and revived Caribbean and Pacific smuggling routes.[24]

More importantly, the initiative looks beyond simple security assistance to emphasize institutional reform and capacity-building—i.e., the "soft-side" of foreign assistance—such as improving the quality of traditional law enforcement and judicial institutions. Mexico has started to address some of the underlying factors fueling the violence, such as poor education, lack of jobs, and corrupt security institutions.[25] Despite these efforts, Mexico and other Central American and Caribbean countries are plagued by large levels of corruption that risk undermining any type of success.

Austerity will not allow for another Plan Colombia. The Merida Initiative and its derivatives do not attempt to mimic Plan Colombia in scale, although they do seem to mimic it in scope. The United States has instead instituted a strategy that focuses on creating enduring partnerships with those states that are willing to share the burden of a rising drug threat. There is, of course, a danger in a strategy that relies on partnering and shared responsibility, given that the partners might not be reliable enough to ensure long-term gains, and their interests do not always align with those of the United States. Given these dangers, should the strategy continue or be adjusted as violence increases in countries such as Mexico and Guatemala?

IV. The Worst Case: The Rise of the Narco-State

What is the worst that could happen in Latin America? Each of the three threats considered so far—economic and political competition from U.S. rivals, the rise of leftist and populist governments hostile to U.S. interests, and instability associated with the drug trade—has been discussed in isolation. The truth is that these threats synergistically destabilize many Latin American countries, which has the potential to affect U.S. security.

For example, Venezuela's deteriorating economic and security situation create incentives for the regime to seek assistance from U.S. rivals or terrorist groups. Trade between Venezuela and China increased from $500 million in 1999 to $23 billion in 2012.[26] Concurrently, Chavez pursued a close relationship with Iranian President Mahmoud Ahmadinejad, though the strength of the relationship is diminishing, given Chavez's death, Ahmadinejad's departure, and U.S. sanctions against Iran. Despite a détente in U.S.-Cuban relations, the Castros continue to support Venezuela's economically dysfunctional police state, setting up an interesting three-way diplomatic relationship.[27] Domestically, links between Venezuela and Colombian drug cartels have emerged: since 2008, high-level Venezuelan officials have been sanctioned for aiding Columbia's FARC with weapons and sanctuaries.[28] Venezuela's continued decline is of chief concern to the United States and the region, although the potential exists for a "perfect storm"—an even more robust confluence of threats to U.S. interests in Latin America.

If a perfect storm were to make landfall, it might well do so closer to U.S. borders. In the Joint Operating Environment (JOE) 2008, the U.S. Joint Forces Command considered "two worst-case scenarios for the Joint Force and indeed the World": the collapse of Pakistan and Mexico.[29] The developments that troubled the authors of JOE 2008 have not vanished. By some measures they appear to have worsened as the Mexican government continues to fight the cartels. Mexican President Calderon's use of soldiers as a domestic police force, quietly continued under President Nieto, has challenged cartel influence, yet raised concerns regarding human rights and civil-military relations. Mexican political and judicial institutions remain weak and open to corruption. The Merida initiative is designed to combat these institutional issues, but as with Colombia, institutional reform takes time and its effectiveness is difficult to measure.

Part of Mexico's strategy is to decapitate cartel leadership in an effort to fracture narco groups into manageable units.[30] Unfortunately, the by-product is an increase in violence along the Mexican-U.S. border and in Mexican states such as Sinaloa and more recently in Guerrero.[31] Mexico's decision to confront the cartels with U.S. support is a step forward, yet the demand generated by the U.S. drug market continues to fuel the cartels' influence, making a strong case for pessimism. This same logic applies to Guatemala, Honduras, El Salvador, the Dominican Republic, and Haiti, where transnational crime organizations threaten to capture the state through corruption.

What would be the consequences for U.S. interests were a series of narco-states to emerge south of the border? The humanitarian consequences—in refugee flows and increased violence—would escalate and overwhelm current border states. The strategic consequences are also worrying. Although even in the worst-case scenario the United States' regional hegemony is unlikely to be challenged in the foreseeable future, instability in Mexico and Central America may strengthen the United States' regional and global rivals. An Iran capable of fostering "wicked problems" in the Western Hemisphere would be capable of raising the costs of U.S. intervention further from its shores. U.S. policymakers have a strong interest in preventing the Mexican state of Chihuahua, for example, from becoming the sort of proximate challenge that Taiwan is for China or Ukraine is for Russia.

What can be done to avert the worst case? As mentioned, the Merida initiative has increased U.S. training and funding for the Mexican military and institutional reform, but the plan faces its challenges and unintended consequences. Institutional reform is difficult to achieve when facing ingrained and rampant corruption, and public salaries cannot compete against either the incentive of bribes or the threat of assassination. Specialized security forces face the same issues and are even at risk of defecting to the cartels, as attested by the U.S. trained and uber-violent Zetas.[32] Professional security forces and independent judiciaries are born out of modern societies, yet stable and durable development is quite difficult without these institutions. Successfully jump-starting these institutions is a paradox that the U.S. is currently attempting to resolve through the selection of vetted partners and increased independent monitoring.

The United States faces a wide range of threats in Latin America, but they are not all created equal. They vary significantly in origin and priority, and not all are as daunting as the "worst case" makes them seem. China and Iran are determined to secure strategic footholds in the region, but both countries face uphill battles. China must surmount overwhelming U.S. economic power as Chinese trade is only now at thirty-eight percent of total U.S. trade in Latin American and the Caribbean. The Chinese have pledged to double this figure by 2017. Is this realistic if the Trans-Pacific Partnership comes to fruition? Iran faces a similar uphill battle in its search for allies, due largely to U.S. efforts to contain its influence through diplomatic pressure and targeted sanctions. Threats originating from within the hemisphere, such as Hugo Chavez's attempt to block U.S. dominance and the proliferation of drug cartels' influence in weak states are being countered by the Merida Initiative and new international security institutions such as the Central America Regional Security Initiative and Caribbean Basin Security Initiative.

The question remains whether a strategy that relies on economic dominance coupled with security partnerships will prevail in a constantly changing world. What is clear in the immediate future is that U.S. grand strategy cannot be wedded to a resource-heavy paradigm. The United States no longer has a big stick to carry. This is nothing new for Latin American strategists.

More than a decade of war in the Middle East has shifted U.S. attention from its southern shores. Strategists must now contend with further belt tightening, necessitating an even leaner strategy. A push for increased economic partnership made possible by diplomatic negotiation favors a U.S. comparative advantage capable of securing long-term interests, and U.S. military partnerships are expanding to counter short-to-intermediate threats that risk destabilizing Latin American countries and sub-regions.

The strategy riddle is made more complex by declining resources, but it is not impossible to solve. Policymakers need only exchange their big stick for a set of arrows.

RECOMMENDED READINGS

Crandall, Russell. 2011. "The Post-American Hemisphere." *Foreign Affairs* 90, no. 3 (May/June): 83–95.
Diamond, Larry, et al. 1999. *Democracy in Developing Countries: Latin America.* 2nd Edition. Boulder, CO.
Dominguez, Jorge I and Rafael Fernandez de Castro. 2010. *Contemporary U.S.-Latin American Relations—Cooperation or Conflict in the 21st Century?* New York.
Holden, Robert H. and Eric Zolov. 2011. *Latin America and the United States—A Documentary History.* 2nd Edition. Oxford.
Isacson, Adam. 2011. "Why Latin America Is Rearming." *Current History: Latin America Edition* 110, no. 133 (February).
Paul, Christopher, Colin P. Clarke, and Chad C. Serena. 2014. *Mexico is Not Colombia.* Santa Monica, CA.
Reid, Michael. 2009. *Forgotten Continent—Battle for Latin America's Soul.* New Haven, CT.
Shirk, David A. 2011. *The Drug War in Mexico: Confronting a Shared Threat.* Council on Foreign Relations (March).
Skidmore, Thomas E. 2014 *Modern Latin America.* 8th Edition. Oxford.
Smith, Peter H. 2008. *Talons of the Eagle, Latin America, the United States and the World.* 3rd Edition. Oxford.
"The Balancing Act." 2011. *The Economist* (August 13).
"Transcript of Monroe Doctrine." 1823.

ADDITIONAL READINGS

Alvarez, Cesar J., and Stephanie Hanson. 2009. "Venezuela's Oil-Based Economy." Council on Foreign Relations.
Beittel, June S. 2012. "Mexico's Drug Trafficking Organizations: Source and Scope of the Rising Violence." Washington, DC.
"Brothers in Arms?" 2012. *The Economist* (January 14).
Cullather, Nicholas. 1994. "Operation PBSUCCESS: The United States and Guatemala, 1952–1954." Edited by CIA History Staff. Langley, VA.
Doyle, Kate. 2003. "Operation Intercept: The Perils of Unilateralism."
Hirst, Joel D. 2010. "The Bolivarian Alliance of the Americas—Hugo Chavez's Bold Plan." *Exchange* 2 (December).
House Armed Services Committee. 2012. Testimony of General Douglas M. Fraser, USAF Commander, USSOUTHCOM, 112th Congress.
JFK Presidential Library. "The Bay of Pigs."
Katzman, Kenneth. 2012. "Iran: U.S. Concerns and Policy Responses." Congressional Research Service. Washington, DC.
Kellog, Paul. 2006. "The Bolivarian Alternative for the Americas: Dawn of an Alternative to Neo-Liberalism?" Annual Meeting of the Canadian Political Science Association. Toronto.
Lyons, John. 2012. "Cocaine: The New Front Lines." *The Wall Street Journal* (January 14).
"Me or Your Own Eyes." 2012. *The Economist* (July 21).
National Intelligence Council (U.S.). 2004. Mapping the Global Future : Report of the National Intelligence Council's 2020 Project, Based on Consultations with Nongovernmental Experts around the World. Washington, DC.

Report to the Honorable Joseph R. Biden, Jr., Chairman, Committee on Foreign Relations, U.S. Senate. 2008. Plan Colombia, Drug Reduction Goals, Were Not Fully Met, but Security Has Improved; U.S. Agencies Need More Detailed Plans for Reducing Assistance.
Seelke, Clare Ribando. 2010. "Mérida Initiative for Mexico and Central America: Funding and Policy Issues." Congressional Research Service. Washington, DC.
Select Committee to Study Governmental Operations With Respect to Intelligence Activities. 1975. Covert Action in Chile 1963–1973.
Sullivan, Mark P. 2012. "Latin America: Terrorism Issues." Congressional Research Service. Washington, DC.
U.S. Department of State. 2012. "Pathways to Prosperity in the Americas, Fact Sheet."
U.S. Senate Committee on the Western Hemisphere, Peace Corps, and Global Narcotics Affairs. 2012. Testimony of Ambassador Roger F. Noriega, "Iran's Influence and Activity in Latin America."
Valenzuela, Arturo. 2011. "U.S.-Latin American Relations: A Look Ahead." U.S. Department of State. Washington, DC.
"Venezuela Sees 'Record Murder Rate' in 2011." 2011. BBC (28 December).
Waddell, Jeffrey. 2003. "United States Army Special Forces Support to 'Plan Colombia.'" U.S. Army War College.
"What Future for US-Backed Plan Colombia?" 2010. BBC (June 13).

NOTES

[1]Fabiola Gutierrez and Chris Kraul, "China Commits $15 Billion in Development Funds for Latin America," *Los Angeles Times* (June 27, 2012), http://latimesblogs.latimes.com/world_now/2012/06/reporting-from-santiago-and-bogota-in-a-bid-to-strengthen-ties-with-an-important-regional-trade-partner-chinese-prime-mi.html.

[2]U.S. Department of Commerce, "U.S. Exports Reach $2.3 Trillion in 2013, Set New Record for Fourth Straight Year" (February 6, 2014), http://www.commerce.gov/news/press-releases/2014/02/06/us-exports-reach-23-trillion-2013-set-new-record-fourth-straight-year.

[3]Office of the United States Trade Representative, "Americas," accessed June 17, 2015, http://www.ustr.gov/countries-regions/americas.

[4]Ibid.

[5]Office of the United States Trade Representative, "North American Free Trade Agreement (NAFTA)," http://www.ustr.gov/trade-agreements/free-trade-agreements/north-american-free- trade-agreement-nafta

[6]"The North American Free Trade Agreement," http://www.export.gov/%5C/FTA/nafta/index.asp.

[7]The White House, "Fact Sheet: The U.S. Economic Relationship With the Western Hemisphere" (April 13, 2012), http://www.whitehouse.gov/the-press-office/2012/04/13/fact-sheet-us-economic-relationship-western-hemisphere.

[8]Ibid.

[9]Office of the United States Trade Representative, "FACT SHEET: The United States in the Trans-Pacific Partnership: Increasing American Exports, Supporting American Jobs," https://ustr.gov/about-us/policy-offices/press-office/fact-sheets/2012/june/us-tpp-increasing-american-exports-supporting-american-jobs.

[10]"Posture Statement of General Douglas M. Fraser, United States Air Force Commander, United States Southern Command, Before the 112th Congress House Armed Services

Committee" (March 6, 2012), http://www.southcom.mil/newsroom/Documents/SOUTHCOM_2012_Posture_Statement.pdf.

[11]"Testimony of Ambassador Roger F. Noriega Before the United States Senate Committee on Foreign Relations, Subcommittee on the Western Hemisphere, Peace Corps, and Global Narcotics Affairs, Hearing on 'Iran's Influence and Activity in Latin America,'" (February 16, 2012), http://www.foreign.senate.gov/imo/media/doc/Roger_Noriega_Testimony1.pdf.

[12]Kenneth Katzman, *Iran: U.S. Concerns and Policy Responses* (Washington, DC: Congressional Research Service, 2012). Mark P. Sullivan, *Latin America: Terrorism Issues* (Washington, DC: Congressional Research Service, 2012).

[13]"Staff Report of the Select Committee to Study Governmental Operations with Respect to Intelligence Activities," http://fas.org/irp/ops/policy/church-chile.htm.

[14]Operation Urgent Fury was launched to stop the Cuban construction of a runway on the island of Grenada. Operation Just Cause was approved in order to oust President Manuel Noriega from power due to his connections with DTOs.

[15]National Intelligence Council (U.S.), *Mapping the Global Future: Report of the National Intelligence Council's 2020 Project, Based on Consultations with Nongovernmental Experts around the World.* Washington, DC: National Intelligence Council (2004), 77.

[16]Paul Kellog, "The Bolivarian Alternative for the Americas: Dawn of an Alternative to Neo-liberalism?" (May 1, 2006), Canadian Political Science Association, York University, Toronto.

[17]William Neuman, "Killing of 10 Soldiers Deals a Setback to Colombian Peace Talks with FARC Rebels," *The New York Times* (April 15, 2015), http://www.nytimes.com/2015/04/16/world/americas/colombia-attack-attributed-to-farc-threatens-peace-talks.html.

[18]"What Future for U.S.-backed Plan Colombia?" *BBC News* (June 13, 2010), http://www.bbc.co.uk/news/10208937.

[19]Jeffrey Waddell, "United States Army Special Forces Support to 'Plan Colombia,'" U.S. Army War College, 2003, 10.

[20]John Lyons, "Cocaine: The New Front Lines," *Wall Street Journal* (January 14, 2012), http://online.wsj.com/article/SB10001424052970204331304577145101343740004.html.

[21]Ibid.

[22]Clare Ribando Seelke, "Mérida Initiative for Mexico and Central America: Funding and Policy Issues," Congressional Research Service. Washington, DC (2010), 20.

[23]Ibid.

[24]Ibid

[25]Ibid.

[26]See Patricia Rey Mallén, "China's Paying Venezuela to Stay Afloat. Now Maduro Wants to Be Friends," *International Business Times* (April 15, 2014), http://www.ibtimes.com/chinas-paying-venezuela-stay-afloat-now-maduro-wants-be-friends-1572022, and China's President Xi Jinping Signs Venezuela Oil Deal," *BBC News* (July 22, 2014), http://www.bbc.co.uk/news/world-latin-america-28414623.

[27]Nick Miroff, "Argument between U.S., Venezuela Puts Cuba in Awkward Position," *Washington Post* (March 10, 2015), http://www.washingtonpost.com/blogs/worldviews/wp/2015/03/10/the-escalating-u-s-venezuela-clash-where-cuba-fits-in/.

[28]Mark P. Sullivan and June S. Beittel, "Latin America: Terrorism Issues," Congressional Research Service Report (August 15, 2014), http://fas.org/sgp/crs/terror/RS21049.pdf.

[29]U.S. Joint Forces Command, "Joint Operating Environment 2008," http://fas.org/man/eprint/joe2008.pdf.

[30]Martin Duran, Elliot Spagat, and Michael Weissenstein, "How Mexican Marines Captured the World's Most Notorious Drug Kingpin," *Business Insider* (February 23, 2014), http://www.businessinsider.com/how-el-chapo-guzman-got-caught-2014–2.

[31]Deborah Bonello, "39 Die in Mexico Police Shootout with Suspected Cartel Members," *Los Angeles Times* (May 22, 2015), http://www.latimes.com/world/mexico-americas/la-fg-three-bodies-found-in-mexico-20150522-story.html.

[32]George W. Grayson, *The Evolution of Los Zetas in Mexico and Central America: Sadism as an Instrument of Cartel Warfare* (Carlisle Barracks, PA: U.S. Army War College Press, April 2014), http://www.strategicstudiesinstitute.army.mil/pubs/display.cfm?pubID=1195.

8

After Genocide

Rwanda and the African Future

BONNIE KOVATCH AND DAVID FREY

Material advance is a hallmark of modernity, as is the unequal distribution of those advances. The modern world order has failed to eliminate the gross disparities between rich and poor. It has created political, military, and economic pressures which, even if intended to pacify, can be inflammatory. Among the more insidious examples of this phenomenon are interventions by the developed world into the developing world. These interventions come with great promise, a panacea for the worst humanitarian crises, including genocide.[1] Yet several centuries of developed world domination have done little to address the structural causes of these humanitarian disasters. Rather, developed world interventions have, by many measures, exacerbated crises and increased the risk of fomenting "the worst that could happen," leading observers to ask if interventions are nothing more than self-serving forms of post-colonial domination meant to preserve, rather than alleviate, the divisions of modernity.[2] By considering the relationship between genocide and the current world order, particularly in reference to Africa, this chapter seeks to characterize as a problem the idea of the "international community" as benevolent policemen. It will suggest that it is possible to conceive of scenarios in which the policemen become tacit perpetrators.

The chapter begins by reviewing the definition of the term "genocide" according to both Raphael Lemkin's original definition and as it is understood in current international law. Then, it puts genocide into the context of Immanuel Wallerstein's World Systems Analysis to consider the preconditions necessary for genocide and explore the effects a catalyst such as climate change would have on the likelihood of genocide occurring. We argue that as climate change, population pressures, and even the development of democratic systems aggravate crises in the developing world (focusing on examples in Africa), they also reduce resources in core states. This produces not only global economic destabilization, but massive refugee flows and political chaos, which can compel elites in the developing world to consider solutions as rash as ethnic cleansing and genocide, and make "core" elites more willing to act instrumentally toward the "periphery" to maintain resource supremacy, state security, and sovereignty. The combined effects make genocide one of the possible outcomes of extreme environmental, political, and economic crisis. We conclude by asking what can be done now to prevent the worst from happening, in light of the challenges of the present day.

I. What is Genocide?

Raphael Lemkin is rightly known as the father of the genocide convention. His advocacy led the United Nations to adopt the Convention on the Punishment and Prevention of Genocide in 1948.[3] Using Nazi actions as his basis for understanding, Lemkin defined genocide as social practice in Axis Rule in Occupied Europe. He argued that the Nazis made a holistic attempt to annihilate Jews and others in eight broad realms: politics, society, culture, economy, biology, the physical world, religion, and morality.[4] Total annihilation in any of the aforementioned domains was not necessary for genocide to occur, but intent to carry out this destruction was. As his notion of genocide was evolving in 1946, Lemkin thus developed a critical equation of "destruction" with what he called permanent "crippling" of a group.[5] This became a critical stipulation of the Genocide Convention, adopted by the U.N. on 9 December 1948, which defined genocide as "acts committed with the intent to destroy, in whole or in part" groups defined by ethnicity, race, nationality, or religion.[6] This provision has stood the test of time, resisting calls for expansion to include class and gender, and it has been reproduced without change in such instruments as the statutes of the ad hoc tribunals for the former Yugoslavia and Rwanda and the Rome Statute of the International Criminal Court.[7] As originally conceived, it should be a beacon of hope for nearly all groups facing mortal threats to their continued existence.

II. Conditions Favoring Genocide[8]

Irresolute Democracies

Samantha Power's "*A Problem from Hell*": *America and the Age of Genocide* (2003), argues that the United States, even while acting as a political and cultural leader of the international community, has dropped the lamp of protection, failing repeatedly to prevent genocide. She concludes that the United States must assert its values with greater conviction and consistency, both intervening in ongoing genocides and, even more importantly, preventing genocides from occurring in the first place. In the last six years, America's political and policy elite have begun to hear Power's call. The opening passage of the executive summary of *Preventing Genocide*, a report by a blue-ribbon American "Genocide Prevention Task Force," chaired by Madeleine Albright and William Cohen, declares that "genocide and mass atrocities threaten American values and interests."[9] Today, detection and prevention of mass atrocity are part of Joint Doctrine, the quadrennial reviews conducted by the State Department and the Department of Defense, and the 2015 National Security Strategy.[10] President Obama continually refers to genocide and mass atrocity prevention as a "core national security interest and a core moral responsibility of the United States."[11] Such approaches seem to hold great promise. They scold, often admitting America's "sins of omission" and suggesting a panacea of prevention.

If we allow that genocide now runs against American values, however, we must also acknowledge history. Genocide has frequently cohered with American interests, not only through sins of omission, but rising, on occasion, to sins of commission. The pre-twentieth century expansion of the United States of America came at indigenous expense. U.S. government support for regimes engaged in genocide in, for example, Latin America, Indonesia, and Iraq in the second half of the last century also stand out as glaring examples. Genocide has been so frequent and so uncontested in the last half century that an epithet more apt in describing recent events than the often chanted "Never Again" is in fact "Again and Again."[12]

Since the Holocaust, the United States has intervened militarily for a variety of purposes: securing foreign ports, removing unpalatable dictators, combating ideologies it opposed, protecting American oil interests, etc. All have provoked vexing moral and legal controversies. Yet, despite an impressive postwar surge in moral resolve and military adventurism, the United States, until recently, rarely engaged in military intervention to prevent what most agree is the worst that could happen, genocide. With a few exceptions of recent vintage, American leaders of all political stripes generally refuse to send military service members to combat genocide.[13] When it came to Cambodia's self-destruction, the Iraqi Anfal Campaign against the Kurds, and Rwandan Genocide, to name a few examples, the United States refrained from condemning the crimes or imposing economic sanctions. In the case of Rwanda, the United States even refused to authorize the deployment of additional U.N. troops or change the rules of engagement. The United States also delayed its promise to provision peace-keepers with World War II-era armored personnel carriers.[14]

Dependency

To answer the question "Can we behave better?" we must consider what all scholars of genocide see as a precondition of mass atrocity: the subordination of one people to another. Colonialism is one manifestation of this subordination. A plastic concept, most scholars agree colonialism exists when a non-indigenous power maintains political, social, economic, and cultural domination over a group of people or country for an extended period of time.[15] Colonial domination established durable patterns of economic exploitation which persisted after colonial territories achieved political independence. Even in the absence of colonies, economic dependence and other forms of foreign domination endure, a condition we call neocolonialism.[16]

Sociologist Immanuel Wallerstein developed what he termed World Systems Analysis, also known as "Dependency Theory," to explain this phenomenon. World Systems Analysis theorizes that there are unequal political and economic relationships in which certain industrialized nations (including the United States) and their global corporations will continue to dominate at the *core* of the world system. At the *semi-periphery* of this system would be countries that have a somewhat marginal economic status. They are somewhere in the middle; they are not dependent countries necessarily; however they do depend on those core states at times. Wallerstein's third category consists of the *peripheral* regions, which include nearly every African state. The core nations and their corporations often control and exploit these peripheral states' economies, natural resources, and labor pools. The division between core and periphery is significant and enduring. It is extremely challenging to move out of any of these categories. The core nations have had decades, if not multiple centuries, to secure their advantages. There are examples of countries that have moved from the periphery into that semi-peripheral state. However, it is extremely challenging for semi-peripheral states to move into the core.[17]

Most free-market economists question Wallerstein's argument that states are relegated to the periphery of the world system. They argue instead that increasing economic integration, like economic growth, generally helps poor and rich nations alike.[18] Yet, despite potential flaws in the economics of Wallerstein's approach, economists of sustainability do admit the basic soundness of his concept, acknowledging that movement from periphery to semi-perhipery is incredibly difficult. Despite predictions to the contrary, the uneven distribution of wealth and power remains, and inequities have been growing, not declining.[19]

Neocolonialism continues the redistribution of human and natural resources from peripheral to core states, a process enabled by continuing cycles of debt. As developing countries borrow from core nations to build infrastructure and capacity, or to import needed goods such as food and energy, debt and trade deficits increase. More debt means more risk, and thus the cost of borrowing tends to increase. The process of wealth extraction thus continues relatively unabated, and the gap between rich and poor, not only between core and periphery but even *within* core and periphery, grows.[20]

Tiered Violence

Mark Levene's exploration of the likely contours of violence in the contemporary world proposes a three-tier schema with a strong semblance to Wallerstein's World Systems Analysis model. The implication of Levene's schema is that there are potential trajectories, patterns, and ultimately forms of violence specific to each tier. In tier one (i.e., core), for example, Levene posits that while these states were directly or indirectly responsible, or at least complicit for much of the conflict or threat of conflict, including genocide in the world at large, they were largely insulated from suffering extreme mass violence within their own domestic contexts. In tier three (i.e., periphery), by contrast, the likelihood of violence was high, often because state authority was insufficient to stop its diffused prevalence and persistence.[21]

It was in tier two (i.e., semi-periphery) that the preconditions of genocide were at their greatest, because it was in these states that the driving forces associated with the developmental imperatives of the international system were at their most intense and urgent. Michael Mann offers an alternative, but complementary theory, arguing that process of becoming a democracy (part of the transition from periphery to semi-periphery, and certainly part of the transition from forms of subordination such as colonialism) is often the catalyst for ethnic cleansing or genocide.[22] Both of these theories present convincing evidence that the conditions of genocide remained closely intertwined with the very building blocks of our contemporary global system.

It has been known for decades that the scope, scale, and relentlessly accelerating pace of development are entirely out of synch with the carrying capacity of the planet.[23] We are exhausting land, depleting resources such as timber and water through means such as clear cutting and pollution, and we are driving up the cost of production. Scarcity, whether material, psychological, or political, can both lead to genocide and be the result of it, creating cycles of violence.[24]

Climate Change

Since the mid-2000s, analysts recognized climate change as a "threat to international peace and security" that was likely to affect Africa more radically than any other part of the world.[25] When resource scarcity (linked to the ongoing demands of the global economic system) combines with population pressures (especially youth bulges) and climate change, a dangerous matrix of destabilizing forces emerges. Jared Diamond states, "severe problems of overpopulation, environmental impact, and climate change cannot persist indefinitely: sooner or later they are likely to resolve themselves, whether in the manner of Rwanda or in some other manner not of our devising, if we don't succeed in solving them by our own actions."[26] The consequences are potentially devastating and likely violent. We have seen examples of this pattern throughout Africa in the last twenty years. Population pressure (density and youth bulges) and drought or other forms of environmental crisis were proximate causes for the genocide in Rwanda, for the breakdown of governance in Somalia, and for the mass atrocities in Darfur, according to some experts.[27] The Sahara is predicted to continue expanding, and thus arable land will decrease while populations grow, exacerbating instability in areas as disparate as Mali, Sudan, Chad, Libya, and even the Central African Republic, all of which have had mass atrocities and either actual or potential genocides in the last ten years.[28]

However, while the relationship between population increase in periphery states and environmental stress is the standard point of entry into this subject, the greatest destroyers of planetary resources in overall global terms are not the poor, but the rich. If everyone's ecological footprint were European, humanity would need 2.1 planet Earths to sustain it, while if all were to follow the United States' lead, we would need nearly five.[29] Let us consider for a moment the implications of core states' efforts to continue a maximized control of periphery mineral and energy supply against a backdrop of resource scarcity. In societies of abundance (i.e., the core) psychological scarcity emerges when there is even a "mild reduction in the availability of goods."[30] This condition will most certainly emerge should the core's access to African raw materials be limited by a host of potential threats. The United Kingdom's Development, Concepts, and Doctrines Centre writes:

> Climate change and HIV/AIDS, scarcity of food and water and regional conflict could lead to Africa becoming a failed continent, where even large, currently self-sustaining states become chaotic. Outside engagement and intervention would effectively be

> limited to a small-number of well-defended entry points and corridors, which would provide access to raw materials essential to the global economy. Nations or corporations wishing to trade with Africa would increasingly be required to provide security for their nationals and necessary support to sustain critical areas of access and security.[31]

What is particularly valuable about this assessment is its remarkably frank assertion of the primacy of the national interest. Africa matters because it has mineral as well as fossil fuel resources. The bottom line, hence, is that under conditions of instability, core states will exert maximum political and military leverage to maintain access to these resources.

One can take this argument a step further and imagine a scenario in which climate change or political instability stimulate the permanent displacement of millions of people, as it has in areas such as Rwanda, the Democratic Republic of the Congo, Syria, and northern Nigeria. In this context, among peripheral states which cannot provide services to their own populations, the question of where will the refugees go arises. Climate change realities, in particular, are pushing all manner of states towards radical measures designed to deny entry to those externally displaced. It would appear to be the richest amongst such states which are most exercised about the threat of environmental refugees, and health crises such as the Ebola pandemic of 2014 raise the stakes even further, amplifying calls for closed borders in core states.

Consider a recent climate change war game conducted under the auspices of the Center for New American Security (CNAS). Game players placed migration-prevention as the number one priority in any long-term framework agreement on climate change, with an emphasis on the repatriation of climate refugees to their country of origin as the necessary outcome. The proposed agreement stated non-coercive repatriation as the "preferred" method toward this purpose, though one might be inclined to ask how exactly that would be accomplished for peoples who are already threatened with early inundation. In fact, the implied policy recommendations offered in the CNAS game are consistent with the general thrust of U.S. security thinking dating back at least to the 2004 Pentagon-commissioned report on "abrupt" climate change. Then, as now, the emphasis has been not on humanitarian assistance to states or societies reeling from climate catastrophe but rather on shoring up "fortress America" against waves of anticipated environmental refugees. Behind such thinking too are major Department of Defense research and development programs whose purpose is to develop a range of hi-tech weapon systems designed to interdict and immobilize "perimeter" intruders. Proclaimed to be non-lethal, what damage such tazers, projectiles, "calmative" chemicals, as well as heat and noise weapons, would actually do to masses of human beings in the event of a major "emergency" is entirely uncharted territory.[32] The scenario which emerges is one of an "attritional" genocide, in which victims are denied health and health care, suffer from man-made famine and malnutrition, and generally fall outside the protection of states.[33] While imaginable in Pakistan, China, and India, the peripheral region most likely to experience this scenario is Africa, where one might argue we are already seeing it play out in Libya, Sudan, and elsewhere.

III. The Worst Case

The overriding implication of the above argument is that the conditions of genocide remain closely intertwined with the very forces driving the contemporary global system. What would happen, however, if the resources upon which our system is dependent were to disappear? Before we consider this scenario, we must warn against a deterministic outlook and acknowledge that Africa and Africans, as well as other peripheral peoples and regions, have taken positive steps, particularly in the last two decades, which have the potential to mitigate against the worst case occurring. For example, the world has seen a heartening decrease in the scope, scale, and frequency of state-led genocides and mass atrocities. Sub-Saharan Africa has had its highest global growth rates over that same period. [34] Grassroots programs like Nobel Laureate Wangari Maathai's Green Belt Movement and the Great Green Wall are attempting to stem the advance of the Sahara through massive tree planting programs which simultaneously empower women and promote democratization.[35]

Despite this, some of these positive trends are fragile and there are signs of persistent problems. Few African states have adopted progressive taxation, and thus inequality has not declined. Of the world's twenty-five most corrupt states, according to Transparency International, thirteen are in Africa.[36] For long-term development plans to succeed, they must be coupled with improved governance, a goal yet unrealized for many African states. Agricultural development schemes are also running into the headwind of climate change. And of course, there remain "massive unresolved arguments" between developed and developing countries over who should bear the primary burden of contending with climate change.[37]

We should expect the acceleration of conflict as environmental blockages increase and natural resource competition becomes more acute. We are already witnessing a rise in lesser atrocities which may be a function of this percolating conflict.[38] Groups under extreme environmental stress, for instance, might make the rational choice to fight for survival in some Hobbesian zero-sum game, as food and water resources diminish, and the values of increasingly rare strategic minerals rise.[39] Great civilizations of the past, famously along the Silk Route, experienced exactly this phenomenon as the wells and oases dried up and raiders pounced.[40] We need look no further than Somalia, Darfur, Rwanda, and the Democratic Republic of the Congo to see similar battles over resource control which ranged from atrocity-based warlordism to outright genocide.

For the substantial (semi-periphery) bloc of states, meaning those fragile states which seek to stay afloat as coherent political entities, the climate change threat operates in political terms from two pincer-like directions. In the first, there is the straightforward fear of being "swamped" by environmental refugees from neighboring states which have already fallen into the lower periphery, or may soon do so. In the second, the threat operates on the level of finding oneself unable to resist other wealthier, more powerful, and militarily stronger states, interfering with or directly appropriating one's own scarce resources, most obviously food, water, and strategic natural resources, including energy. Should democracy spread and semi-peripheral countries become more responsive to the needs of their peoples, the stakes will rise. The anxiety felt by each state's elites of having to navigate between the pincers of climate change and the political imperative to carry their countries forward to ever higher levels of development to fulfill the wants of their populations may lead to the consideration of increasingly radical alternatives. That said, democracy is not necessary for this dynamic to occur. Most models of conflict risk assessment or prediction, in fact, see state instability and autocracy as highly correlated with the potential for war or genocide.[41]

Where do the leading core states fit into this darkening scene? Expert Western opinion generally grafts a map of already existing global economic poverty onto any forward-looking plot of vulnerability to climate conflict, and thus the risks for Africa are particularly high.[42] Rich core countries intensely fear mass refugee "invasions." In circumstances in which standard front-line public services find themselves overwhelmed or unable to cope, core populations may perceive these realities as existential threats. It is in such emergency conditions that core-state elites might contemplate responses which would be unforgivable.

IV. The Antidote?

The endemic nature of the risk of genocide means that solutions to it will be multivalent. The invasion of Iraq, the controversies over Libya and more recently Syria, the vexing problem of Ukraine, and the multiple areas at risk in Africa (Mali, Central African Republic, South Sudan, the Democratic Republic of the Congo, Nigeria, and the Ebola-affected states of West Africa, to name a few) muddy the debates about when it is acceptable to intervene in a sovereign country to protect civilians and how that intervention should occur. When developing policy options, at a minimum we should consider all of the following categories of questions.

Detection: What are the practical steps that might be taken to identify where and when genocide might occur? What are the universal warning signs? Would it help to view climate change as a humanitarian rather than an economic problem?

Prevention: How might we prevent genocide? How do we build resilience? Are women the key to the prevention of genocide? What are the range of prevention and response options—not only boots on the ground, but soft power tools, etc.—available to leaders, particularly to U.S. policymakers, to counteract developing genocide? If we intervene, are we inviting accusations of aggressive neocolonialism? What forms of intervention produce net positives, and by what metrics do we evaluate this question? If we do agree on trouble spots, how do international leaders influence communities at risk? What other strategies and tactics should policymakers consider? How do we empower the periphery and expand African agency? Should we empower states or strive to diminish state sovereignty? Are the answers in international organizations, multi-state regions, localities, or some other polity? Can we be serious about prevention without addressing how the current global system perpetuates the unequal distribution of wealth and resources on the planet, particularly since this is a structural problem that will worsen due to climate change and scarcity? Should we consider a massive redistribution of wealth, in the form of a global Marshall Plan, for international and national security? Do our national security interests require us to invest in environmental management and climate adaptation measures in countries on the periphery? Can these capacity-building efforts in environmental affairs be accomplished without acting imperially? Must we concede that we may need to force others to accept the antidote to genocide, particularly those in Africa who remain perpetually on the cusp of the worst that could happen?

Political Will: Are the world's governments any more prepared than they were twenty years ago to set aside selfish interests—or lack of interest—and act to protect civilians from mass atrocity? How do you create incentives for leaders to act to prevent potential harm when there are few political rewards for stopping something that does not happen? For whom do you create incentives—government leaders, non-governmental organizations, or individual activists? What new levers—legal, technological, or political—exist to encourage proactive action? How do we create civil societies, or constituencies in civil societies, capable of encouraging positive action? Can prevention occur without improvements in governance?

The challenges before us are significant, but no problem is insurmountable. While we now stand at the apex of a particular human trajectory, we also possess sufficient analytical tools and material evidence to survey the broad landscape of human history and experience which preceded it. The historical record is replete with examples of human proclivities for mass atrocity. What is distinct about this current epoch is that the disparity between material overreach and the limits of the planetary carrying capacity seem to be leading us all (the core included) into a totalizing mode of exterminatory behavior. Mahatma Gandhi put the case even more tersely: there is "enough for everybody's need but not for everybody's greed." To prevent the worst from happening, creative, inclusive, and sustainable solutions are required so that we are not always acting *after* genocide.

RECOMMENDED READINGS

Gourevitch, Philip. 2009. "The Life After." *The New Yorker* (May 4).

------. 1998. *We Wish to Inform You That Tomorrow We Will be Killed with Our Families: Stories from Rwanda.* New York.

Levene, Mark. 2010. "From Past to Future: Prospects of Genocide and its Avoidance in the Twenty-First Century." In Donald Bloxham and A. Dirk Moses, eds., *The Oxford Handbook of Genocide Studies.* New York and Oxford.

Power, Samantha. 2013 [2002]. *A Problem from Hell: America and the Age of Genocide.* New York.

Totten, Samuel, and Paul Bartrop, eds. 2009. *The Genocide Studies Reader.* New York.

NOTES

[1]Gary Bass, *Freedom's Battle: The Origins of Humanitarian Intervention* (New York: Knopf, 2008).

[2]Benjamin Valentino, "The Perils of Limited Humanitarian Intervention: Lessons from the 1990s," *Wisconsin International Law Journal* 24 (October 1, 2006). While Valentino does not argue that all intervention is self-serving, he argues that interventions through the 1990s lacked efficacy. They were often poorly planned, poorly executed, too late to prevent harm, or not undertaken when most warranted.

[3]A. Dirk Moses, "Raphael Lemkin, Culture, and the Concept of Genocide," in *The Oxford Handbook of Genocide Studies*, eds. Donald Bloxham and A. Dirk Moses (New York and Oxford: Oxford University Press, 2010), 19.

[4]For a complete discussion of the eight techniques see Raphael Lemkin, *Axis Rule in Occupied Europe* (Washington, DC: Carnegie Endowment for International Peace, 1944), 82–90.

[5]Ibid., 79.

[6]"No. 1021: Convention on the Prevention and Punishment of the Crime of Genocide," United Nations Treaty Series (1951), 280, https://treaties.un.org/doc/Publication/UNTS/Volume%2078/volume-78-I-1021-English.pdf.

[7]William A. Schabas, "Introductory Note: Convention on the Prevention and Punishment of the Crime of Genocide," *Audiovisual Library of International Law, United Nations*, accessed October 3, 2014, http://legal.un.org/avl/ha/cppcg/cppcg.html.

[8]"Framework of Analysis for Atrocity Crimes: A Tool for Prevention," United Nations Office on Genocide Prevention and the Responsibility to Protect (2014), accessed May 25, 2015, http://www.un.org/en/preventgenocide/adviser/methodology.shtml.

[9]Madeleine Albright, William Cohen, et al., "Preventing Genocide"(Washington, DC: United States Holocaust Memorial Museum, The American Academy of Diplomacy, and the Endowment of the United States Institute of Peace, 2008), accessed October 23, 2014, http://www.ushmm.org/m/pdfs/20081124-genocide-prevention-report.pdf.

[10]Appendix B, "Mass Atrocity Response Operations," in *Peace Operations,* Joint Publication 3-07.3 (August 1, 2012), B1–B10, accessed October 23, 2014, http://www.fas.org/irp/doddir/dod/jp3-07-3.pdf. Barack Obama, "National Security Strategy," (February 2015), accessed 10 March 2015, https://www.whitehouse.gov/sites/default/files/docs/2015_national_security_strategy.pdf.

[11]The White House, Office of the Press Secretary, "Presidential Study Directive on Mass Atrocities (PSD-10)" (August 4, 2011), accessed October 23, 2014, http://www.whitehouse.gov/the-press-office/2011/08/04/presidential-study-directive-mass-atrocities.

[12]An early title to Samantha Power's 2002 book, "A Problem from Hell," which addresses American responses to genocide since the Holocaust was "Again and Again." See Samantha Power, "Never Again: The World's Most Unfulfilled Promise," *Frontline*, accessed October 3, 2014, http://www.pbs.org/wgbh/pages/frontline/shows/karadzic/genocide/neveragain.html.

[13]With the exception of interventions in Kosovo (1999), Libya (2011) and Iraq (2014), the United States has stood by as some of the worst genocides of the twentieth century took place.

[14]Samantha Power, "Never Again"; Frontline, "Ghosts of Rwanda" (dir. Greg Barker, 2004).

[15]John McCormick, *Comparative Politics in Transition* (7th Edition) (Boston, MA: Wadsworth, 2012), 43–4.

[16]Two indicators of atrocity crimes are relevant here, namely "Economic interests, including those based on the safeguard and well-being of elites or identity groups, or control over the distribution of resources" and "Discovery of natural resources or launching of exploitation projects that have a serious impact on the livelihoods and sustainability of groups or civilian populations." See the United Nations' "Framework of Analysis for Atrocity Crimes," 13, 17.

[17]See Immanuel Wallerstein, *The Capitalist World-Economy* (Cambridge: Cambridge University Press, 1979).

[18]"Growth is Good," *The Economist* (May 25, 2000), accessed October 20, 2014, http://www.economist.com/node/334693.

[19]According to a 2013 U.N. report, "The World is more unequal today than at any point since World War II." "Many studies have shown that inequality between nations is growing… and that has been accompanied by growing inequality within most countries." Lance W. Garner, ed., *Humanity Divided: Confronting Inequality in Developing Countries* (New York: United Nations Development Programme, 2013), 1, 64.

[20]According to the International Monetary Fund, "Sub-Saharan Africa's remarkable growth over the past two decades has not translated into shared prosperity. The subcontinent remains marred by inequality, despite being one of the world's fastest growing regions." Francis Gouahinga, "New Revenues Can Offset Africa's Rising Income Inequality," *IMF Survey Magazine* (October 21, 2014), http://www.imf.org/external/pubs/ft/survey/so/2014/car102114a.htm.

[21]Mark Levene, "Connecting Threads: Rwanda, the Holocaust and the Pattern of Contemporary Genocide," in Roger W. Smith, ed., *Genocide: Essays toward Understanding, Early Warning and Prevention* (Williamsburg, VA: Association of Genocide Scholars, 1999), especially 46–9. See also Risk Factor 3, Weakness of State structures in the U.N. "Framework of Analysis for Atrocity Crimes," 12.

[22]Michael Mann, *The Dark Side of Democracy* (Cambridge: Cambridge University Press, 2005), esp. 1–54.

[23]Donella Medows, Jorgen Randers, and Dennis Meadows, *The Limits to Growth: The 30 Year Update* (Chelsea, VT: Chelsea Green Publishing Company, 2004).

[24]Roger W. Smith, "Scarcity and Genocide," in Samuel Totten and Paul Bartrop, eds., *The Genocide Studies Reader* (New York: Routledge, 2009), 120–7.

[25]Oli Brown, Anne Hammill, and Robert McLeman, "Climate Change as the 'New' Security Threat: Implications for Africa," *International Affairs* 83, no. 6 (2007): 1141–54, 1141.

[26]Jared Diamond, *Collapse: How Societies Choose to Fail or Survive* (London: Penguin, 2005), 328.

[27]Amy R. Krakowka, Natalie Heimel, and Francis A. Galgano, "Modeling Environmental Security in Sub-Saharan Africa," *Geographic Bulletin* 53 (2012): 21–38. See also Julie Flint and Alex De Waal, *Darfur: A New History of a Long War* (London and New York: Zed Books, 2008), 44–6.

[28]The United Nations admits that "Sudden changes that affect the economy or the workforce, including as a result of financial crisis, natural disasters or epidemics" stands as a triggering factor for atrocity crimes. See the United Nations' "Framework of Analysis for Atrocity Crimes," 17.

[29]Mark Levene, "From Past to Future: Prospects of Genocide and its Avoidance in the Twenty-First Century," in Donald Bloxham and A. Dirk Moses, eds., *The Oxford Handbook of Genocide Studies* (New York and Oxford: Oxford University Press, 2010), 644.

[30]Smith, "Scarcity and Genocide," 121.

[3]From DCDC (Development, Concepts, and Doctrines Centre, MOD), "Strategic Trends, 2030," quoted in Mark Levene, "From Past to Future," 644.

[32]Center for a New American Security (CNAS), "Climate Change Wargame," 28–30 July 2008, http://www.cnas.org/sites/default/files/uploads/CNAS_ClimateGame_FinalAgreement.pdf.

[33]Sheri Rosenberg and Everita Silina, "Genocide by Attrition," in Joyce Apsel and Ernesto Verdeja, eds., *Genocide Matters. Ongoing Issues and Emerging Perspectives* (New York: Routledge, 2013), 113–18.

[34]International Monetary Fund, *Regional Economic Outlook, Sub-Saharan Africa: Staying the Course*, (Washington, DC: International Monetary Fund, 2014), ix.

[35]Public Radio International/Living on Earth, "Africa's Great Green Wall of Trees," (March 30, 2012), www.loe.org/shows/segments.htlm?programID=12-P13-00013&segmentID=3. The concept behind the Great Green Wall is to plant 4,300 miles of trees through 11 countries in Africa's Sahal region, from Senegal to the Red Sea. Many of the planters are rural women, and frequently environmental advocacy has bled into advocacy for more open and accountable governance.

[36]Transparency International, "Corruptions Perception Index 2013," (Berlin: Transparency International, 2014), accessed October 20, 2014, http://www.transparency.org/cpi2013/results.

[37]Alex Evans, "Climate, Scarcity and Sustainability in the Post-2015 Development Agenda," (New York: New York University Center on International Cooperation, 2012), 4. http://sustainabledevelopment.un.org/content/documents/767evans.pdf.

[38]For statistics on genocide, atrocity and mass atrocity, see C.H. Anderton, "Datasets and Trends of Genocide, Mass Killing, and Other Civilian Atrocities," in C.H. Anderton and J. Brauer, eds., *Economic Aspects of Genocide, Mass Killing, and Their Prevention* (Oxford and New York: Oxford University Press, 2016).

[39]Much of the world's most acute food insecurity, for example, is in the Saharan or Sahel regions of Africa. See the Famine Early Warning Systems Network (FEWS NET), "Acute Food Insecurity" map, Near and Medium Term (April-September 2015), accessed June 5, 2015, www.fews.net.

[40]See Rob Johnson, "Climate Change, Resources and Future War: The Case of Central Asia," in *History at the End of the World? History, Climate Change and the Possibility of Closure*, eds. Mark Levene, Rob Johnson, and Penny Roberts (Penrith: Humanities E-Books, 2010).

[41]Genocide Prevention Advisory Network, *Guiding Principles of the Emerging Architecture Aiming at the Prevention of Genocide, War Crimes, and Crimes Against Humanity*, (The Hague: Ministerie van Buitenlandse Zaken/George Mason University, 2012), 5–42, esp. 6, 15–16, accessed June 3, 2015, http://www.gpanet.org/webfm_send/134.

[42]See Dan Smith and Janani Vivekananda, *A Climate of Conflict: The Links between Climate Change, Peace, and War* (London: International Alert, 2007), 18–19; and Brown, Hammel, and McLeman, "Climate Change as the 'New' Security Threat," 1145–8.

9

Avoiding the Next Great Recession

Lessons Learned from the Crash of 2008

LOUIS L. BONO

The Great Recession of 2008 had devastating effects on markets around the world that continue to be felt to this day. In its wake, policymakers have attempted redress the systemic risks that led to the crisis. This chapter outlines causes of the crisis and considers three disparate issues that have been the target of reform efforts: the role of the U.S. Federal Reserve, executive compensation, and global governance. My goal is not to argue that some reform efforts are better than others, but to frame a discussion of which reforms might avoid (or at least abate) the next great recession.

I. Too Big To Fail

The investment banking crisis that rocked global finance markets and developed into a full-blown economic crisis officially occurred in September 2008, but the first major indicator that a crisis was imminent occurred a year earlier, not on Wall Street but across the Atlantic in European markets. On August 7, 2007, the giant French bank BNP Paribas suspended transaction on three relatively obscure money market funds that were heavily leveraged in U.S. mortgage-backed securities. The bank had to deny its depositors withdrawals from these accounts, because it could not valuate the assets of the funds.[1]

Mortgage-backed securities were first developed in the 1980s. A form of financial engineering, they were designed to mitigate the risk that borrowers—home owners—would repay their lenders prematurely (thus avoiding interest fees lenders expected to receive).[2] To limit this risk, investment bankers took large numbers of mortgages and pooled them into bonds. The bonds typically combined a range of safe-to-risky mortgages and offered investors tiers of risk: those willing to take on more risk would realize a higher interest rate whereas those seeking a safer investment would yield a lower return.[3] It was not until the early 2000s, however, that mortgage-backed securities became a popular investment vehicle.

In the late 1990s, several Asian economies began to overheat, causing downward pressure on their currencies in relation to the dollar. Governments in the region tried to preserve the value of their currencies by liquidating their dollar reserves, but they did not have enough to weather the storm. As a result, their currencies and economies collapsed, impoverishing an estimated twenty-two million people.[4]

The lesson learned in the wake of the Asian financial crisis, for governments and investors in both developed and developing economies, was the need for safe investments to hedge against a crisis, and no investment was safer than the U.S. dollar. Increasing demand for dollars and a loose monetary policy by the Federal Reserve, which sought to revive the U.S. economy from the dot-com bubble and then the 9/11 attacks, combined to put downward pressure on interest rates. Lower interest rates were a boon for consumers, who took advantage of cheap money to purchase homes and cars, and for businesses, which undertook capital investments. But low interest rates handicapped investors seeking safe havens and financial institutions relying on interest rates to generate income.

However, one person's liability is another's asset, and the boom in real estate transactions fueled a windfall for Wall Street. By bundling risky with sound mortgages into mortgaged-backed securities, Wall Street firms could mitigate the overall risk of individual mortgages and offer investors a range of risk-interest options. The credit rating agencies loved these collateralized debt obligations, which they considered ultra-safe investments.[5] It was a win-win-win situation: investors had a safe vehicle with a higher rate of return, interest rates remained low so consumers could borrow greater amounts to purchase homes and/or pay off higher interest credit card debt, and investment bankers reaped enormous fees from assembling and trading the securities.

Or so it seemed. To keep this good thing going, investment bankers needed more mortgages to bundle; to get more mortgages, they had to expand the applicant pool. Lenders were already under pressure to increase minority home-ownership, having long been criticized by the Congress and presidential administrations for discriminatory lending practices.[6] So lenders relaxed the requirements for mortgages offering zero-money down terms; liar loans, in which applicants were not required to verify credit-worthiness, income, or assets; and negative-amortization loans, in which the payments were insufficient to cover the interest rate, meaning the principle rose, rather than declined over time.[7] But that did not matter, because the extension of easy credit to this subprime market, coupled with low interest rates that led existing homeowners to speculate on investment properties, caused housing prices to soar.[8] Borrowers were enticed by attractive, "teaser" rates on adjustable rate mortgages (ARMs) that would adjust upwards after two years.[9] For borrowers and lenders this was not a problem: as long as home values continued to appreciate, borrowers could refinance their loans—e.g., roll over their ARMs. Moreover, lenders had no incentive to be diligent; they were getting paid by Wall Street bankers who needed the loans to package into securities, while policymakers and politicians were happy with the rise in home-ownership.

In the meantime, financial engineers found new ways to exploit the market for mortgage-backed securities and subprime loans. They repackaged some of the riskiest portions of several mortgaged backed securities—the subprime mortgages—into new bonds to attain a higher rating.[10] These CDO2s (collateralized debt obligations) were very complex and opaque securities.[11] They also engineered CDOs that were comprised of credit default swaps on the riskier mortgage bonds.[12] Credit default swaps were the mechanism used by investors to short the mortgage-backed securities. For a relatively low premium, investors could take out insurance on—essentially bet against—the mortgage bonds. For an insurance company like AIG, it seemed like easy money; after all, the ratings agencies loved the bonds and besides, what were the chances that the entire U.S. housing market would go bust?[13] AIG was so confident in this venture that it did not take precautions to ensure that it had enough collateral to cover its losses.[14] AIG and others credit default swap issuers would soon realize the swaps on bonds carried the same risk of ownership in the event the bonds crashed.[15] In the meantime, the financial engineers earned handsome fees for packaging and trading the CDO2s and credit default swaps. Solvency was of no concern to Wall Street.[16]

In 2005, nearly one-trillion dollars' worth of mortgage-backed securities were issued.[17] That is also the year that U.S. housing prices peaked. In October 2006, the housing market experienced its greatest decline in thirty-five years.[18] So in 2007, when all those ARM teaser rates issued in 2005 increased suddenly, subprime borrowers and real estate speculators could not refinance at a lower rate, because the values on their homes were less than the amount owed on their mortgages. They were financially underwater, and many defaulted on their mortgages. The rise in defaults and the decline in housing prices worried investors and prompted them to cash out their mortgaged-backed securities, causing prices to fall. This led to huge losses for the mortgage-backed security market—so much so that large institutional holders such as BNP Paribas could no longer valuate the complex bonds.

In late 2007, there was a series of runs on financial institutions, and by December the economy was officially in a recession.[19] In March 2008 the investment bank Bear Stearns, which was heavily invested in mortgage-backed securities, could not obtain short-term financing in the overnight market—the market through which banks borrow and lend money from each other to manage liquidity—because other banks feared Bear's potential losses. This rendered Bear "functionally bankrupt."[20] The Federal Reserve brokered a deal with JP Morgan/Chase to purchase Bear. Under the deal, the Fed took on $30 billion of Bear's toxic assets.

The problem for Bear and other investment institutions was not the lack of assets but the fact that their mortgage-backed assets could not be valuated and used as collateral. By the summer of 2008, credit risks were increasing, and the storm was brewing.[21] Lehman Brothers, the fourth largest investment bank, had about $60 billion in toxic securities that could not be valuated and only $25 billion in capital. With insufficient collateral, Lehman Brothers could not borrow in the overnight market, and attempts by the federal regulators to arrange a buyout failed.

On September 15, 2008, the storm hit: Lehman brothers, the fourth largest investment bank with over $600 billion in assets and 25,000 employees, filed for bankruptcy, the largest in U.S. history.[22] The following day AIG was on the verge of collapse, hemorrhaging money trying to cover its $400 billion of credit default swaps.[23] Contagion was spreading; billions of dollars in assets were tied up in Lehman's bankruptcy and banks were refusing to lend to other banks—"one of the most essential functions of the banking system."[24] A credit crisis would evolve into a financial crisis, which would ultimately turn into a global economic crisis. The Great Recession of 2008 had begun.

II. The Federal Reserve: A Systemic Risk In and Of Itself?

> "Do you have $80 billion?" Representative Barney Frank asked Fed Chairman Ben Bernanke whether he could bail out AIG.
>
> "I have $800 billion," replied Bernanke.[25]

Before his appointment as Chairman of the Federal Reserve in 2006, Ben Bernanke was best known as a scholar of the Great Depression. He documented that when trouble strikes the financial sector, lending is cut back. Because the U.S. economy is premised on credit, reductions in lending impair growth.[26] It was thus fortuitous, if not fortunate, for Bernanke to be at the helm of the Fed when the Great Recession hit.

Like Roosevelt during the Great Depression, Bernanke took the "try everything" approach to see what would work, and like Roosevelt, Bernanke had his own alphabet soup of new programs.[27] Bernanke's aggressive, experimental approach had actually begun in late 2007 when the Fed introduced credit facilities to provide liquidity for the markets.[28] Throughout 2008, the Fed aggressively lowered interest rates, until they reached zero by year end.[29] A facility launched on September 22, 2008—a week after the Lehman collapse—lent $24 billion on its first day.[30] By 2010, the Fed had over $1.1 trillion in securities on its books.[31]

Bernanke was employing an unconventional, somewhat controversial policy known as "quantitative easing," using newly created money to purchase mortgage-backed securities.[32] His goal was to expand the money supply and liquidate the cash-strapped mortgage sector.[33] In 2010, Bernanke launched his second round of quantitative easing, known as QE2, with the Fed announcing that it was purchasing $600 billion in long-term U.S. Treasury bonds.[34] By taking these bonds off the market, which, while difficult to value, were not necessarily worthless, Bernanke was crowding out investors, forcing them into other investments such as corporate bonds or mortgage-backed securities. A year later, the Fed sold $400 billion in shorter-term U.S. bonds for $400 billion in longer-term bonds. This time, Bernanke was trying to lower long-term interest rates to encourage mortgage borrowing and capital investments.[35]

By almost all accounts, Bernanke's innovative, all-out approach, which also included currency swaps with foreign central banks and stress tests for banks, mitigated the crisis and put the U.S. economy on a path to recovery.[36] A year after the Lehman crash, he commented "'we came very close in [2008] to Depression 2.0.'"[37]

While it is generally accepted that Bernanke's actions, along with the Troubled Asset Relief Program (TARP) that bailed out banks, helped stave off disastrous consequences, praise for the Fed has not been universal. The Federal Reserve is the third, albeit most successful, attempt at a central bank in a nation with deep-rooted suspicions of concentrated, unchecked power. Critics contend that the Fed, under Bernanke's predecessor Alan Greenspan, created the conditions for the crisis by keeping interest rates too low for too long and ignoring the signs of systemic risk.[38] Greenspan even admitted that he and his team did not understand the complexities of CDO.[39] Bernanke, for his part, acknowledged that the Fed should have intervened to address risky lending practices and protect consumers in the years prior to the crisis.[40] That the Fed failed to foresee the crisis, however, is understandable, as central banks do not have a great track record of recognizing and preventing bubbles.[41] More troubling for the Fed was that the crisis brought to light its immense, unchecked powers, notably its ability to create money.

The American polity is premised on the fear of an all-powerful government that acts contrary to the rights and interests of the citizens. That the Fed (and the Administration) rescued the very institutions that caused the crisis, at a time when U.S. unemployment rates were among the highest since the Great Depression, created a populist backlash. Economists and even Fed whistleblowers alleged "backdoor deals" between the Fed and Wall Street, and calls by "Main Street" to reform the Fed have been heard loud and clearly in the current Republican-controlled Congress.[42]

According to one economist: "Monetary policy works a lot better when it is transparent, predictable and keeps to well-established traditions and limitations, than if the Fed shoots from the hip following the passions of the day."[43] Even former Fed Chairman Paul Volcker cautioned that the Fed has "got so much authority, used so much authority, [and] made up some authority."[44]

The most controversial of the reform proposals, the ability of Congress to audit the Fed, is unlikely to gain hold, but other proposals to increase Congressional oversight, shift the balance of power within the Fed, and increase monetary policy transparency could provide a basis for compromise between the White House, the Fed, and the Hill. As they negotiate Federal Reserve reform proposals, policymakers are left to wrestle with these questions:

1. Would restrictions on the Fed render the United States more vulnerable to a future crisis?
2. Is limited power the price of political independence?[45]

III. Executive Compensation: Moral Hazard or Obligation?

> "If you do something very risky and it pays off, you benefit, but if you do something very risky and it doesn't pay off you may lose.... Otherwise the structure of compensation over-incentivizes risk taking."
>
> —CONGRESSMAN BARNEY FRANK[46]

> "I owe the public nothing."
>
> —JOHN PIERPONT MORGAN[47]

Despite efforts by some members of Congress to restrain the Fed, Congress actually vested the central bank with the additional authority to oversee the financial sector just a few years earlier via the Dodd-Frank Act. The Dodd-Frank Wall Street Reform and Consumer Protection Act is a comprehensive legislative package designed to regulate the financial industry and mitigate the systemic risks that caused the Great Recession. One issue addressed by the act is executive pay and compensation, which was considered to have exacerbated the crisis by creating incentives for extraordinary risks.[48]

Payment schemes among the investment banks were premised on not only short-term gains but highly-leveraged bets, with investment bankers insulated from shareholder losses.[49] One study determined that senior managers "profited handsomely" while their clients lost "virtually everything."[50] Wall Street's attitude toward Main Street in the wake of the crisis seemed one of indifference, if not sheer arrogance; with unemployment rates near ten percent and retirement plans tanking, thousands of employees of the largest TARP bailout recipients received bonuses in excess of $1 million.[51]

The ensuing public outrage led the Treasury Department to restrict compensation schemes of TARP recipients and sent a clear message to Congress to address what was considered a perverse incentive structure.[52] Dodd-Frank seeks to mitigate moral hazard by expanding executive accountability in three primary categories.[53] The first requires shareholder input on compensation—a non-binding "say on pay" vote a minimum of every three years. The second mandates additional public disclosures, including the relationship between executive compensation and the firm's performance, the relationship between pay incentives and share price, and a comparison of executive compensation with the firm's median employee income—the "shaming" provision. The third provision imposes checks and balances to ensure the independence of the firm's compensation committee and includes a two-year "clawback" provision on compensation in cases of failure or errors in performance.[54]

A major criticism of Dodd-Frank is that it distorts the risk-reward relationship. Executives by nature are risk averse, to the extent their jobs are on the line. Thus, investors seeking large gains typically create incentives for risk through compensation.[55] Conversely, the "say on pay" requirement could impel some executives to take on greater risk than they otherwise would to placate the near-term expectations of shareholders at the expense of the firm's long-term viability.[56] There is also the issue of who takes on the risk. Dodd-Frank addresses executive compensation, not the packages for the "rain-makers"—the star traders who are actually more likely to cause catastrophic losses to the firm.[57] Finally, compensation restrictions could induce the brightest financial minds to take their talents overseas, much the way high corporate taxes encourage corporations to relocate offshore.

- While July 2015 marked the fifth anniversary of Dodd-Frank, the SEC is still issuing rules for implementation. Thus, the jury is still out as to the efficacy as well as the sagacity of this attempt to regulate financial executives.
- Should the government inhibit financial risk taking? Will regulation of executive compensation undermine growth potential?
- Do executives of financial firms have a fiduciary responsibility to the nation's economic well-being?

IV. A New or an Alternative Form of Global Governance?

> "The whole world is moving to the American model of free enterprise and capital markets."
>
> —SANDY WEILL, CITIGROUP (2007)[58]

The impacts of the Great Recession were not confined to the U.S. economy; contagion spread throughout the world. Global GDP growth dropped from 4 percent in 2007 to 1.5 percent in 2008 to negative 2.1 percent in 2009, causing Ben Bernanke to declare this "the worst financial crisis since the 1930s." Two months after the Lehman collapse, President Bush convened the first Group of 20 (G-20) summit of the world's largest economies in Washington, D.C.

The meeting was symbolic in that it projected a united effort to address the crisis and its systemic roots, but it also marked a change in global governance structures, as the emerging economies were included at a table that had traditionally been reserved for the industrialized economies. The initial meetings—there were two in 2009—were largely successful, not just because their actions were instrumental in stemming global economic contraction, but because the leaders from these twenty disparate economies and cultures put aside their differences to forge a consensus. Thus, these initial meetings raised the specter of a new global architecture for the twenty-first century.[59]

It is said that in crisis, there is opportunity, and as the crisis receded, so did the ability of the G-20 to take meaningful action. At their June 2009 inaugural summit, the leaders of Brazil, Russia, India, and China (the "BRIC" countries) demanded greater voice and representation in international financial institutions (IFIs). Frustrated by the slow pace of IFI reforms, the BRICS (the BRIC group plus South Africa) have opted to establish their own structures. In July 2014, the five BRICS members announced their own development bank, and most recently, China established the Asian Infrastructure Investment Bank (AIIB), which four of the G-7 have joined—a fifth is contemplating membership—despite doubts over the AIIB's governance structures, lending standards, and its ultimate objectives under Chinese leadership.

The BRIC leaders also called for "a stable, predictable and more diversified international monetary system" in June 2009. The dollar's role as the global currency is a tremendous instrument of power, both economic and political, for the U.S. government. It allows the United States not only to borrow money at low interest rates across the globe, but to impose crippling sanctions against foreign regimes and enterprises by cutting off access to dollar-denominated transactions.

Following their 2009 summit, Russia's president declared that "there can be no successful currency system, and particularly a global system, if the financial instruments that are used are denominated in only one currency."[60] And in October 2013, China's official news media *Xinhua* published a commentary entitled: "U.S. fiscal failure warrants a de-Americanized world." In it the author charged a "self-serving Washington ha[d] abused its superpower status and introduced even more chaos into the world by shifting financial risks overseas."[61] Further, by undermining the dollar's hegemony, emerging and some existing powers sought to thwart—or at a minimum check—the ability of the United States to deploy the dollar as a sword, such as through sanctions regimes imposed on Iran and later Russia. Nevertheless, despite the 2008 crisis and subsequent rhetoric, recent trends such as the PRC's August 2015 abrupt devaluation of the RMB, the ruble's decline occasioned by the drop in oil prices and sanctions over Ukraine, and the continuous struggles of the Eurozone contrasted with the gradual U.S. recovery, are likely to reinforce market sentiment for the dollar's long-term preeminence. Moreover, the PRC's currency manipulation has led the IMF to signal that it will not add the RMB to the basket of official currencies in 2015—a status that would provide the RMB greater clout in global markets.

- Is the G-20 a viable forum for global governance or is it better suited to crisis management?
- Are the days of the dollar's dominance numbered? Should the United States actively seek to preserve its role as the global economic superpower

at all costs, should it hedge its bets and expand multilateral, financial governance, or will global markets continue to preserve the sanctity of the dollar?

We study history to avoid the mistakes of the past. If there is any upside to economic crises, it is that they enable policymakers, regulators, economists, and businesses to identify their causes and develop safeguards and tripwires to prevent their recurrence. Have we learned the right lessons from the 2008 financial crisis? What, if any, steps should be taken now to prevent the next great recession?

RECOMMENDED READINGS

Blinder, Alan S., and Mark Zandi. 2010. "How the Great Recession Was Brought to an End." https://www.economy.com/mark-zandi/documents/End-of-Great-Recession.pdf.

Cho, Sungjoon, and Claire R. Kelly. 2012. "Promises and Perils of New Global Governance: A Case of the G20." *Chicago Journal of International Law* 12: 491–562.

Coffee, John C., Jr. 2011–12. "The Political Economy of Dodd-Frank: Why Financial Reform Tends to be Frustrated and Systemic Risk Perpetuated." *Cornell Law Review* 97: 1019–82.

Dunning, Andrew. 2011–12. "The Changing Landscape of Executive Compensation after Dodd-Frank." *Review of Banking and Financial Law* 30: 64–72.

Irwin, Neil. 2013. *The Alchemists.* New York.

Lewis, Michael. 2010. *The Big Short.* New York.

Mishkin, Frederic S. 2010. "Over the Cliff: From the Subprime to the Global Financial Crisis." *NBER Working Paper Series* (December 2010).

Sorkin, Andrew Ross. 2009. *Too Big to Fail.* New York.

NOTES

[1]Neil Irwin, *The Alchemists* (New York: Penguin Books, 2013), 1–2, and Frederic S. Mishkin, "Over the Cliff: From the Subprime to the Global Financial Crisis," *NBER Working Paper Series* (December 2010), 1. The assets did not lose all of their value; it is just that BNP Paribas could not determine what the exact values were. To avoid insolvency—when total liabilities exceed total asset—the bank had to freeze the accounts.

[2]Ibid., 5. Also see Michael Lewis, *The Big Short* (New York: W.W. Norton & Co., 2010), 7.

[3]Lewis, *The Big Short*, 7; Irwin, *The Alchemists*, 102.

[4]Benn Steil and Robert E. Litan, *Financial Statecraft* (New Haven, CT: Yale University Press, 2006), 83–4; Irwin, *The Alchemists*, 101.

[5]See Lewis, *The Big Short*, 98–9. Lewis adds: "In 2008, the rating agencies would claim that they never intended for the ratings to be taken as such precise measurements. Ratings were merely the agencies' best guess at a rank ordering of risk" (51).

[6]See, e.g., Steven A. Holmes, "Fannie Mae Eases Credit To Aid Mortgage Lending," *The New York Times* (September 30, 1999), http://www.nytimes.com/1999/09/30/business/fannie-mae-eases-credit-to-aid-mortgage-lending.html, and Jeff Jacoby, "Frank's Fingerprints are All

Over the Financial Fiasco," *The Boston Globe* (September 28, 2008), http://www.boston.com/bostonglobe/editorial_opinion/oped/articles/2008/09/28/franks_fingerprints_are_all_over_the_financial_fiasco/.

[7]Irwin, *The Alchemists,* 99–100.

[8]Andrew Ross Sorkin, *Too Big to Fail* (New York: Viking, 2009), 4–5.

[9]Lewis, *The Big Short,* 66.

[10]Ibid., 73 and 140. According to Lewis, "the CDO was, in effect a credit laundering service for… Lower Middle Class America. For Wall Street it was a machine that turned lead into gold" (73).

[11]See Sorkin, *Too Big to Fail,* 90.

[12]Lewis, *The Big Short,* 140.

[13]Sorkin, *Too Big to Fail,* 157.

[14]Ibid. Also see Irwin, *The Alchemists,* 145.

[15]Lewis, *The Big Short,* 206.

[16]Ibid., 143–4.

[17]Irwin, *The Alchemists,* 102–3.

[1]8Lewis, *The Big Short,* 189.

[1]9Irwin, *The Alchemists,* 132.

[2]0Ibid., 132–3.

[21]Ibid., 132–4; also see Mishkin, "Over the Cliff," 3.

[22]Mishkin, "Over the Cliff," 4.

[23]Ibid., 6.

[24]Andrew Ross Sorkin et al., "36 Hours of Alarm and Action as Crisis Spiraled," *The New York Times,* A1. (October 2, 2008).

[25]Irwin, *The Alchemists,* 146. See also Sorkin, *Too Big to Fail,* 407.

[26]Irwin, *The Alchemists,* 119.

[27]Ibid., 149, 151; see also, Mishkin, "Over the Cliff," 11, 13.

[28]Alan S. Blinder and Mark Zandi, "How the Great Recession Was Brought to an End," (July 27, 2010), 2, https://www.princeton.edu/~blinder/End-of-Great-Recession.pdf.

[29]Ibid.

[30]Irwin, *The Alchemists,* 150.

[31]Ibid., 263.

[32]"Quantitative easing" is the purchase of government securities or other securities from the market conducted by a central bank in order to reduce interest rates and increase the money supply by flooding financial institutions with capital in an effort to stimulate lending and increase liquidity. It is considered when short-term interest rates are at or approaching zero.

[33]Irwin, *The Alchemists,* 263, and Mishkin, "Over the Cliff," 12–13.

[34]Irwin, *The Alchemists,* 255.

[35]Ibid., 331.

[36]Mishkin, "Over the Cliff," 13.

[37]Blinder and Zandi, "How the Great Recession Was Brought to an End," 7.

[38]See, e.g., Lewis, *The Big Short,* 229.

[39]Sorkin, *Too Big to Fail,* 90.

[40]Irwin, *The Alchemists,* 177.

[41]John H. Cochrane, "The Danger of an All-Powerful Federal Reserve," *The Wall Street Journal* (August 26, 2013), http://online.wsj.com/articles/SB10001424127887323906804579036571835323800.

[42]Perianne Boring, "Call Your Congressman In Favor of Rand Paul's Fed Audit," *Forbes* (November 29, 2013), http://www.forbes.com/sites/perianneboring/2013/11/29/call-your-congressman-in-favor-of-rand-pauls-fed-audit/.

[43]Cochrane, "The Danger of an All-Powerful Federal Reserve."

[44]"The Federal Reserve at 100; Age Shall Not Weary Her," *The Economist* (December 21, 2013), http://www.economist.com/news/finance-and-economics/21591857-americas-central-bank-has-become-ever-more-powerful-over-past-century-age-shall; Gene Epstein, "Volcker: Fed is Too Big for Its Britches," *Barron's* (June 15, 2013), http://online.barrons.com/articles/SB50001424052748704878904578537312919247172.

[45]Cochrane, "The Danger of an All-Powerful Federal Reserve."

[46]Barney Frank, Interview with Mark Haines of CNBC (June 11, 2009).

[47]Quoted in *The New York World* (May 11, 1901).

[48]Andrew Dunning, "The Changing Landscape of Executive Compensation after Dodd-Frank," *Review of Banking and Financial Law* 30 (2011–12): 64–72, 64.

[49]John C. Coffee, Jr., "The Political Economy of Dodd-Frank: Why Financial Reform Tends to be Frustrated and Systemic Risk Perpetuated," *Cornell Law Review* 97 (2011–12): 1019–82, 1019, 1051.

[50]Ibid.

[51]Louise Story and Eric Dash, "Bankers Reaped Lavish Bonuses during Bailouts," *The New York Times* (July 30, 2009), http://www.nytimes.com/2009/07/31/business/31pay.html?_r=0; Coffee, "The Political Economy of Dodd-Frank," 1068. See also Sorkin, *Too Big to Fail*, 532.

[52]Dunning, "The Changing Landscape," 65–6.

[53]"Moral hazard" occurs when a party insured or otherwise insulated from risky activity, engages in more of it, often to the detriment of another party. See Steil and Litan, *Financial Statecraft*, 131.

[54]Ibid., 66–9.

[55]Coffee, "The Political Economy of Dodd-Frank," 1053.

[56]Dunning, "The Changing Landscape," 70.

[57]Coffee, "The Political Economy of Dodd-Frank," 1071–2.

[58]Louis Uchitelle, "The Richest of the Rich, Proud of a New Gilded Age," *The New York Times* (July 15, 2007), http://www.nytimes.com/2007/07/15/business/15gilded.html?pagewanted=all&_r=0.

[59]See Sungjoon Cho and Claire R. Kelly, "Promises and Perils of New Global Governance: A Case of the G20," *Chicago Journal of International Law* 12 (2012): 491–562, 547.

[60]Andrew Kramer, "Emerging Economies Meet in Russia," *The New York Times* (June 16, 2009), http://www.nytimes.com/2009/06/17/world/europe/17bric.html.

[61]Liu Chang, "U.S. Fiscal Failure Warrants a de-Americanized World," *Xinhua* (October 13, 2013), http://news.xinhuanet.com/english/indepth/2013-10/13/c_132794246.htm.

10

After the Cyber Pearl Harbor

Vulnerability and Resiliancy in a Networked World

AARON BRANTLY

> I fear all we have done is to awaken a sleeping giant and fill him with a terrible resolve.
>
> —ADMIRAL ISOROKU YAMAMOTO, IN *TORA! TORA! TORA!*

When the last of the fires had been put out and the final screams from the sunken USS Arizona had been forever silenced, the United States rose from an act of strategic and tactical surprise unlike any it had previously experienced. Less than a day after the attacks on Pearl Harbor, President Roosevelt was able, with the support and approval of Congress, to declare war. In the following weeks, months, and years, millions of citizen soldiers would be mobilized and the entire industrial base of a nation would be placed on war footing. An isolationist nation became a nation reinvigorated by a warrior's resolve. A sleeping giant had risen to action.

Seventy-three years later the image of a nation caught unawares haunts us and forces us to consider the implications similar attacks. But post-World War-II conflicts have rarely been so straightforward. Since World War II the United States has not formally declared war on another country. War carries unprecedented risk in the nuclear age, and what constitutes an act of war is not always clear.

What follows is a conflict scenario followed by a discussion of policy issues that would need to be addressed during and after a catastrophic cyber attack on the United States. The conflict scenario, while extreme, is nevertheless plausible. How U.S. policymakers would respond, however, is uncertain.

I. Operation Rockets Red Glare

At 12:00 EST on July 3, 2016 a link is posted to the Facebook page of five of the nation's top music artists, each of whom is holding a concert in a different U.S. city on July 4th. The link entices visitors with an offer of free concert tickets as well as special backstage passes. Less than twenty seconds later the first user has clicked on the link and is taken to a false domain website that serves malware. This website is mobile, tablet, and desktop enabled. Each device that accesses this website is served a customized virus designed to do several things: first, it reposts the link to the user's own Facebook page without their permission; second, it scans their contacts and sends an email to all of their contacts with a brief message telling them to look at some recent photos; finally, it installs a botnet script that allows a remote computer to activate a Distributed Denial of Service attack on this device.[1] The email that has been sent to all of their contacts contains a copy of the virus disguised to look like an image that, when clicked, installs the same virus on whatever device they are using.

By 18:00 EST on July 3, the Facebook links alone have generated nearly one million clicks, and the fake image in the email has been clicked ten million times. Less than six hours after introduction, without anyone knowing, the virus has infected eleven million devices. By 24:00 EST the count is upwards of fifty million devices. At the same time this mysterious virus is spreading, one hundred prepositioned Federal government employees with previously unknown associations to the Chinese government have logged onto their computers in twenty cities and thirty different federal agencies, and they have inserted thumb drives into their computer workstations. Leaving their computers turned on but their monitors turned off, all one hundred employees exit their buildings. Meanwhile, employees of the Yankee Nuclear Power Station, Calvert Cliffs Nuclear Power Plant, the Edwin I. Hatch Nuclear Plant, Turkey Point Station, and the Diablo Syn Nuclear Power Plant, show up to work and insert Bluetooth-enabled USB thumb drives into their work stations.

By 06:00 EST on July 4, more than one hundred million network-connected devices have been infected in the United States alone. At this time applications start appearing in the Android Play Store and the Apple App Store for the Fireworks displays in New York, Washington, D.C., San Francisco, Chicago, Dallas, and Atlanta. The stores describe these applications as unofficial guides to the day's festivities in each of these cities. As the country wakes up on the 4th of July each of these applications is downloaded thousands of times.

During the days preceding the 4th of July, news agencies release reports indicating the U.S. intelligence community's efforts to thwart all possible terrorist attacks from Islamist extremists. The U.S. government has not seen any additional signals chatter to indicate problems from any nation state or non-state groups in the days and weeks preceding the 4th of July.

At 12:00 EST on July 4, all Bluetooth-enabled USB sticks have been successfully installed on nuclear power station computers, and on one hundred different computers at fifty different Federal agencies. Although some security researchers have started to pick up on the rapid spread of a new virus, by this time the virus has spread to more than two hundred million connected devices worldwide. The number of devices is growing rapidly.

Just as people are sitting down for fireworks across the United States, the virus, embedded now in more than four hundred million devices globally, goes active. The virus is programmed to force infected devices to participate in a DDoS attack against various network-connected infrastructures. Once a DDoS attack reaches maturation, subsequent devices begin pinging other pre-identified targets. Within minutes all credit card transactions in the United States grind to a halt. ATMs are inoperable. Cell networks are clogged with data traffic making voice calls difficult if not impossible. Of the nearly four hundred million connected devices approximately one hundred million are programmed to attack networked Industrial Control Systems for major mass transportation systems in New York, Washington, Chicago, and Philadelphia.[2] Within minutes a dozen subway and metro trains have crashed, resulting in several hundred casualties. First responders are called, but by now the DDoS attack has changed its focus to target networked city traffic grids, creating gridlock as people head downtown to watch fireworks displays. All subway systems nationwide are shut down due to an inability to safeguard riders. Thousands of passengers are stranded in tunnels, and emergency personnel are unable to reach them. Mobile phone networks are clogged with traffic and few calls are going out.

As chaos begins to spread in major cities, the virus implanted on each of the USB sticks at the fifty different Federal Agencies begins spreading across Federal networks. The virus, modeled after CryptoLocker, is designed to encrypt and make all data on targeted computers inaccessible.[3] Thousands of computers are affected; quickly the call goes out to shut down all networked federal computers. Many agencies with limited duty staffs are ordering a complete disconnect of their buildings from the Internet. All digital Federal communications move towards a complete standstill, and all processing of payments, payrolls, health benefits, verifications of identities at border crossings, and hundreds of other systems become inoperable.

As the virus spreads through Federal networks, individuals sitting in cars outside the five nuclear power plants point with powerful directional Bluetooth antennas at the facilities. Leveraging intelligence gained through the Edward Snowden intelligence leaks of 2013–14, these individuals begin systematically breaking into the computer control systems regulating the temperature of the reactors. They do not change the temperatures of the core; instead, they manipulate the output to indicate overheating. This sets off alarms and immediately all five reactors begin emergency shutdown procedures. As these reactors shut down, the power grid is strained and rolling blackouts start occurring. The blackouts cause panic in cities where subway systems are shut down and traffic is already snarled. At 20:00 EST the President activates the emergency alert system and all TVs and radios begin broadcasting a message for people to return to their homes in a safe and orderly fashion. The minute the Emergency Alert Broadcast begins, all infected digital devices target defense networks simultaneously. The virus that has spread through Federal networks now penetrates and disrupts classified Command, Control Computers, Communications and Intelligence Surveillance and Reconnaissance (C4ISR) network capabilities. The U.S. defense establishment is under the most severe and sustained attack it has ever experienced.

As code enters the classified networks, C4ISR services begin to degrade. The ability for PACCOM, the Pacific Fleet, and Washington to communicate is severely degraded; by 22:00 EST on July 4, communications between them have come to a virtual standstill. Isolated, Carrier Strike Group 1, currently stationed in the East China Sea, establishes a war-time footing and begins preparations for an imminent attack. Because it has lost communications with PACCOM and with Washington, its C4ISR is severely degraded; it maintains only an analog radio range defensive perimeter.

At 23:59 EST China, which had been conducting naval drills in the South China Sea, immediately changes course and sends most of its naval and air assets towards Taiwan. China deploys one hundred JH-7 fighter-bombers accompanied by one hundred J-11 air superiority fighters to take out all surface-to-air Radar installations. The initial wave of attacks are followed immediately by one hundred H-6 bombers and an additional fifty J-11 fighters with designated targets, including Air Force and Army installations, across Taiwan. The air defenses of Taiwan are immediately overwhelmed. Carrier Strike Group One is unable to respond. Within six hours Elements of the South China Sea and East China Sea Fleets begin an assault on Taiwan with support from several hundred ships, 12,000 PLA Marines, and 10,000 Paratroopers from the 15th PLA Airborne Corps. Within twenty-four hours the fighting has all but stopped on Taiwan, its defense forces having been caught by surprise and overwhelmed. The United States is unable to respond. Instead of participating in the defense of Taiwan U.S. forces would now be required to liberate Taiwan, necessitating significant assets and risking a nuclear conflict.

By July 6, China has possession of Taiwan, U.S. critical infrastructure has been severely damaged by widespread chaos on public transportation, roads, and electric grids, U.S. government computers are inaccessible as a result of the encryption of their contents, and U.S. commerce has reverted to cash alone as a result of the inability to process credit cards. The penetration of nuclear power plants has resulted in all nuclear power plants nationwide being shut down until their security can be ensured. Internet-connected devices are still engaging in DDoS attacks and the volume of devices affected is unable to be diminished as people continue to attempt to use their devices that they had come to depend upon.

Events of the previous days are in line with China's cyber strategy.[4] China has invested a significant amount of time and resources developing what it refers to as "informationization" strategy. *China National Defense News*, in February 2007, defined *informationization* or cyber warfare as the struggle for the information advantage in the realms of politics, military affairs, economics, and technology and utilizes a broad array of cross-functional areas of applicability in which it desires to make its efforts succeed.[5] The focus of Chinese information warfare development is not the ability to wage network-centric warfare as the United States has demonstrated in previous conflicts, but rather to attack and significantly degrade the ability of an enemy to wage effective combat operations.[6] Much of China's cyber capability development to date has been focused on obtaining a wide array of capabilities as part of a broad process of military modernization.[7] Of seven cases of economic or industrial espionage prosecuted between 2009 and 2011, six were of individuals with links to China.[8]

The President, sitting in the situation room, looks at representatives from the National Security Council and asks what he should do. The room is silent. This crisis, both military and civilian in nature, has already impacted almost every Federal agency and department. How should policymakers respond?

II. Policy Problems in the Digital Age

On February 16, 2010, the Bipartisan Policy Center ran a simulation similar to the scenario described above. Analysis of the scenario, called "Cyber Shock-Wave," revealed that in a severe cyber crisis the legal authorities and functions of U.S. government agencies and officials would be ambiguous, at best. The subsequent report divided its key findings into four areas where weaknesses were discovered: government organization, legal authorities, international protocols, and public education and awareness.[9] The specific weaknesses include the inability of government officials to deal with issues outside of .mil and .gov networks, the lack of clear lines of authority, the inability to provide timely and accurate decision-making, policy, legal and organizational constraints, missing or underdeveloped statutory authorities, international response mechanisms, a significant lack of public education on proper behavior in cyberspace, and general network security issues.[10]

Attempts to resolve these weaknesses are ongoing. Policy and strategic frameworks that comprise any potential response to significant cyber incidents are being formulated at virtually every level of government. For more than a decade the U.S. Government has been researching, formulating, and reformulating its national and international cybersecurity strategy to stay in step with this rapidly evolving domain of interaction. Deputy Secretary of Defense William J. Lynn III noted in 2010 that the creation of U.S. Cyber Command was a direct result of challenges faced by the pervasiveness of information technology across the U.S. Government.[11] Policy documents including the 2003 *National Strategy to Secure Cyberspace*, the 2009 *Cyberspace Policy Review*, the 2011 Department of Defense *Strategy for Operating in Cyberspace*, and the 2011 *International Strategy for Cyberspace*, have all become roadmaps for cross-governmental and cross-societal integration of a fuller and more comprehensive approach to dealing with the multitude of issues arising from cyberspace.

Any substantive debate focusing on the aftermath of a major cyber incident necessarily focuses four phases of political reaction.[12] These phases constitute a decision matrix upon which to build policy recommendations at each stage of a crisis. These phases of reaction include triage, treatment, risk mitigation, and response.

Stage One: Triage

Triage occurs after an incident has occurred or has been identified as in progress. As in the case above, a fast-moving incident might only be recognizable after initial losses have occurred. Triage involves identifying the type of incident(s) and prioritizing treatments. As in a medical emergency, different specialists might be required to respond to different situations; different aspects of government and society might be called upon to respond following a major cyber incident. Triage asks the question: "how can we minimize further damage in the most efficient manner?"

During the triage phase, immediately following a significant cyber incident, the first priority of the government is to maintain the security of the homeland. The incident is a cyber and kinetic incident, yet the cyber incident poses the greatest challenge to the homeland. Therefore, policymakers identify national territorial integrity, economic stability, and civil order as the initial treatment areas.

Stage Two: Treatment

Treatment involves the application of the specific organizational and functional units to halt, slow, and repair damage. Treatment could involve private, local, state, federal, and international assets all with the goal of halting further losses and repairing those that have already occurred. The treatment phase requires significant levels of coordination, escalation processes, legal and statutory authorities, and leadership.

Treatment should include, but is not limited to, the activation of all National Guard units nation-wide to ensure territorial integrity and provide additional resources for civil order, the elevation of the national alert status military installations, the grounding of all air-traffic, the closure of all public transportation, and suspension of the markets. Lastly, all nuclear power stations should be shut down and begin a software-reset process. Although initial treatments do not solve the broader problems caused by the cyber incident, they facilitate an organized approach and enable subsequent treatments.

Stage Three: Risk Mitigation

Risk mitigation occurs in tandem with treatment and can occur during and after response phases. Because an incident in cyber occurs within a system of systems environment, a nesting of networks and computing devices, it can be vital to shut down assets prior to their manipulation, corruption, or degradation. Risk mitigation comes into play as soon as triage occurs. It can be both a short-term and a long-term process; often, it is best examined in a lessons learned or after action report. Risk mitigation is a crucial aspect of facilitating resilience and minimizing vulnerabilities.

Risk mitigation in this scenario requires the shutting down of all mobile networks and the dissemination of Public Service Announcements (PSAs), on the national emergency alert system requesting all citizens reinstall their phone software and shut down their computers until such time as an antivirus solution can be developed. Federal networks should be shut down and each computer should be removed from the network and independently verified. Those devices found to contain malicious programs should be immediately erased, re-imaged and inspected before returning them to the network. Long-term risk mitigation includes policy changes and incentive programs to increase cybersecurity across civilian and military infrastructure.

Stage Four: Response

A response is a highly political action and often forms the center of the political debate associated with a particular incident. A response can serve as a deterrent to dissuade future actions; it can be punitive, to demonstrate resolve; or it can be defensive, to pre-empt future attacks. A response can take many forms and can be sought through legal, criminal, military, formal, and informal mechanisms. A response is often the product of a bureaucratic decision-making process.

The degradation of command and control capabilities makes most forms of military response difficult; additionally, China's nuclear status complicates any potential response. Economic interdependencies with China make any potential economic sanctions difficult if not equally harmful to the United States. A diplomatic démarche through the United Nations is likely to have little effect on China, but is a clear first step. Second, as U.S. capabilities return, the U.S. should forcefully re-establish its Pacific position in control of key shipping lanes and should work to foster increased military and diplomatic ties with Asian nations to counterbalance Chinese aggression. Last, the United States should institute a policy of controlled interdependence to ensure all strategic goods can be produced within the continental United States to alleviate potential supply constraints with an increasingly belligerent nation.

A significant cyber incident can theoretically achieve as much damage, destruction, and confusion as many conventional kinetic attacks. For policymakers, it is important to move quickly and efficiently to reestablish control over a situation before it spirals too far. How, then, should policymakers respond to a "Cyber Pearl Harbor" like the one described here?

As noted in a February 2013 Government Accountability Office report, "no integrated, overarching strategy exists that articulates priority actions, assigns responsibilities for performing them, and sets time frames for their completion."[13] Therefore, to address vulnerability and resiliency in a networked world following a cyber Pearl Harbor first requires addressing specific policy and statutory issues hindering an adequate response. Whereas the original Pearl Harbor attack necessitated rapid after-incident coordination and response, it is possible that anticipatory policy and statutory developments might reduce the potential severity of a significant cyber incident.

Networks are always going to have vulnerabilities, yet the ability of a government to respond and adapt to changes as they arise will foster resilience and minimize bureaucratic vulnerabilities.

RECOMMENDED READINGS

Bronk, Christopher. 2011. "Blown to Bits: China's War in Cyberspace, August-September 2020."

Cyber ShockWave: Simulation Report and Findings. 2010. Bipartisanpolicy.org (February).

Lynn, William J. 2010. "Defending a New Domain." *Foreign Affairs* (September 1).

Masters, Jonathan. 2011. "Confronting the Cyber Threat." Council on Foreign Relations Backgrounder (May 23).

Thomas, Timothy L. 2009. "Nation-state Cyber Strategies: Examples from China and Russia." In Kramer, Franklin D, and Stuart H Starr, eds. *Cyberpower and National Security*. Washington, DC.

GOVERNMENT DOCUMENTS RELATED TO CYBER

Carter, Ashton. 2015. The Department of Defense Cyber Strategy. http://www.defense.gov/home/features/2015/0415_cyber-strategy/Final_2015_DoD_CYBER_STRATEGY_for_web.pdf.

Obama, Barack H. 2013. Cyberspace Policy Review: Assuring a Trusted and Resilient Information and Communications Infrastructure.

Obama, Barack H. 2011. International Strategy for Cyberspace: Prosperity, Security, and Openness in a Networked World.

U.S. Government Accountability Office. 2013. Cybersecurity: National Strategy, Roles, and Responsibilities Need to Be Better Defined and More Effectively Implemented. Washington, DC.

Wortzel, Larry M. 2013. Testimony in "U.S.-China Economic and Security Review Commission 2013 Report to Congress: China's Military Modernization, U.S.-China Security Relations, and China's Cyber Activities." United States House of Representatives, 113th Congress 26. Washington, DC.

NOTES

[1]Distributed Denial of Service attacks (DDoS) is the process by which a networked connected computing device or multiple devices are used to overwhelm a target with a flood of external communications requests causing the target system to become inaccessible, unusable or simply fail. The more nodes or bots attached to a DDoS attack the more powerful and distributed the attack.

[2]Industrial Control Systems (ICS) are automated systems that manage industrial processes including subway, transportation, electrical and other systems. Failures of these types of systems have been linked to accidents involving various industrial processes. The STUXNET virus was a virus designed to manipulate various ICS systems.

[3]Cryptolocker is a form of ransomware (subset of malware) that targeted windows computers via email attachments. Once activated the malware encrypts certain files on the target system using RSA public-key cryptography making the files inaccessible until a ransom is paid and the files are unlocked).

[4]Timothy L. Thomas, "Nation-state Cyber Strategies: Examples from China and Russia," in *Cyberpower and National Security*, eds. Franklin D. Kramer and Stuart H Starr (Washington, DC: Potomac Books, 2009), 466.

[5]Ibid.

[6]Ibid., 467.

[7]Larry M. Wortzel, Testimony to the U.S. House of Representatives Armed Services Committee Hearing on "2013 Report to Congress of the U.S.-China Economic Security Review Commission" (November 12, 2013), http://origin.www.uscc.gov/sites/default/files/WortzelL-20131120_2013%20Annual%20Report.pdf.

[8]Office of the National Counterintelligence Executive, "Foreign Spies Stealing U.S. Economic Secrets in Cyberspace: Report to Congress on Foreign Economic Collection and Industrial Espionage, 2009–2011" (October 2011), http://www.ncix.gov/publications/reports/fecie_all/Foreign_Economic_Collection_2011.pdf.

[9]"Cyber ShockWave: Simulation Report and Findings," Bipartisanpolicy.org, Washington, DC (February 2010), 4.

[10]Ibid.

[11]William J. Lynn III, "Defending a New Domain," *Foreign Affairs* (September 1, 2010), accessed August 6, 2014, http://www.foreignaffairs.com/articles/66552/william-j-lynn-iii/defending-a-new-domain.

[12]This should be distinguished from the responses of a computer emergency response team (CERT) or other network specific security protocols.

[13]U.S. Government Accountability Office, "Cybersecurity: National Strategy, Roles, and Responsibilities Need to Be Better Defined and More Effectively Implemented," (Washington, DC: GPO, 2013).

11

Globe, Warmed

Coping with a Hotter Planet

ADAM J. KALKSTEIN, WILEY C. THOMPSON, AND JOHN MELKON

Global climate change is one of the preeminent environmental issues currently affecting the planet. Although many uncertainties remain, virtually all climate scientists are in agreement that increased greenhouse gas emissions are primarily responsible for an observed surface warming on Earth. The potential impacts of climate change are extensive and are likely to affect billions of people in the future through a continued rise in sea level, an increased risk of potentially deadly heat waves, an increase in the severity and duration of crippling drought, and beyond. As greenhouse gas concentrations continue their upward trend, global average temperatures are forecast to rise well into the future, further exacerbating the problem.

The goal of this chapter is to outline a variety of worst-case scenarios regarding future climate change through a discussion of potential impacts to the Earth system, global security, and policy. Although the scenarios presented here are all plausible, it is important to note that this summary does not present the most likely outcomes of climate change but rather the worst potential outcomes with the greatest impact to human well-being.

I. Models

Forecasting future climate is an inherently difficult task due to the complexities of the climate system and the uncertainties surrounding future greenhouse gas emissions. In an attempt to produce the most accurate models possible, numerous modeling organizations from around the world have collaborated as part of the fifth phase of the Climate Model Intercomparison Project (CMIP5).[1] The CMIP5 output represents some of the most sophisticated future climate data available and was recently used as guidance in the Intergovernmental Panel on Climate Change (IPCC) 5th Assessment Report (AR5).[2] Likewise, a variety of greenhouse gas emission scenarios have also been developed; after all, uncertainty exists not only within the climate system itself, but also how humans will impact the planet in the future. To predict the contribution of human activity on climate change, the Representative Concentration Pathways (RCP) examine emissions, land use changes, energy, pollution, technology, and socio-economic status to develop future radiative forcing (excess energy) estimates. In all, four pathways were created to estimate this excess energy by 2100.[3]

The worst of these scenarios assumes a "high-emission business as usual" future, in which fossil fuels continue to dominate the energy sector, population rise continues, and only modest technological advancements occur.[4] When used as input in the CMIP5 models, a dramatic warming is forecast across much of the globe (Figure 11.1). Most land masses are expected to experience an average warming in excess of 4 degrees C (7.2 degrees F), with some locales in the high latitudes approaching 10 degrees C (18 degrees F). Although some scientists raise important questions concerning the accuracy of CMIP5 models[5] and the specific impact of greenhouse gases,[6] the worst-case climate change scenarios outlined by the IPCC remain a distinct possibility.

II. Impacts

Sea Level Rise

Beginning with the retreat of the Laurentide Ice Sheet and overall climatic warming approximately fifteen thousand years ago, global sea level has risen. In some cases, the increase in sea level has been dramatic, possibly exceeding twenty meters in less than five hundred years.[7] Presently, sea level continues to rise, albeit at a much lower rate (approximately 2.5 to 3.2 mm per year), primarily caused by a combination of thermal expansion and glacial melt.[8] However, there is mounting evidence that the rate of sea level rise has once again started to increase, likely due to the corresponding rise in global surface temperature.[9] As a result of these increasing rates, scientists are becoming more alarmed about a potential "tipping point," in which an era of rapid sea level rise will return.[10] In fact, observed sea level rise has outpaced most model predictions in recent years, likely a result of accelerating ice loss across Greenland and portions of Antarctica.[11]

Western Antarctica is particularly susceptible to changes in global temperature, and numerous studies suggest that the West Antarctic Ice Sheet has already begun a period of irreversible and rapid disintegration. In fact, there is new evidence that such a collapse would occur even more rapidly than previously thought, possibly in a matter of several centuries.[12] These changes would likely have an increasingly large impact on global sea level in future decades and centuries.[13] To summarize the scope of the problem, one study ominously concludes:

> At the end of the last ice age, the Earth slowly warmed by 4–7 °C globally and lost almost two-thirds of its land ice in the process. That raised sea level by 120 metres, at rates often exceeding a metre per century. It seems that nothing in the present ice-sheet configuration would rule out similar rates in future. How much of the remaining 65 metres worth of land ice will humans melt if we warm the planet by a further several degrees?[14]

Clearly, sea level rise has the potential to be a serious problem in the future by reshaping coastlines and threatening coastal cities and ecosystems.

Floods

As global temperatures increase, the atmosphere's ability to contain water vapor increases as well. In other words, in a warmer planet, when it rains, it pours. When the increased intensity in precipitation is combined with land use changes which increase the amount of run-off (e.g., the creation of impermeable surfaces such as parking lots), it is likely the occurrence of floods will increase across much of the planet. In fact, there is evidence that climate change is already having such an impact. Recent research suggests that human activity is responsible for more frequent extreme precipitation events that have been observed. Further, there is the potential that global climate models might be underestimating the actual impact of anthropogenic warming on such precipitation events, with the threat that extreme events might become more intense sooner than anticipated, with more severe impacts.[15]

Other scientists have reached similar conclusions with two separate studies concluding that future extreme precipitation events will approximately double in frequency.[16] Interestingly, the increase in extreme events comes at the expense of periods of light-to-moderate precipitation, which are likely to decrease.[17] Another potential impact of climate change is that regions with distinct wet and dry seasons are likely to experience an even larger annual range in their precipitation.[18] Thus, wet seasons are likely to get wetter while dry seasons are likely to get dryer.

Drought

Severe drought is forecast to increase in the future, particularly in marginal climate regions already susceptible to drought conditions. Locations most at risk include North Africa, the Middle East, and the Mediterranean.[19] The forecast of increased drought conditions is based on several variables and does not contradict the prediction of increased flooding discussed above. First, heightened temperatures correspond with higher levels of evaporation. Further, although total precipitation is forecast to remain the same or even increase across the planet, much of this precipitation will fall during extreme events in which water is more likely to run off the surface rather than soaking into the ground. In fact, as noted earlier, the highly beneficial light-to-moderate precipitation events are likely to decrease in the future.

While many of the regions most susceptible to drought are within developing countries, rapidly-growing locations such as the southwest United States are also at risk. Independent of any anthropogenic climate change, numerous studies outline historical "megadroughts" across the Southwest, sometimes lasting decades, centuries, or even millennia.[20] Unfortunately, much of the population and urban growth in this region over the past hundred years has occurred during one of the wettest periods in the last 1200 years.[21] Thus, with elevated temperatures, reduced snowpack, and a northern shift in storm track likely to occur due to human-induced climate change, most scientists conclude that the Southwest United States will be even more susceptible to extended drought in the future, making already stretched water supplies even more difficult to maintain.[22]

Heat

Heat is currently the leading weather-related killer in the United States,[23] and recent heat waves across the planet have killed tens of thousands of people. For example, the 2010 Russian Heat Wave had in excess of fifty thousand fatalities, while the 2003 European Heat Wave resulted in at least forty thousand deaths.[24] Heat is often known as a "silent killer"; unlike severe storms, there is no lasting impact on infrastructure, and as a result, the true impacts of heat are often underestimated or overlooked.

There is mounting evidence that climate change will result in more severe, longer lasting, and more frequent heat waves,[25] and that human health will be negatively affected with increases in both human morbidity and mortality.[26] One worst-case scenario offered suggests that over two thousand excess deaths per year will occur in Chicago alone by 2100[27] while another study finds that if heat waves similar to those experienced in Europe and Russia occurred in the United States, cities such as New York City could see in excess of three thousand additional fatalities.[28]

Security

How will climate change impact global security? Taken individually, each impact may seem a singular and geographically-isolated event, but collectively they are likely to worsen existing civil strife and a number of already-precarious security scenarios. As institutions fail to respond to the human need for security, these events can develop into what Abala-Bertrand calls a "complex humanitarian emergency."[29] Climate change will act as a "'threat multiplier,' amplifying existing vulnerabilities among populations and existing threats to security."[30] The negative impact on society may manifest in the form of humanitarian crises or state-on-state conflict. A simple model illustrating the nexus of climate and instability through a series of casual linkages between climate change and armed conflict was suggested by Buhaug et al. (See Figure 2).[31] In their model, adverse climate change can result in an increase in natural disasters, rising sea level, and/or resource scarcity. When mitigating factors like good governance or societal equality are not present to buffer adverse climatic effects, the result can be the manifestation of negative socio-political factors (drivers) and as their model suggests, there may be an increased risk of armed conflict.

U.S. policymakers have a number of tools with which to respond to crises linked to climate change. Given the likelihood of growing insecurity, it is possible that the U.S. military will play a role in these responses. U.S. military forces might be deployed to meet a humanitarian gap or to intervene in an escalating conflict. President Obama has already called attention to this possibility. In his 2010 National Security Strategy, the President warns that "a changing climate portends a future in which the United States must be better prepared and resourced to exercise robust leadership to help meet critical humanitarian needs."[32] This call for leadership may manifest as aid or programs to create more resilient societies or, when governmental systems fail to respond appropriately or in adequate measure, the introduction of U.S. military assets into the disaster-stricken area.

As discussed above, water insecurity is among the most prevalent concerns related to climate change. Incidence of drought may increase in severity and geographic expanse. At present, drought influences security in arid regions like the Sahel, but in the future, drought may also influence security in South America, portions of Africa, South-East Asia and the Mediterranean region.[33] Changes in snow pack accumulation may have significant impacts on water availability to agricultural communities on the lowland watersheds. Of particular concern is the Tibetan Plateau.[34] Snowpack in this area feeds the Ganges, Indus, and Brahmaputra rivers. Because the populations of Pakistan, India, Bangladesh, Nepal, and Bhutan draw on these riverine systems for their livelihoods, changes in these systems will impact them significantly. There are dams being built and still others which are planned that, while intended to regulate flow and provide power, may further decrease the flow to downstream consumers and provide a shock to these agricultural communities. But climate change's influence on water resources is not limited to populations in need of water, and some communities may find they have to plan for and accommodate large episodic increases in water. According the United Nations Environment Programme, half the world's population lives within 60 km of the sea, and three-quarters of all large cities are located on the coast.[35] Elevated birthrates and migration make it likely that the number of people living on or near the coast will increase.

III. Worst-Case Scenario

To see how water insecurity related to climate change can cause insecurity, consider a fictional but plausible complex humanitarian emergency scenario. A sub-equatorial coastal country, Calania has experienced violence against a number of districts in the country's mountainous interior. These mountainous, interior districts share a porous border with the conflict-prone, land-locked neighboring country of Seionia. Many communities from Seionia have crossed the border, seeking more secure conditions in Calania. With little land available to settle and fearing a lack of opportunity and acceptance, these groups continue their movement, along with other interior Calanians to the coastal capital of Coastdell.

Coastdell is a rapidly growing urban expanse of twenty-one million with one of the highest growth rates (3.2 percent) and population density (20k/km2) on the continent. Elevations in the area range from zero to forty meters above sea level. The upland residential areas and the business district are reasonably well developed, benefitting from infrastructure left by recently departed colonial authorities and continued investment, but the greatest population densities and areas of poverty consist of unincorporated informal settlements (slums) in the lowland areas. These slum residents, while also Calanians, are not well integrated into society, are poorly accounted for in census estimates and are certainly not a part of any disaster response plan. Now consider the Seionians, who have arrived in Coastdell as they have fled violence in their own country.

They are occupying marginal lowland areas on the periphery of the Coastdell city boundary along the coast and along the riverbanks of drainage systems leading from the interior mountains to the coast. Many Seionians have become victims of crime and also abuse by police and military forces.

It is now early September, peak tropical cyclone season in the region. This has many non-governmental agencies concerned as they anticipate responding to disasters in the region. The Calanian government has been criticized for failing to develop a comprehensive national disaster response plan. A very intense tropical cyclone, fueled by unusually warm ocean waters and a particularly moist atmosphere, makes landfall at high tide with Coastdell falling in the most severe quadrant of the storm. The rains that have been falling on the inland high ground for some days now have flooded drainage systems as they make their way to the coastal swamps. The discharge in the rivers has displaced informal settlements. As the storm surge moves inland it meets the swollen rivers. With nowhere to go, the waters rise.

One can imagine that the damage from a storm as described above would be significant, even in developed regions (e.g., Hurricane Katrina). In developing regions, such storms produce less damage from a financial standpoint, but often lead to greater numbers of dead, injured, and displaced. The fictitious government of Calania, having failed to develop a disaster response plan ahead of time and lacking existing support systems in place, may be compelled to rely upon the assistance provided by responding foreign governmental, non-governmental, and private entities to meet gaps in humanitarian and response capacity. The complexity of the urban operating environment, poorly planned and controlled urban growth, lack of building codes and code enforcement, the failure to incorporate and account for all residents, and the dominance of criminal elements across the urban fabric will create significant challenges for outside and domestic responders both.

When we add the multiplier of climate change to our past experiences, challenges like those facing the government of Calania will become more common. And given the pressure on states and non-governmental organizations in the developed world to intervene in humanitarian crises of this sort, the effects of these challenges are not isolated to countries like Calania. How might Calania have better prepared for this crisis, and what role (if any) should U.S. policymakers play in encouraging states like Calania to plan for the worst case? How can U.S. policymakers use models like the "pathways to conflict" model above as a framework to find those casual pathways and intervene as early as possible and in the most culturally appropriate and sustainable manner?

IV. Policy Considerations

In May 2014 the CNA Corporation Military Advisory Board (MAB) released a report titled "National Security and the Accelerating Risks of Climate Change," sparking a debate over the same issues that the above scenario highlighted. In the summary, the report's authors declared:

> We who have served on the MAB are concerned that while the causes of climate change and its impacts continue to be argued or ignored in our nation, the linkage between changes in our climate and national security has been obscured. Political concerns and budgetary limitations cannot be allowed to dominate what is essentially a salient national security concern for our nation.[36]

Senator James Inhofe dismissed the report as a publicity stunt. "There is no one in more pursuit of publicity," he said, "than a retired military officer." Inhofe continued:

> I look back wistfully at the days of the Cold War. Now you have people who are mentally imbalanced, with the ability to deploy a nuclear weapon. For anyone to say that any type of global warming is anywhere close to the threat that we have with crazy people running around with nuclear weapons, it shows how desperate they are to get the public to buy this.[37]

In light of the continued scientific debate regarding the severity of climate change, the disparity in multilateral engagement and commitment within the international system, and considering the domestic policy discord on the costs of implementing a clean energy economic policy, what steps should the United States take to lead on this issue? How should a policymaker, hoping to serve the collective best interests, respond to the security challenges that climate change might raise?

Policymakers should focus on a set of six key questions, based on the key recommendations of the CNA report:

1. How can the U.S. promote cooperation with other nations, as well as nongovernmental and intergovernmental stakeholders, to address the projected impacts of climate change?

2. How should the U.S. military's Combatant Commanders influence stakeholders in their areas of responsibility to build capacity and lower risk in those areas where the effects of climate change could be a cause of conflict?
3. To expedite crisis response and requirements generation, should the Arctic region be assigned to one combatant command? If so, to which combatant command should it be assigned and what underlying facts and assumptions support that decision?
4. Increased population, urbanization, and changing weather can affect production and distribution of water, food, and energy. How can policy makers work to gain cooperation from host nations to ensure that adaptive planning is performed that considers the interrelation of these critical resources?
5. The imprecise nature of climate change makes it hard to determine the actual costs of investment to promote resilience in U.S. infrastructure. In a time of austerity, what other primary considerations should policymakers promote in lieu of such investments, or what budget items can be cut to counteract the costs of adaptive changes?
6. Going forward, how can the Department of Defense develop innovative solutions such as public-private partnerships to build climate change-resilient facilities in bases and their communities? What industries can support this effort, and how can policymakers properly create incentives for participation?

Climate change is an exceedingly complex and far-reaching issue. It has already started to have considerable impacts on physical processes such as heat and drought which have raised some alarming security and humanitarian concerns. In a worst-case but highly plausible scenario, greenhouse gas emissions will continue to rise unchecked well into the future with some dramatic consequences. Unfortunately, there is no simple fix, and any potential solution would take a global effort spanning many years, something that has thus far eluded scientists and policymakers alike. In the meantime, U.S. policymakers, including those in the Department of Defense, are faced with some challenging decisions regarding how to best prepare for and adapt to a warming planet.

RECOMMENDED READINGS

Cayan, D. R., et al. 2010. "Future Dryness in the Southwest U.S. and the Hydrology of the Early 21st Century Drought." *Proceedings of the National Academy of Sciences* 107, no. 50: 21271–6.

CNA Military Advisory Board. 2014. *National Security and the Accelerating Risks of Climate Change*. Washington, DC.

King, W. 2014. *Understanding Environmental Security and Climate Change*. Fort Leavenworth, KS.

Meehl, G. A., & C. Tebaldi. 2004. "More Intense, More Frequent, and Longer Lasting Heat Waves in the 21st Century." *Science* 305, issue 5686: 994–7.

Stocker, T.F., et al., eds. 2013. *Climate Change 2013: The Physical Science Basis. Contribution of Working Group I to the Fifth Assessment Report of the Intergovernmental Panel on Climate Change*. Cambridge and New York.

NOTES

[1]K. E. Taylor, R. J. Stouffer, and G. A. Meehl, "An Overview of CMIP5 and the Experiment Design," *Bulletin of the American Meteorological Society*, 93, no. 4 (2012): 485–98.

[2]IPCC, *Climate Change 2013: The Physical Science Basis. Contribution of Working Group I to the Fifth Assessment Report of the Intergovernmental Panel on Climate Change.* Stocker, et al., eds. (Cambridge and New York: Cambridge University Press, 2013).

[3]D. P. Van Vuuren, et al., "The Representative Concentration Pathways: An Overview," *Climatic Change* 109: 5–31.

[4]K. Riahi, et al. "RCP 8.5—A Scenario of Comparatively High Greenhouse Gas Emissions," *Climatic Change* 5; R. Knutti and J. Sedláček, "Robustness and Uncertainties in the New CMIP5 Climate Model Projections," *Nature Climate Change* 3, no. 4 (2013):369–73.

[5]R. Knutti and J. Sedláček, "Robustness and Uncertainties in the New CMIP5 Climate Model Projections," Nature Climate Change 3, no. 4 (2013):369–73.

[6]R. H. Moss, et al., "The Next Generation of Scenarios for Climate Change Research and Assessment," *Nature* 463.7282: 747–56.

[7]P. Deschamps, et al., "Ice-sheet Collapse and Sea-level Rise at the Bolling Warming 14,600 [thinsp] Years Ago," *Nature* 483 (2012): 559–64.

[8]A. Cazenave, et al., "Sea Level Budget Over 2003–2008: A Reevaluation from GRACE Space Gravimetry, Satellite Altimetry and Argo," *Global and Planetary Change* 65, no. 1 (2009): 83–8.

[9]J. A. Church, and N. J. White, "Sea-level Rise from the Late 19th to the Early 21st Century," *Surveys in Geophysics* 32, no. 4–5 (2011): 585–602.

[10]D. E. Smith, et al., "The Early Holocene Sea Level Rise," *Quaternary Science Reviews* 30, no. 15 (2011): 1846–60.

[11]E. Rignot, et al., "Acceleration of the Contribution of the Greenland and Antarctic Ice Sheets to Sea Level Rise," *Geophysical Research Letters* 38, no. 5 (2011).

[12]I. Joughin, B., E. Smith, and B. Medley, "Marine Ice Sheet Collapse Potentially Under Way for the Thwaites Glacier Basin, West Antarctica," *Science* 344, issue 6185 (2014): 735–8.

[13]E. Rignot, et al., "Widespread, Rapid Grounding Line Retreat of Pine Island, Thwaites, Smith, and Kohler Glaciers, West Antarctica, from 1992 to 2011," *Geophysical Research Letters* 41, issue 10 (2014): 35029.

[14]S. Rahmstorf, "A New View on Sea Level Rise," *Nature Reports Climate Change* 4 (April 2010): 44–5.

[15]S. K. Min, et al., "Human Contribution to More-intense Precipitation Extremes," *Nature* 470, issue 7334 (2011): 378–81.

[16]P. Pall, et al., "Anthropogenic Greenhouse Gas Contribution to Flood Risk in England and Wales in Autumn 2000," *Nature* 470, issue 7334 (2011): 382–5. C. J. Shiu, et al., "How Much Do Precipitation Extremes Change in a Warming Climate?" *Geophysical Research Letters* 39, issue 17 (2012).

[17]K. E. Trenberth, et al., "The Changing Character of Precipitation," *Bulletin of the American Meteorological Society* 84, no. 9 (2003): 1205–17.

[18]C. Chou and C. W. Lan, "Changes in the Annual Range of Precipitation under Global Warming," *Journal of Climate* 25, no. 1 (2012): 222–35.

[19]M. G. Sanderson, D. L. Hemming, and R. A. Betts, "Regional Temperature and Precipitation Changes under High-end (≥ 4 C) Global Warming," *Philosophical Transactions of the Royal Society A: Mathematical, Physical and Engineering Sciences* 369, no. 1934 (2011): 85–98.

[20]P. J. Fawcett, et al., "Extended Megadroughts in the Southwestern United States during Pleistocene Interglacials," *Nature* 470, issue 7335 (2011): 518–21.

[21]E. R. Cook, et al., "North American Drought: Reconstructions, Causes, and Consequences," *Earth-Science Reviews* 81, no. 1 (2007): 93–134.

[22]D. S. Gutzler and T. O. Robbins, "Climate Variability and Projected Change in the Western United States: Regional Downscaling and Drought Statistics," *Climate Dynamics* 37, no. 5–6 (2011): 835–49. D. R. Cayan, et al., "Future Dryness in the Southwest U.S. and the Hydrology of the Early 21st Century Drought," *Proceedings of the National Academy of Sciences* 107, no. 50 (2010): 21271–6.

[23]National Oceanic and Atmospheric Administration (NOAA), "Natural Hazard Statistics" (2014), http://wwwnws.noaa.gov/om/ehazstats.shtml, accessed September 2, 2014.

[24]B. A. Revich, "Heat-wave, Air Quality and Mortality in European Russia in Summer 2010: Preliminary Assessment," *Yekologiya Cheloveka/Human Ecology* 7 (2011): 3–9. R. García-Herrera, et al., "A Review of the European Summer Heat Wave of 2003," *Critical Reviews in Environmental Science and Technology* 40, no. 4 (2010): 267–306.

[25]G. A. Meehl and C. Tebaldi, "More Intense, More Frequent, and Longer Lasting Heat Waves in the 21st Century," *Science* 305, no. 5686 (2004): 994–7. G. Luber and M. McGeehin, "Climate Change and Extreme Heat Events," *American Journal of Preventive Medicine* 35, no. 5 (2008), 429–35. E. M. Fischer and C. Schär, "Consistent Geographical Patterns of Changes in High-impact European Heatwaves," *Nature Geoscience* 3, no. 6 (2010): 398–403.

[26]M. A. McGeehin and M. Mirabelli, "The Potential Impacts of Climate Variability and Change on Temperature-related Morbidity and Mortality in the United States," *Environmental Health Perspectives* 109, supplement 2 (2001): 185.

[27]R. D. Peng, et al., "Toward a Quantitative Estimate of Future Heat Wave Mortality under Global Climate Change," *Environmental Health Perspectives* 119, no. 5 (May 2011): 701–6.

[28]L. S. Kalkstein, et al., "Analog European Heat Waves for U.S. Cities to Analyze Impacts on Heat-related Mortality," *Bulletin of the American Meteorological Society* 89, no. 1 (2008): 75–85.

[29]J. Albala-Bertrand, "Responses to Complex Humanitarian Emergencies and Natural Disasters: An Analytical Comparison," *Third World Quarterly* 21, no. 2 (2000): 215–27.

[30]W. King, *Understanding Environmental Security and Climate Change* (Fort Leavenworth, KS: The Simon Center, 2014); "Climate Change: Implications for Defence" (2014), Cambridge Institute for Sustainability Leadership.

[31]H. Buhaug, N. Gleditsch, and O. Theisen, "Implications of Climate Change for Armed Conflict," Presented at the World Bank Workshop on Social Dimensions of Climate Change, Washington, DC, 5–6 March 2008.

[32]Barack Obama, *National Security Strategy* (Washington, DC: The White House, 2010).

[33]A. Shepard, et al., *The Geography of Poverty, Disasters and Climate Extremes in 2030* (London: Overseas Development Institute, 2013).

[34]King, *Understanding Environmental Security and Climate Change*, and "Climate Change: Implications for Defence."

[35]UNEP, "Cities and Coastal Areas," accessed August 24, 2014, http://www.unep.org/urban_environment/issues/coastal_zones.asp.

[36]CNA Military Advisory Board, "National Security and the Accelerating Risks of Climate Change," May 2014.

[37]M. Galucci, "Climate Change 2014: House Bills Would Make It Harder To Fight The National Security Threats Posed By Global Warming," *International Business Times* (July 16, 2014).

12

Plagues, Peoples, and Power

The Globalization of Disease Control

JON MALINOWSKI

> There was no one who wept for any death, for all awaited death. And so many died that all believed that it was the end of the world.
>
> —AGNOLO DI TURA, FOURTEENTH CENTURY

Epidemics alter history. The Plague of Athens in 430 B.C. devastated the Athenian Empire and led to its defeat in the Peloponnesian War. The Plague of Justinian that began in A.D. 541 and returned periodically for two centuries afterwards so weakened the Eastern Roman Empire and adjacent areas that some scholars suggest new Islamic states were able to more easily gain a foothold, creating a new world order.[1] The Black Death of the fourteenth century killed as many as 50 million people or more and rewove the economic and social fabric of Europe.[2]

Infectious disease already takes a tremendous toll on human populations each year and should always be a concern of global leaders. Tuberculosis (TB) killed 1.5 million people in 2013 alone.[3] Another 584,000 people died of malaria in the same year.[4] Diarrheal disease affects 1.7 billion people annually and kills 760,000 children under five each year.[5] AIDS-related deaths, although declining, killed 1.5 million people in 2013.[6] By contrast, as of this writing the war in Syria has killed approximately 230,000 people in four years.[7]

Although humanity lives with deadly disease already, a globalizing world raises the specter of new outbreaks affecting areas that have, in recent history, largely escaped catastrophic epidemics.[8] In a connected world, planes that carry goods and services to every corner of the world also transport infected humans. The notion that emerging diseases can be isolated to far-away regions is foolish. Even a century ago, in an era of ocean liners and railroads, between twenty and forty percent of the entire global population became ill from the 1918 flu.[9] How much faster might similar diseases spread today?

I. Understanding Human Disease

Before considering the impact of globalization on pandemic disease, policymakers must understand how infectious disease spreads. Typically, infectious disease can be thought of in terms of a triangle of agent, host, and environment. A biological *agent* is a pathogen, typically a bacteria, virus, fungus, protozoa, or worm, that causes a disease (see Figure 12.1). For example, Ebola is a virus, while malaria is caused by a protozoa. It is nearly impossible for humans to eradicate agents from the environment. There are simply too many places for them to inhabit.

The *host* for a disease is a person or other living thing that is infected by an agent. Diseases are often combated by changing the biology or behavior of a host. Vaccines, for example, create antibodies to diseases that help a host fight later infections. Behavioral changes might include, for example, encouraging hand-washing and the proper locating of latrines to combat cholera. A host, once infected, can become a reservoir for a disease that could then be transmit-

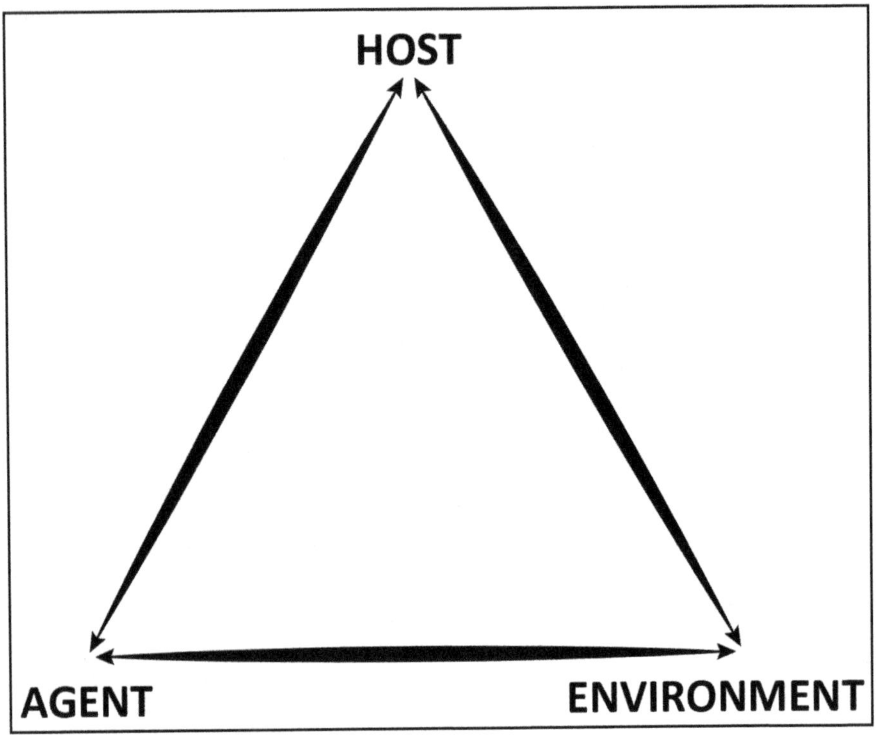

Figure 12.1

ted to another organism, such as when a person suffering from the flu sneezes in a crowded room.

The *environment* vertex of the triangle refers to conditions that allow a disease to exist or to be transmitted. These can be biological, cultural, or social. For example, an environment that is wet may harbor infected mosquitoes while a crowded urban setting may speed up transmission of an airborne pathogen. The recent Ebola epidemic highlights one aspect of the environment that is often overlooked in the discussion of epidemics, the destruction of natural habitat. Ebola outbreaks often begin in newly cleared areas on the edge of forests where human populations come into contact with infected animals.[10] Because rural-to-urban migration is so common, the disease can be carried to urban areas if an afflicted person moves soon after infection.

Because diseases require hospitable environments to spread, social and cultural changes can help to limit and even eliminate certain diseases. Consider, for instance, the near-eradication of Guinea worm. This disease, also known as dracunculiasis, is on the verge of eradication in the world not because of a new vaccine or high-tech pesticide, but because water usage habits were modified through education and simple safety steps. Guinea worm infects a person when contaminated water is consumed. Over the course of a year, a female Guinea worm can grow to a meter in length inside a human before painfully emerging through lesions commonly found on the legs or feet. To alleviate the pain of the worm, which can take up to a month to emerge, people often go into cool water, at which point larvae are released back into the water supply. Through the efforts of NGOs led by the Carter Center, people in endemic areas were taught to filter water, sometimes by using straws with filters inside them, to prevent ingestion of Guinea Worm larvae. These behavioral changes have reduced the disease from 3.5 million cases in 1986 to only 126 cases in 2014.[11]

Of course, for a disease to actually occur, an agent must get into a host. This can be achieved in many ways. *Direct transmission* involves the airborne spread of an agent, ingestion in water or food, direct contact with an agent (think athlete's foot on a locker room floor), or though sex.[12] Measles, for instance, passes only from human-to-human and is highly contagious. Quarantine or isolation has been used for centuries to prevent person-to-person transmission.

Indirect transmission involves infection by means of a *vector*, such as an insect or an animal that transmits the disease to other organisms. Arthropods, such as ticks, mosquitoes, flies, lice, and mites are common vectors of infectious agents. Animals can also be vectors for diseases such as rabies, which can be spread through the bite of a bat or raccoon.[13] From a public health perspective, diseases are often targeted by controlling vectors. For example, mosquito breeding areas, such as swamps, can be drained to reduce exposure to malaria, as was done with great success throughout the American South. Global warming, however, may roll back some of this progress. When temperatures rise, mosquitoes or ticks may thrive in areas that were previously inhospitable. For example, global warming may be allowing dengue fever, traditionally a tropical disease, to spread into new areas of the United States. A mosquito that spreads dengue is already found in twenty-eight states. If the world warms in coming decades, the habitat of the mosquito will likely increase. Warmer weather allows adult mosquitos to mature more quickly, causes female mosquitos to bite more frequently, and insures more mosquitos will survive a winter. Dengue fever already kills 22,000 people per year. If warming continues, billions more may be exposed to this deadly virus.[14]

II. Globalization and Disease

Globalization refers to the increased flow of people, capital, information, and products among people and places of the world. In the past few decades, the pace of globalization has increased dramatically.[15] What happens in local areas can now affect the world quickly, and vice versa. The beheading of a journalist in a remote corner of the Middle East, for example, can almost instantaneously impact the foreign policy and cultural attitudes of a country a hemisphere away. The strengthening of the local-global nexus increases the likelihood of pandemics. Consider the impact of transportation, trade, information technology, and urbanization on disease.

Transportation

The rapid increase in the speed of transportation is a considerable concern to public health officials. In the past, diseases such as the plague traveled slowly along overland and sea routes. Pathogens could take years to spread across a continent. For example, the Black Death (bubonic plague) may have taken nine years to travel from Central Asia to Italy.[16] Today, someone infected with a disease in Africa can be in New York City in just nine hours. This raises the possibility that an undetected disease could cross continents in just hours and spread widely before detection. The ability of a disease to spread in this way was illustrated by the Toronto outbreak of severe acute respiratory syndrome (SARS) in 2003. A Canadian woman contracted the disease in a Hong Kong hotel room, traveled back to Canada in late February, became ill, and died in early March.

A family member also became sick and was treated in a hospital, where numerous workers and patients were infected. Over the next three months, over 250 cases and forty-four deaths were recorded from one initial victim, a case fatality rate of eighteen percent.[17] The 2010–2013 cholera outbreak in Haiti provides another example of continent-jumping disease. After the earthquake of January 2010, the country struggled to rebuild. In October of that year, cholera broke out; to date, it has claimed over eighty-five hundred lives.[18] There is some evidence that the disease was introduced by United Nations' aid workers from Nepal through sewage leaking from a U.N. facility, although the organization denies this claim. Victims of the outbreak are suing the U.N.[19]

The increase in short-stay tourism in tropical areas has also raised new risks. International travelers, including vulnerable populations such as children and the elderly, routinely venture to remote, tropical areas because they can get there quickly, easily, and (by historical standards) inexpensively. But such travel can easily introduce tropical pathogens into populated areas outside the tropics. Because vacations tend to be short, travelers often do not become sick until after they return and resume their everyday lives. In 1996, for example, ten thousand cases of malaria were reported in the European Union; all were related to international travel.[20]

The ability of a disease to spread rapidly by modern transportation raises considerable challenges for policy makers. How and when should travel be restricted to areas with particular infections? Should passengers from disease-source areas be monitored? During the SARS outbreak, some passengers were scanned with infrared sensors to check for infection.[21] Is this approach feasible worldwide? In addition, how are economic losses balanced with health concerns? A boycott on travel to a certain area can cause millions of dollars in losses for local economies that rely on the tourist dollar.

Trade

Economic globalization can also impact diseases. For example, the global trade in food means that a contaminated facility can spread a disease across a whole continent, as in the case of numerous *E. coli* outbreaks in the U.S. hamburger industry. In the United Kingdom, bovine spongiform encephalopathy (BSE), commonly known as mad cow disease, became such a problem in the 1980s and 1990s that it led to a ten-year ban on British beef imports by the European Commission. More devastating is the sad story of hemophiliacs around the world who were contaminated by HIV-tainted blood products between 1982 and 1984. Even after at-risk populations were identified, some unscrupulous producers still collected blood from infected donors.[22] As an example of the consequences, a study of U.S. hemophiliacs born in 1978 who received blood products as children from 1982–84 showed that 45 percent were HIV-positive.[23]

As the world becomes more connected by trade flows and more reliant on international supply chains, how should policy makers address safety and public health? Do governments need to do more? If so, who should pay for the increased costs of inspections and monitoring? Can wealthy countries expect poorer trade partners to be equally vigilant? Does the responsibility for safety rest with producers, distributors, governments, or consumers?

Communications

A positive aspect of globalization for disease control is the rapid development of communications technology and the Internet. Global communication systems allows researchers and decision makers around the world to get early information about new epidemics and emerging diseases. Furthermore, the wealth of information available on the Internet can be used to educate healthcare workers in remote areas about how to treat and contain epidemics and thus, with hope, prevent pandemics. Geographic information systems (GIS) also allow for better mapping of diseases and their spread.[24] In the years ahead, what should governments do to further the development of technologies that aid the detection, containment, and treatment of diseases? What are some potential dangers of social media and disease? For example, in the current Ebola outbreak in West Africa, social media has been used to unify groups, but many myths, quack cures, and conspiracy theories are also circulating.[25] Should governments censor misinformation in a time of epidemic? If not, how can it be combated?

Urbanization

A final aspect of globalization impacting disease is the movement of millions of people in migration streams bringing rural residents to cities. Population mobility and disease are related because the conditions that push people from rural areas, such as poverty, the breakdown of social systems, and environmental degradation, also contribute to epidemics.[26] In addition, migrants are often impoverished and malnourished, increasing their risk for infection. Housing in urban areas can be ideal for diseases such as tuberculosis, and the diversity of urban settings can subject migrants to new pathogens to which they may have little or no resistance. With cities in areas such as South Asia and sub-Saharan Africa likely to double in coming decades, we can expect disease to be neighbors of the poor. Even middle-class housing can be a prime habitat for the spread of disease. In the 2003 SARS outbreak in Hong Kong, a high-rise housing complex known as Amoy Gardens had 321 cases of SARS. The density of living and possibly the pipe system contributed to the high numbers of infected. Aggressive isolation of residents and quick public health efforts are cited as saving lives.[27] Policymakers should seriously assess the ability of domestic and international public health organizations to respond to the challenges of urbanization in the twenty-first century. The historical examples of urbanization contributing to epidemics are almost countless.

III. What's the Worst that Could Happen?

Hollywood would suggest that the worst thing that could happen in terms of pandemic disease would be an outbreak of something such as Ebola or a similar hemorrhagic disease. While this certainly would be horrible, it is relatively unlikely. For one thing, Ebola kills quickly and thus the infected are rarely able to travel very far. Second, Ebola is transmitted through direct contact with body fluids. Third, the horrible condition under which people die of Ebola makes it hard for the disease to hide. Ebola victims, in the late stages of the disease, bleed from the eyes, nose, ears, and other body openings. It is hard to misdiagnose the severity of the disease.

The worst that could happen is likely a virulent strain of influenza that passes easily from person-to-person. A likely candidate is Influenza A (H5N1), often called avian influenza or "bird flu." It is enzootic in many bird populations around the world and can be contracted by humans if they come into contact with an infected bird or its meat or fluids.[28] Over six hundred people have become sick with H5N1 in the past decade. About sixty percent of those infected have died, which is a very high case-fatality rate.[29] The 1918 influenza pandemic had a case fatality rate of about 2.5 percent, while the 1957 and 1968 flu pandemics were in the 0.1 percent range. A 2007 study suggests that the actual case-fatality rate for an H5N1 outbreak might be closer to 14 to 33 percent, but even this number is horrifying if this strain became global and easily transmittable.[30] An H5N1 pandemic similar to the 1918 flu could cause 142 million deaths and a loss of $4.4 trillion in global GDP.[31]

The good news is that H5N1 cannot, at this time, be passed from human to human. But studies suggest that mutations of the virus could make that possible.[32] If a highly lethal strain of H5N1 emerged, or if H5N1 was weaponized and released, the results could be disastrous.[33] While vaccines are being developed, they are never a certain thing with influenza, and even if they were to prove effective they could take months to produce and distribute.

The potential for a pandemic of this lethality prompts many questions for leaders in the health, political, and business realms. What strategies should policy makers take now to lessen the impact of an H5N1 or similar outbreak? When a pandemic emerges, how aggressive should countries be in imposing public health measures? At what point must the rights of individuals get pushed aside in the name of the collective well-being? What structures might be put in place or strengthened to help early detection of new influenza strains or diseases?

It would be naïve foolishness to assume that modern scientific and technological advancements in the fields of medicine and public health will prevent another altering of human history by pandemic disease. Policymakers must be vigilant because globalization makes pandemics more likely and disease agents have proven they can survive centuries of human attempts to defeat them. The worst thing that can happen is not necessarily a zombie apocalypse. Nor is it a Hollywood movie that begins with a beaker breaking in a secluded government lab. Rather, the worst case might begin with a butcher in an urban market cutting up a chicken. What happens after that, though, depends on how well policymakers anticipate—and prepare for—the public health challenges that globalization raises.

RECOMMENDED READINGS

Barry, John M. 2005. *The Great Influenza: The Story of the Deadliest Pandemic in History*. New York.
Doherty, Peter C. 2013. *Pandemics: What Everyone Needs to Know*. New York.
Gupta, Sunetra. 2013. *Pandemics: Our Fears and the Facts*. Kindle Edition. Seattle, WA.
Osterholm, Michael T. 2007. "Unprepared for a Pandemic." *Foreign Affairs* 86, no. 2: 47–57.
Saker, Lance, et al. 2004. *Globalization and Infectious Diseases: A Review of the Linkages*. Geneva.

NOTES

[1]S. Sabbatani, R. Manfredi, and S. Florino, "The Justinian Plague (part two). Influence of the Epidemic on the Rise of the Islamic Empire," *Infez Med* 20, no. 3 (2012): 217–32.

[2]Ole J. Benedictow, "The Black Death: The Greatest Catastrophe Ever," *History Today* 55, no.3 (2005).

[3]World Health Organization (WHO), "Tuberculosis," Fact Sheet No. 104 (March 2015), http://www.who.int/mediacentre/factsheets/fs104/en/.

[4]WHO, "Factsheet on the World Malaria Report 2014" (December 2014), http://www.who.int/malaria/media/world_malaria_report_2014/en/.

[5]WHO, "Diarrheal Disease," Fact Sheet No. 330 (April 2013), http://www.who.int/mediacentre/factsheets/fs330/en/.

[6]UNAIDS, "Fact Sheet," accessed June 17, 2015, http://www.unaids.org/en/resources/campaigns/2014/2014gapreport/factsheet.

[7]"Syrian Rebel Forces Seize Major Military Base from Government," *The Guardian* (June 9, 2015), http://www.theguardian.com/world/2015/jun/09/syrian-rebel-forces-seize-major-military-base-government-forces.

[8]An *epidemic* refers to a disease outbreak that spreads to more people than usual. This is contrasted with an *endemic disease*, one that is always within a population at a certain level. Chicken pox is an infection that is endemic in the United States. Malaria is endemic in some areas or the world, but if it suddenly broke out in the United States, it would be called an epidemic because it is not common. A *pandemic* is an epidemic that spreads worldwide or, by some definitions, across international boundaries or throughout a large region.

[9]Jeffrey Taubenberger and David Morens, "1918 Influenza: the Mother of All Pandemics," *Emerging Infectious Diseases* 12, no. 1 (2006): accessed September 2, 2014, doi: 10.3201/eid1201.050979.

[10]Terrence McCoy, "How Deforestation Shares the Blame for the Ebola Epidemic," *The Washington Post* (July 8, 2014), accessed September 2, 2014, http://www.washingtonpost.com/news/morning-mix/wp/2014/07/08/how-deforestation-and-human-activity-could-be-to-blame-for-the-ebola-pandemic/.

[11]The Carter Center, "Guinea Worm Eradication Program," accessed June 17, 2014, http://www.cartercenter.org/health/guinea_worm/index.html.

[12]Kenneth J. Rothman, *Epidemiology: An Introduction* (Oxford: Oxford University Press, 2012), 112–14.

[13]The term *zoonotic* refers to diseases that can pass from animals to humans through contact with animal fluids or meat. A 1967 outbreak of the deadly Marburg virus in Germany was linked to exposure to infected monkeys. Similarly, the 2002 outbreak of SARS in China was connected to exposure to dead civets, a small mammal.

[14]Kim Knowlton, Gina Solomon, and Miriam Rotkin-Ellman, "Fever Pitch: Mosquito-Borne Dengue Fever Threat Spreading in the Americas," NRDC Issue Paper (New York: National Resources Defense Council, July 2009). Accessed on September 2, 2014, http://www.nrdc.org/health/dengue/files/dengue.pdf.

[15]Manfred B. Steger, *Globalization: A Very Short Introduction* (Oxford: Oxford University Press, 2013).

[16]David Herlihy, *The Black Death and the Transformation of the West* (Cambridge, MA: Harvard University Press, 1997).

[17]The *case fatality rate* (CFR), or "fatality rate," is the proportion of deaths in a population infected with a disease. "SARS in Canada: Anatomy of an Outbreak," Public Health Agency of Canada, Accessed on September 3, 2014, http://www.phac-aspc.gc.ca/publicat/sars-sras/naylor/2-eng.php.

[18]Randal C. Archibald and Somini Sengupta, "U.N. Struggles to Stem Haiti Cholera Epidemic," *The New York Times* (April 19, 2014), accessed September 15, 2014, http://www.nytimes.com/2014/04/20/world/americas/un-struggles-to-stem-haiti-cholera-epidemic.html.

[19]Ed Pilkington, "Haitians Launch New Lawsuit against UN over Thousands of Cholera Deaths," *The Guardian* (March 11, 2014), accessed September 3, 2014, http://www.theguardian.com/world/2014/mar/11/haiti-cholera-un-deaths-lawsuit.

[20]Lance Saker, et al., *Globalization and Infectious Diseases: A Review of the Linkages* (Geneva: World Health Organization, 2004), accessed September 2, 2014, http://apps.who.int/iris/handle/10665/68726.

[21]Sunetra Gupta, *Pandemics: Our Fears and the Facts* (Seattle, WA: Amazon, 2013). Kindle Edition.

[22]Ann Marie Kimball, *Risky Trade: Infectious Disease in the Era of Global Trade* (Burlington, VT: Ashgate, 2006).

[23]B.L. Evatt, "The Tragic History of AIDS in the Hemophilia Population, 1982–1984," World Federation of Hemophilia Occasional Papers 4, no. 6 (2007).

[24]Saker et al., *Globalization and Infectious Diseases.*

[25]Satta Sarmah, "Fighting the Endless Spread of Ebola Misinformation on Social Media," *Fast Company* (August 19, 2014), accessed September 2, 2014, http://www.fastcompany.com/3034380/fighting-the-endless-spread-of-ebola-misinformation-on-social-media.

[26]Saker et al., *Globalization and Infectious Diseases.*

[27]Peter Shadbolt, "SARS 10 Years on: How Dogged Detective Work Defeated an Epidemic," *CNN* (February 21, 2013), accessed September 3, 2014, http://www.cnn.com/2013/02/21/world/asia/sars-amoy-gardens/.

[28]*Enzootic* means endemic in an animal population. *Endemic* is used for human populations.

[29]"Highly Pathogenic Avian Influenza A (H5N1) in People," Centers for Disease Control and Prevention, updated January 8, 2014, accessed September 4, 2014, http://www.cdc.gov/flu/avianflu/h5n1-people.htm.

[30]Felix Li, et al., "Finding the Real Case-Fertility Rate of H5N1 Avian Influenza," *Journal of Epidemiology and Community Health* 62 (2008): 555–9.

[31]Michael T. Osterholm, "Unprepared for a Pandemic," *Foreign Affairs* 86, no. 2 (2007): 47–57.

[32]Flu viruses can mutate through a process of recombination. If an animal and human version of the flu infect the same human cell, they can swap genetic material, creating an animal virus that can be spread from human to human.

[33]Stephanie Schorow, "Fears of Bioterrorism or an Accidental Release," *Harvard Gazette* (February 16, 2012), accessed on September 4, 2014, http://news.harvard.edu/gazette/story/2012/02/fears-of-bioterrorism-or-an-accidental-release/.

13

Coping with Nuclear Terrorism and Nuclear Weapons Proliferation

CYNTHIA ROBERTS

Imagine the day after 9/11 if instead of flying planes into the Twin Towers, terrorists had detonated a 10 kiloton nuclear weapon (about the size of the Hiroshima bomb) in midtown Manhattan. A catastrophe of untold death and destruction would still be unfolding. Nothing would have saved the hundreds of thousands, possibly more than a million, New Yorkers murdered by the initial blast, fireball, and radiation.[1] Millions more would survive, only to face fires, as well as lethal and spreading radioactive fallout, among other hazards. These living victims could not depend on first responders to help them in the crucial minutes and hours after the blast. Power, phones, and access to the Internet would be knocked out in the area. Emergency personnel outside the affected zone would need time to mobilize and respond in chaotic and dangerous conditions. Contemplating the day after *this* 9/11 makes one grateful that the real 9/11, though catastrophic, was not worse than it was. This scenario of a nuclear attack resulting from nuclear weapons falling into the wrong hands of terrorists or "rogue state" actors has steeled U.S. policymakers' resolve to prevent such an event from happening.[2]

A terrorist nuclear attack is the paradigmatic low-probability, high-cost event,[3] but nuclear dangers and risks have been increasing in recent years.[4] North Korea tested its first nuclear weapon in 2006 after withdrawing from the Non-Proliferation Treaty (NPT) in 2003; Iran refused to stop its uranium enrichment program and was placed under United Nations Security Council sanctions (scheduled to be removed under the terms of the July 2015 nuclear agreement that delays for more than a decade Iran's nuclear "breakout" time); Al-Qaeda and other jihadist groups are known to be interested in acquiring nuclear weapons and materials; suspected nuclear facilities in Pakistan have been attacked; nuclear technology has been transferred by Pakistan and North Korea; illegal nuclear programs were exposed in Iraq (1991), Iran (2002), Libya (2003), and Syria (2007); and a long list of nuclear security and control incidents and failures has been documented. According to a recent study, four of the nine states (or nearly 50 percent) that built nuclear arsenals have experienced "severe political crises affecting nuclear security and/or control of use."[5]

The threat of nuclear terrorism differs markedly from the spectre of nuclear Armageddon in the Cold War when the superpowers developed assured destruction postures and capabilities that deterred nuclear use. Because terrorists are not easily or fully deterrable, preventing their acquisition of nuclear weapons and other weapons of mass destruction (WMD) and employment, if acquired, are leading policy objectives. Potential nuclear proliferation to nonstate terrorists and rogue actors involves factors relating both to the supply of nuclear materials and technologies and demand from groups that are motivated to acquire nuclear weapons and exploit available opportunities to do so. Although it would not be easy, a motivated terrorist group might be able to steal a nuclear warhead and overcome the security safeguards blocking its operational use. Or more likely, terrorists could acquire nuclear materials in the form of plutonium or highly enriched uranium (HEU) to produce a weapon of approximately 10 kilotons, similar to the Hiroshima device, by gaining design plans from a proliferation smuggling ring like the one started by A.Q. Khan in Pakistan.[6]

The low probability of a terrorist nuclear attack constrains policy planning and encourages public complacency. But the difficulties terrorists and rogue actors encounter are also numerous, many the result of policies which collectively have helped to prevent a nuclear 9/11 on American soil or in other countries.[7] Even if policymakers effectively extend and adapt existing measures, there is still no guarantee that terrorists will not succeed in striking with nuclear or other weapons of mass destruction (WMD). In this event, civil defense measures could play a vital role in limiting the extent of the damage. The 2014 "National Defense Strategy for Countering Weapons of Mass Destruction" summarizes the comprehensive objectives to "reduce incentives to pursue, possess, and employ WMD; increase barriers to the acquisition, proliferation, and use of WMD; manage WMD risks emanating from hostile, fragile, or failed states and safe havens; and deny the effects of current and emerging WMD threats through layered, integrated defenses."[8] This chapter explores the challenges inherent in limiting the spread of nuclear weapons while pursuing other U.S. strategic interests, and considers policies to achieve this objective and mitigate the effects of failures. In particular, it examines the role of the international nuclear nonproliferation regime and counterproliferation mechanisms in the context of American strategic objectives. At the end it returns to the question of civil defense in the event of a terrorist nuclear attack on American soil.

I. Proliferation, Terrorism and Policy Responses

The threat posed by nuclear weapons has been at the forefront of international security since their advent and first use by the United States during World War II. American presidents have consistently sought to limit nuclear proliferation, starting with a 1946 statute that prohibited the transfer of nuclear weapons to other states. President Harry Truman declared that the United States alone "must constitute ourselves trustees of this new force" and even the subsequent Baruch Plan to invest control over all nuclear materials with a new U.N. body insisted that the United States would retain its nuclear bombs until the new agency created reliable mechanisms for international control and intrusive inspections.[9]

After the Soviet Union crossed the nuclear threshold, attention turned to other cooperative methods of limiting their spread. President Dwight Eisenhower's 1953 "Atoms for Peace" proposal, which envisioned redirecting nuclear research from military requirements to peaceful, economic development, eventually produced the authorization in 1956 for the International Atomic Energy Agency (IAEA). The IAEA was tasked with providing information and assistance to countries to use nuclear energy for peaceful purposes and conducting inspections of their nuclear facilities to guard against diversion of uranium fuel and plutonium produced by reactors to military pursuits. A 1961 U.N. resolution unanimously authorized negotiation of a treaty that would ban countries without nuclear weapons from acquiring them and require IAEA inspections. This process resulted in a set of international agreements anchored by the Nuclear Nonproliferation Treaty (NPT) which was signed on July 1, 1968, and entered into force on March 5, 1970.[10] Since their inception these legal agreements have faced challenges, especially Pakistan's test of a nuclear weapon in 1998, North Korea's nuclear test in 2006, and Iran's covert nuclear program.

In retrospect, although Eisenhower's Atoms for Peace initiatives contributed to the norm of nuclear nonproliferation and eventual NPT regime, they also had the negative impact of accelerating the international diffusion of scientific and industrial nuclear technology. In the 1950s, the United States actively promoted nuclear energy exports and technological agreements with more than 24 states. Enforcement of safeguards by Washington, other nuclear suppliers, and the IAEA, was inadequate. Perhaps inevitably, U.S. nuclear assistance was diverted to military purposes, notably by Israel, India, and Pakistan.[11]

Trade and technological globalization lower the threshold for the development or acquisition of WMD not only for states, but also possibly for substate or nonstate groups. Discussions about supply-side issues, opportunities for nuclear programs to develop, and opportunities for terrorists to acquire nuclear materials and weapons, must take into consideration the large and growing nuclear power industry throughout the world. The risks associated with nuclear power, which include those pertaining to facility safety, the availability of nuclear material, and the spread of nuclear engineering know-how, are a critical component of the nuclear-power debate. The nuclear power industry is also the source of many dual-use materials, which are components that can be used for both licit and illicit nuclear programs.[12] There is also an industry around nuclear and radiological materials in science and medicine that creates concerns for smaller-scale threats.

India had used the technology and materials acquired under the Atoms for Peace process to build and test its first nuclear device in 1974 and become a nuclear weapons state in 1998.[13] However, the Pakistani test, in particular, ushered in a new series of concerns about nuclear weapons in international security and raised questions about the value of the NPT regime.[14] Pakistan's nuclear weapons program took many observers by surprise, despite the fact that the country had been seeking to achieve technological parity with its regional adversary India. The source of surprise did not lie with Pakistan's intent, because the country had never signed the NPT, but in their ability to develop a weapon with minimal support from the existing nuclear powers.[15] Pakistan's capacity to cross the nuclear threshold by using informal networks and dual-use material made it clear that cooperative measures like the NPT represented only one approach to the problem—and one that would not be sufficient to stem the spread of nuclear weapons in the future.

The detonation of Pakistan's nuclear weapon also coincided with an increase in militant Islamic terrorism marked by the African embassy bombings in 1998, the USS Cole bombing in 2000, and the September 11 attacks against the United States in 2001.[16] Concerns about the spread of nuclear technology fused with those of increased large-scale terrorist activity, rekindling discussions of the threat from nuclear terrorism. The George W. Bush administration, which perceived intense homeland vulnerability while overrating the benefits of an aggressive use of U.S. military power,[17] responded with a strategy that emphasized preemptive and preventive strikes against both terrorists and rogue states, notably Iraq.[18] The idea of preventive war harkened back to the Cold War, and Bismarck is often quoted as saying "preventive war is like committing suicide for fear of death." In 1994 the Clinton administration came close to launching preventive strikes against North Korea to prevent its development of a nuclear capability.[19] Although the Obama administration has backed away from preventive war against rogue states, the emphasis on *counter*proliferation and preemptive strikes against terrorists remains a central element of American policy. President Obama recently reaffirmed in the 2015 National Security Strategy, "No threat poses as grave a danger to our security and well-being as the potential use of nuclear weapons and materials by irresponsible states or terrorists."

Two of the United States' most pressing national security issues, the nuclear programs in Iran and North Korea, lie at the intersection of nonproliferation and counterproliferation. Both states have challenged the principles that undergird the cooperative approach of the NPT by signing the convention and then either withdrawing from or violating the agreement. Since both countries appear undeterred in their quest for nuclear weapon capabilities, U.S. and international policymakers often resort to countervailing measures such as denying resources, stifling technological advancement, and imposing costs as inducements for international negotiations to achieve compliance.

II. The Nuclear Nonproliferation Treaty and the Small Number of Determined Proliferators

The NPT is the centerpiece of international efforts to limit the spread of nuclear weapons. One theory behind nuclear arms control and the NPT comes from the idea of rational cooperation under anarchy.[20] The treaty only works when countries feel they are better off not having nuclear weapons, as long as other countries (excluding the five nuclear weapons states) do not have them as well. Institutionalized cooperation assumes strategic interaction with other states: country A may be better off with nuclear weapons provided their neighbor country B does not have them, but once country B acquires nuclear weapons then country A would have been better off had neither pursued that course. Mutual cooperation becomes a stable state over an infinite number of plays. The treaty and associated regime is built on mutual or multilateral cooperative interests, information to identify violations, and enforcement mechanisms or punishments should a signatory violate its obligations. However, the NPT also has elements best explained by two other international relations theories. According to constructivism, norms reflect the logic of appropriateness of particular types of international behavior, such as a taboo against using nuclear weapons or the value placed by many members of the international community on a world without nuclear weapons.[21] Realism also has explanatory power to the extent that the most powerful actors prefer to create institutions that advance their interests and bind others while permitting maximum flexibility for the rule-makers and first movers.[22]

The three mainstays of the NPT are non-proliferation, disarmament, and the peaceful use of nuclear energy. The five recognized nuclear powers in the treaty correspond to the five permanent members of the United Nations Security Council: China, France, Russia, the United Kingdom, and the United States. The NPT embodies the norm of nuclear abstinence, excluding the five nuclear powers, which are supposed to be on the path of arms reductions. Moreover, the NPT's requirements for safeguards, including IAEA inspections of nuclear power facilities, remain a requirement for receiving peaceful nuclear assistance and have caught cheaters and countries pursuing suspicious weapons-related activities (e.g., Iran, North Korea, South Korea, and Egypt).[23]

It is undeniable that the NPT has *not* prevented the most determined proliferators from getting the bomb and helped shield violators that joined to conceal their illegal nuclear programs. However, measured against the larger sample of about 200 countries that could have become nuclear weapons states but chose not to, or reversed initial programs, its role should not be discounted.[24] For example, South Africa abandoned its nuclear weapons program while the three former Soviet republics of Ukraine, Belarus, and Kazakhstan agreed to give up their stockpiles after the collapse of the Soviet Union and joined the NPT.

In addition to the five countries identified in the NPT as nuclear weapons states, three additional states, as mentioned above, possess nuclear weapons and are unwilling to relinquish their nuclear status. India successfully tested a nuclear weapon in 1974; Pakistan followed in 1998, and India then tested a more advanced fusion weapon in 1998. Israel also has an undeclared nuclear capability. None of these countries signed the NPT, meaning that their nuclear activities were not violations of treaty obligations. As a rising regional power with growing energy needs, India's challenge to the NPT regime is perhaps the most significant. In recent years, Delhi has shown responsible behavior, complying with the 2006 U.S.-India civil nuclear agreement that requires India to separate its civil and military nuclear facilities and place the former under IAEA safeguards. Aiming to supply 25 percent of its electricity from nuclear power by 2050, India seeks to join the Nuclear Suppliers Group (as well as the Missile Technology Control Regime), but still prefers to remain outside the NPT.

Beyond these eight countries, the two states with active nuclear programs at different stages of development are North Korea and Iran, both of which were signatories of the NPT at one time. Their activities have put them in violation of their obligations and they are widely considered rogue regimes. North Korea has an ongoing nuclear weapons program, is capable of enriching uranium and producing weapons-grade plutonium, and has tested nuclear explosive devices in 2006, 2009, and 2013. Pyongyang withdrew from the NPT in 2003, but previously managed to subvert international inspections by running parallel programs for both plutonium and highly-enriched uranium with most of the international attention focused on the Yongbyon plutonium reactor. It is believed to possess up to ten nuclear weapons.

Unlike North Korea, Iran has not withdrawn from the NPT and claims that its current nuclear activities are consistent with the treaty in permitting development of nuclear energy. Iran, a leading oil-producing state, argues that it wishes to reserve its petroleum stock for export and meet its domestic energy needs through nuclear power. Despite this claim, Iran has blocked inspections of many nuclear facilities, and the IAEA found Iran in violation of their treaty obligations. The 2015 landmark agreement between Iran and the P-5 permanent members of the U.N. Security council plus Germany (whose implementation was verifed by the IAEA on January 16, 2016) significantly restricts Iran's path to acquiring nuclear weapons for ten years but could leave Tehran in the position of a breakout capability when the treaty expires. Partly related to these cases, there is concern that a new nuclear weapons cascade could occur, particularly in the Middle East and Asia, with demand-side dynamics tied in with geopolitical tensions and other factors.

III. Nuclear Capable States

Two final categories of states also play an important role in nuclear proliferation. Many states have the nuclear material and scientific capabilities to develop nuclear weapons in a matter of months, putting them in the category of latent nuclear weapons states. Germany and Japan, for example, could probably become nuclear weapons states in less than a year. Other countries that could probably cross the weapon threshold quickly include Canada, South Korea, and Taiwan.

Several officials and analysts have warned of the security risks arising from the spread of uranium enrichment and plutonium fuel-production facilities and the emergence of many "virtual nuclear weapons states" with the capacity to develop nuclear weapons in a very short time period.[25]

The final category is composed of "nuclear reversal" states that have voluntarily given up nuclear ambitions after investing in weapons programs or seriously explored the nuclear option but reconsidered. Some of the notable examples include South Africa, Libya, Brazil, and Argentina. Three former Soviet states (Ukraine, Belarus, and Kazakhstan) opted to relinquish nuclear weapons left from the Soviet occupation after a lengthy negotiating process in the early 1990s. Why states forego nuclear weapons programs or give them up after initially pursuing them is a puzzle with many possible explanations (ranging from inducements to dissuasion, coercion and economic sanctions) that may vary from case to case[26]

IV. U.S. Strategy and Nuclear Nonproliferation Policy

The policy of nonproliferation has been the diplomatic and legal cornerstone of American nuclear policy since the 1950s. The U.S. gains strategic benefits from promoting nonproliferation norms and mechanisms, including arms control, to demonstrate its compliance with NPT provisions and lessen perceptions of American hegemony and hypocrisy. President Obama's promulgation of a Global Zero policy is widely credited with attempting to elevate the goals of the nonproliferation regime, although this campaign is not unique and it is doubtful it makes an impact on strongly committed terrorists. All U.S. presidents, except George W. Bush, have advocated the eventual elimination of nuclear weapons[26] and developed nonproliferation and counterproliferation mechanisms to prevent the further spread of other actors' nuclear weapons. The United States has also pursued nuclear arms control with the Soviet Union and Russia to reduce their arsenals despite adversarial or conflictual relations. In both cases, the practical benefits accrue to the United States, above all in military mission requirements given its dominance in global conventional strike capabilities.

The reality of American nuclear policy is complicated and not without contradictions and associated risks. For example, the 2010 U.S. Nuclear Posture Review identified the "fundamental role" of U.S. nuclear forces was to deter the use of nuclear weapons against itself, its allies or its partners and also gave "assurance" that the United States would not use nuclear weapons against non-nuclear weapons states "that are party to the NPT and in compliance with their non-proliferation obligations." Yet in its nuclear employment policy, the United States has sought strategic nuclear primacy through warfighting and damage-limitation strategies that rely on counterforce capabilities, i.e., those with sufficient payloads and accuracy to strike the adversary's nuclear weapons.[27] This approach defies the logic of mutual vulnerability that underpins deterrence[28] and the normative logic of reducing nuclear weapons while pursuing their elimination.

Robust American counterforce capabilities may be needed to ensure the credibility of extended deterrence (the ability of a nuclear power to deter an attack on its non-nuclear allies)[29] while the United States has actively dissuaded several allies that have demonstrated interest in acquiring nuclear weapons or threshold capability, including Germany, Taiwan, South Korea, and Japan. The United States has employed both inducements and coercion to limit the spread of nuclear weapons to allies.[30] Security guarantees can serve as the basis for coercive leverage to ensure allies forego their nuclear aspirations. Many allies are recipients of U.S. security guarantees including the "nuclear umbrella," and in NATO there are "nuclear-sharing" arrangements, through which non-nuclear states (such as Germany, Italy and Turkey) maintain a capability to use their attack aircraft in a nuclear role, employing American nuclear warheads stored in Europe. This arrangement, while problematic for nonproliferation, may offer other strategic advantages. It should bolster the reassurance of allies against fears of abandonment, mitigate alliance entrapment problems for the United States, and also reduce the dangers of catalytic nuclear postures in which a nuclear state—such as Israel, South Africa, or Pakistan—might threaten to use nuclear weapons to draw the United States into a conflict in which it does not want to be involved.[31]

The United States is not the only nuclear weapons state that has sought to limit the spread of nuclear weapons while simultaneously advancing other strategic objectives that may lead to the opposite outcome. In some cases, such competing objectives have led states or subnational actors to provide sensitive nuclear assistance, as France did to Israel to advance Paris' goal of constraining Egypt, and the Khan network did in multiple instances with the apparent connivance of Pakistani authorities, in part to complicate and burden U.S. strategic behavior.[32] One of the principal resulting problems is that even small nuclear arsenals in the hands of states or nonstate actors could threaten U.S. security and interests by bolstering beliefs that nuclear weapons would make aggressive moves less risky. America's ability to coerce weaker actors could also be impaired. Some observers have suggested that this was one reason the United States could invade Iraq, but not North Korea, and that Iran appreciated the difference.[33]

V. Counterproliferation

Because nonproliferation relies on a cooperative framework where the underlying assumption is that the parties will opt to forgo nuclear weapons, other mechanisms have been needed to cope with actors that nonetheless pursue nuclear capabilities. States may opt out or withdraw from the NPT, while sub-state or transnational actors like terrorists are not a party to such agreements. Counterproliferation attempts to combat the spread of unconventional weapons through the active process of combating efforts to acquire WMD, with nuclear weapons at the top of the list.

As the debate over how to respond to a potential Iranian nuclear capability demonstrates, the threat to use force preventively to destroy or degrade a developing nuclear program remains an important policy instrument for counterproliferation, although as shown in the cases of the North Korean and Chinese nuclear weapons programs, political leaders have been reluctant to resort to preventive strikes given the likely costs and unintended consequences. Besides the use of force, the counterproliferation toolbox includes coercive diplomacy and dissuasion as well as economic pressure, including sanctions to raise the costs to states that may want to get the bomb. American leadership and global power are central to the development and implementation of counterproliferation initiatives in partnership with other governments and international organizations.

The concept of counterproliferation to prevent nuclear weapons and materials from falling into the wrong hands gained traction in the early 1990s with the collapse of the Soviet Union.[34] The Soviet Union had maintained nuclear arsenals in many of the former Soviet republics, such as Ukraine and Belarus and these countries had an extensive nuclear architecture. Although the newly independent states would ultimately accede to the NPT, there were concerns about unsecured nuclear materials and warheads. The possibility that terrorists, rogue regimes or subnational actors would acquire those materials or gain control over "loose" nuclear weapons motivated an active stance towards preventing such outcomes.[35] Recognizing the need for American assistance to mitigate the threats, senior American policymakers quickly undertook important initiatives, starting with the Nunn-Lugar Act (1991), which created the Cooperative Threat Reduction (CTR) Program that became embedded within the Defense Threat Reduction Agency (DTRA). Four objectives were specified: (1) to dismantle WMD in the former USSR; (2) consolidate and secure remaining WMD and related technology and materials; (3) increase transparency and encourage higher standards of conduct; and (4) support defense cooperation with the objective of preventing proliferation. According to DTRA, the program has deactivated more than 7,500 nuclear warheads, neutralized chemical weapons, safeguarded fissile materials, converted weapons facilities for peaceful use, among other initiatives, and was subsequently expanded outside the former Soviet Union.[36] A new bilateral cooperative framework was signed with Russia in 2013 to supercede the CTR, but implementation was halted by the Russian government in 2015 in protest over Western sanctions and renewed conflictual relations associated with the war in Ukraine.

Nuclear smuggling below the state level has been rare, but it represents a serious challenge that could grow because of the global market in dual-use technologies and demand from both states and non-state actors. The largest known case of nuclear smuggling involved the A.Q. Khan network, which supplied weapon designs, centrifuges, and other materials to rogue states like Libya and North Korea.[37] A.Q. Khan was considered the father of Pakistan's nuclear program. After Pakistan acquired nuclear weapons, Khan repurposed the network for smuggling nuclear technologies. It took a number of years to identify the activity and dismantle the network. Khan was placed under house arrest in Pakistan until 2009 when he was released, despite strong protests from the United States.

Although the total quantity of unsecured nuclear sources is unclear, the IAEA identified 1,080 cases of illicit trafficking and other unauthorized use of nuclear and radiological materials from 1993 through 2006.[38] Although the IAEA discontinued public updates of highly enriched uranium and plutonium thefts and other incidents in 2008, they have continued to an unknown degree. Georgian authorities confirmed seizing nuclear material in 2010 from smugglers entering Georgia from Armenia. In 2011, Moldovan authorities arrested smugglers possessing 4.4 grams of weapon-grade highly enriched uranium taken from a larger ring that reportedly possesses one kilogram of uranium.[39] To date, the only known instances of nuclear material used in terrorist bombs occurred in connection with Chechen separatists, though these devices were never detonated.[40]

Following the creation of the CTR, the U.S. promoted several additional international and national counterproliferation initiatives, including the Proliferation Security Initiative (PSI), which involves a group of countries taking active steps to prohibit the sale of dual-use materials and invest in nuclear detection capabilities. Both counterproliferation and deterrence may also be strengthened through progress in the evolving science of nuclear forensics. The United States and partner countries are constructing a database of nuclear signatures to trace the origins of nuclear materials in the event smuggled materials are seized or a nuclear explosion occurs. Multiple branches and agencies of the U.S. government, located mainly in the Departments of Defense and Energy, are involved in counterproliferation initiatives focused on combatting the spread of WMD and defensive measures to ensure nuclear security against a variety of threats including the worst case of a nuclear attack.

VI. Concluding Policy Issues

To return to the opening scenario, is the United States prepared to deal with the threat of nuclear terrorism if nonproliferation and counterproliferation policies fail? What would happen if terrorists or a subnational group clandestinely detonated a nuclear weapon in a major American city? During the Cold War, plans for civil defense against attack by thousands of thermonuclear warheads were unrealistic. However, in addition to federal policies for homeland defense, such as improved screening for nuclear materials and weapons concealed in commercial shipping containers and similar delivery modes, civil defense measures against a small-scale terrorist nuclear or other WMD attack would be prudent.[41] National and local authorities (including New York City's counterterrorism officials) are reluctant to promote civil defense education partly to avoid frightening people after 9/11. Such dodging, however, seems misguided in major American cities, such as New York, Washington, and Los Angeles, given how routinely and efficiently other disaster preparation information is disseminated, for example about hurricanes and the spread of Ebola or deadly flu viruses. Japan engages in extensive public education and preparedness for earthquakes, and indisputably its approach saves lives.

Information and basic disaster preparation is especially relevant in the case of a nuclear attack because what the shocked and injured survivors of a nuclear explosion do in the first 48 hours after a detonation will determine whether they live or die. Just as informed people watching the ocean water recede right before a tsunami hits know to run immediately to high ground, city dwellers need to react rapidly and instinctively to shelter themselves from the initial radioactive fallout. Radioactive particles begin to deposit in the first fifteen minutes after a nuclear detonation, and fallout spreads in a localized area over the next twenty-four to forty-eight hours. Depending on prevailing weather and wind patterns, the fallout plume from a ten kiloton improvised nuclear device will likely extend a few tens of miles downwind in a relatively narrow, cigar shape with a width of a few miles. With telecommunications out or unreliable in affected and nearby zones, individuals must know ahead of time what they should do and in what order.

For instance, it makes sense to get out of the path of an approaching mushroom cloud and smoke by heading perpendicular to the plume. Underground shelters offer an appropriate place to shelter from deadly gamma rays, for example in a basement behind thick walls. Schools, businesses, and apartment buildings could resurrect the practice of identifying designated shelters. Wind patterns also impact the spread of lethal radiation (in the Northeast the wind usually blows west to east) putting city dwellers at greater risk of contamination if they head out in the open in the wrong direction. Such civil defense awareness facts, like fire drills, can save lives, and in times of austerity are cost effective.

Reflecting the stark reality of the nuclear threat, President Obama in his 2009 Prague speech declared that nuclear terrorism "is the most immediate and extreme threat to global security." To counter this threat, the President urged that "we act with purpose and without delay." He unveiled a new international effort to secure vulnerable nuclear materials around the world, which Washington inaugurated with a Global Summit on Nuclear Security in 2010. This first Nuclear Security Summit was followed by others in 2012 and 2014. America's global cities could join this effort by undertaking prudent and affordable civil defense measures against the WMD threat.

RECOMMENDED READINGS

Allison, Graham T. 2004. *Nuclear Terrorism: The Ultimate Preventable Catastrophe.* New York.

Kroenig, Matthew. 2010. *Exporting the Bomb: Technology Transfer and the Spread of Nuclear Weapons.* Ithaca, NY.

Narang, Vipin. 2014. *Nuclear Strategy in the Modern Era: Regional Powers and International Conflict.* Princeton, NJ.

Sagan, Scott D., and Kenneth N. Waltz. 2002. *The Spread of Nuclear Weapons: A Debate Renewed.* New York.

Tannenwald, Nina. 2007. *The Nuclear Taboo: The United States and the Non-use of Nuclear Weapons since 1945.* Cambridge.

ADDITIONAL READINGS

Brands, Hal, and David Palkki. 2011. "Saddam, Israel, and the Bomb: Nuclear Alarmism Justified?" *International Security* 36, no. 1 (Summer): 133–66.

Carter, Ashton B., and William J. Perry. 2000. *Preventive Defense: A New Security Strategy for America.* Washington, DC.

Flynn, Stephen. 2004. *America the Vulnerable: How Our Government is Failing to Protect Us from Terrorism.* New York.

Fuhrmann, Matthew. 2009. "Spreading Temptation: Proliferation and Peaceful Nuclear Cooperation Agreements." *International Security* 34, no. 1: 7–41.

Fuhrmann, Matthew and Sarah E. Kreps. 2010. "Targeting Nuclear Programs in War and

Peace: A Quantitative Empirical Analysis, 1941–2000." *Journal of Conflict Resolution* 54 (December): 831–59.
Hymans, Jacques E. C. 2006. *The Psychology of Nuclear Proliferation.* Cambridge.
Kemp, Scott R. 2014. "The Nonproliferation Emperor Has No Clothes: The Gas Centrifuge, Supply-Side Controls, and the Future of Nuclear Proliferation." *International Security* 38, no. 4 (Spring): 39–78.
Khan, Feroz H. 2012. *Eating Grass: The Making of the Pakistani Bomb.* Redwood City, CA.
Monteiro, Nuno P., and Alexandre Debs. 2014. "The Strategic Logic of Nuclear Proliferation." *International Security* 39, no. 2 (November): 7–51.
Singh, Sonali, and Christopher R. Way. 2004. "The Correlates of Nuclear Proliferation: A Quantitative Test." *Journal of Conflict Resolution* 48 (December): 859–85.
Stulberg, Adam N., and Matthew Fuhrmann, eds. 2013. *The Nuclear Renaissance and International Security.* Palo Alto, CA.
Wirtz, James J., and Peter R. Lavoy, eds. 2012. *Over the Horizon Proliferation Threats.* Palo Alto, CA.

NOTES

[1]The sections of this chapter on a nuclear terrorist incident first appeared in Cynthia Roberts and Andrew Sherlock, "The Day After," available at http://cynthiaaroberts.com. Based on daytime population estimates, if terrorists detonate a 10 kiloton weapon, our model estimates the effects of the blast, shock wave, and prompt nuclear radiation would kill approximately 560,000 people or about 85 percent of those within a radius of 1.3 kilometers, (about 16 city blocks). The subsequent thermal radiation and effects from accumulated fallout could be expected to kill another 500,000 people, about half of the survivors within a 2 kilometer radius (roughly 25 city blocks). Samuel Glasstone and Philip J. Dolan, eds. *The Effects of Nuclear Weapons* (Washington, DC: U.S. Department of Defense and the U.S. Department of Energy, 1977). See also Ashton B. Carter, Michael M. May, and William J. Perry, "The Day After: Action in the 24 Hours Following a Nuclear Blast in an American City" (Cambridge, MA.: Preventive Defense Project, Harvard and Stanford Universities, May 2007).

[2]Since the 1990s, "rogue states" have been considered by many U.S. officials as those that flout international law and threaten international peace and security. After 9/11, the Bush administration conflated the threat from terrorists and rogue states or "outlaw regimes that seek and possess nuclear, chemical, and biological weapons." By contrast, despite not signing the NPT, India was recognized in 2005 as a "responsible" nuclear weapons state.

[3]Some scholars emphasize the low probability and argue the risks are exaggerated. See for example, John Mueller and Mark G. Stewart, "The Terrorism Delusion: America's Overwrought Response to September 11," *International Security* 37, no. 1 (Summer 2012): 81–110; and John Mueller, *Atomic Obsession: Nuclear Alarmism from Hiroshima to Al-Qaeda* (Oxford: Oxford University Press, 2009).

[4]Graham Allison, *Nuclear Terrorism: The Ultimate Preventable Catastrophe* (New York: Henry Holt, 2004); Henry D. Sokoski and Bruno Tertrais, eds. *Nuclear Weapons Security Crises: What Does History Teach?* (Washington, DC: Strategic Studies Institute and U.S. Army War College Press, 2013); Scott D. Sagan, *The Limits of Safety: Organizations, Accidents, and Nuclear Weapons* (Princeton, NJ: Princeton University Press, 1993); Leonard S. Spector, with Jacqueline R. Smith, *Nuclear Ambitions: The Spread of Nuclear Weapons, 1989–1990* (Boulder, CO: Westview Press, 1990).

[5]Sokolski and Tertrais, *Nuclear Weapons Security Crises*, 7–12. In the last decade, there were more than a dozen terrorist plots against New York City, and documents found in Abbottabad show that Bin Laden never abandoned his goal of attacking New York again and other U.S. cities. Multiple sources also attest to al Qaeda's nuclear ambitions. See for example, David Albright, Kathryn Beuhler, and Holly Higgins, "Bin Laden and the Bomb," *Bulletin of the Atomic Scientists* 58 (January/February 2002) and Yossef Bodansky, *Bin Laden: The Man Who Declared War on America* (Rocklin, CA: Forum Press, 2001). No one knows for sure, but some experts after 9/11 estimated the chances of a deliberate terrorist nuclear explosion in an American metropolis to be between 29 and 50 percent. Allison, *Nuclear Terrorism.* See also Richard L. Garwin, "Nuclear or Biological Megaterrorism," 27th Session of the International Seminars on Planetary Emergencies, August 21, 2002; Homeland Security Council. "National Planning Scenarios: Created for Use in National, Federal, State, and Local Homeland Security Preparedness Activities," ver. 20.1, April 2005; "The U.S-Russia Joint Threat Assessment on Nuclear Terrorism," *Belfer Center for Science and International Affairs and Institute for U.S and Canadian Studies* (2010); Stuart Casey-Maslen, "Armed Non-State Actors and 'Nuclear Terrorism,'" in Gro Nystuen, et al., eds. *Nuclear Weapons Under International Law* (Cambridge: Cambridge University Press, 2014); Carson Mark, et al., "Can Terrorists Build Nuclear Weapons?" *International Task Force on the Prevention of Nuclear Terrorism—Nuclear Control Institute* (Washington, DC, 1996); and Peter D. Zimmerman and Jeffrey G. Lewis, "The Bomb in the Backyard," *Foreign Policy* (October 16, 2009), 5–9.

[6]Matthew Bunn and Anthony Wier, *Securing the Bomb: An Agenda for Action*, Harvard University, Project on Managing the Atom, May 2004; Richard L. Garwin and Georges Charpak, *Megawatts and Megatons: A Turning Point in the Nuclear Age?* (New York: Alfred A. Knopf, 2001); Spector, *Nuclear Ambitions*; and Chaim Braun and Christopher F. Chyba, "Proliferation Rings: New Challenges to the Nuclear Nonproliferation Regime," *International Security* 29, no. 2 (Fall 2004): 5-49. For the argument that states are unlikely to share nuclear weapons, see Keir A. Lieber and Daryl G. Press, "Why States Won't Give Nuclear Weapons to Terrorists," *International Security* 38, no. 1 (Summer 2013): 80–104.

[7]Michael Levi, *On Nuclear Terrorism* (Cambridge, MA: Harvard University Press, 2007).

[8]Department of Defense Strategy for Countering Weapons of Mass Destruction (June 2014).

[9]Peter R. Lavoy, "The Enduring Effects of Atoms for Peace," *Arms Control Today* 33, no. 10 (2003): 26–30.

[10]Treaty on the Non-Proliferation of Nuclear Weapons available online at www.state.gov/www/global/arms/treaties/npt1.html. India, Israel, and Pakistan never joined the NPT. North Korea announced its withdrawal from the NPT in January 2003. The Statute of the IAEA may be accessed here: https://www.iaea.org/about/statute.

[11]Lavoy, "The Enduring Effects of Atoms for Peace."

[12]Matthew Fuhrmann, "Spreading Temptation: Proliferation and Peaceful Nuclear Cooperation Agreements," *International Security* 34, no. 1 (Summer 2009): 17–41.

[13]Peter R. Lavoy, *Learning to Live with the Bomb: India, the United States, and the Myths of Nuclear Security* (New York: Palgrave Macmillan, 2004).

[14]Richard K. Betts, "Universal Deterrence or Conceptual Collapse? Liberal Pessimism and Utopian Realism," in *The Coming Crisis: Nuclear Proliferation, U.S. Interests and World Order*, ed. Victor A. Utgoff (Cambridge, MA: MIT Press, 2000), 51–85; Richard K. Betts, "The New Threat of Mass Destruction," *Foreign Affairs* 77, no. 1 (January/February 1998): 26–41; and Ashton B. Carter and William J. Perry, *Preventive Defense: A New Security Strategy for America* (Washington, DC: Brookings Institution Press, 1999).

[15]Pakistan received from China uranium and technical designs. See Bates Gill, "The Growing Challenge of Proliferation in Asia," in *Strategic Asia 2003–2004: Fragility and Crisis*, eds. Richard J. Ellings and Aaron L. Friedberg (Seattle, WA: National Bureau of Asian Research), 365–97, and Leonard Weiss, "Pakistan: It's Déjà Vu All Over Again," *Bulletin of the Atomic Scientists* 60, no. 3 (May/June 2004): 52–9.

[16]Daniel Benjamin and Steven Simon, *The Age of Sacred Terror: Radical Islam's War Against America* (New York: Random House, 2003).

[17]Jack Snyder, "Imperial Temptations," *The National Interest* (2003): 29–40; Hal Brands, "The Dangers of Being Grand: George W. Bush and the Post-9/11 Era," chap. 4 in *What Good is Grand Strategy? Power and Purpose in American Statecraft from Harry S. Truman to George W. Bush* (Ithaca, NY: Cornell University Press, 2014).

[18]White House, *National Security Strategy of the United States of America* (September 17, 2002); White House, *National Strategy to Combat Weapons of Mass Destruction*, December 2002; President George W. Bush, "Address to the Nation, March 17, 2003."

[19]Marc Trachtenberg, "Preventive War and U.S. Foreign Policy," *Security Studies* 16, no. 1 (January/March 2007): 1–31, and David J. Karl, "Proliferation Pessimism and Emerging Nuclear Powers," *International Security* 21, no. 3 (Winter 1996/97): 87–119. See also Alexandre Debs and Nuno P. Monteiro, "Known Unknowns: Power Shifts, Uncertainty, and War," *International Organization* 68, no. 1 (January 2014): 1–31; Matthew Fuhrmann and Sarah E. Kreps, "Targeting Nuclear Programs in War and Peace: A Quantitative Empirical Analysis, 1941–2000," *Journal of Conflict Resolution* 54, no. 6 (December 2010): 831–59.

[20]Robert Axelrod, *Evolution of Cooperation* (New York: Basic Books, 1984).

[21]Maria Rost Rublee, *Nonproliferation Norms: Why States Choose Nuclear Restraint* (Atlanta, GA: University of Georgia Press, 2009); Nina Tannenwald, *The Nuclear Taboo: The United States and the Non-Use of Nuclear Weapons* (Cambridge: Cambridge University Press, 2007); and Jacques E.C. Hymans, *The Psychology of Nuclear Proliferation: Identity, Emotions and Foreign Policy* (Cambridge: Cambridge University Press, 2006).

[22]For the theoretical argument about hegemonic privileges and major powers creating institutions that serve their interests, see Michael Mastanduno, "System Maker and Privilege Taker," *World Politics* 61, no. 1 (January 2009): 121–54; Stephen D. Krasner, "Global Communications and National Power: Life on the Pareto Frontier," *World Politics* 43, no. 3 (April 1991): 336–66; and John J. Mearsheimer, "The False Promise of International Institutions," *International Security* 19, no. 3 (Winter 1994–1995): 5–49. As applied to nonproliferation, see Betts, "Universal Deterrence or Conceptual Collapse?"

[23]Scott D. Sagan, "The Causes of Nuclear Weapons Proliferation," *Annual Review of Political Science* 14 (2011): 225–44; James M. Acton, "Nuclear Power, Disarmament, and Technological Restraint," *Survival* 51, no. 4 (August-September 2009):101–26.

[24]Sagan, "The Causes of Nuclear Weapons Proliferation," and "Why Do States Build Nuclear Weapons? Three Models in Search of a Bomb," *International Security* 21, no. 3 (Winter 1996/97): 54–86.

[25]See Mohamed ElBaradei, "Addressing Verification Challenges," Statements of the Director General: Symposium on International Safeguards, October 16, 2006, http://www.iaea.org/NewsCenter/Statements/2006/ebsp2006n018.html; George Perkovich and James M. Acton, "Abolishing Nuclear Weapons," Adelphi Paper 396 (London: International Institute for Strategic Studies, 2008); and James Wirtz and Peter Lavoy, eds. *Over the Horizon Proliferation Threats* (Palo Alto , CA: Stanford University Press, 2012).

[26]Sagan, "The Causes of Nuclear Weapons Proliferation." See also the citations in note 31 and Etel Solingen, *Nuclear Logics: Contrasting Paths in East Asia and the Middle East* (Princeton, NJ: Princeton University Press, 2007); Erik Gartzke and Matthew Kroenig, "A Strategic Approach to Nuclear Proliferation," *Journal of Conflict Resolution* 53, no. 2 (April 2009): 151–60; and Scott Helfstein, "Friends Don't Let Friends Proliferate," *Political Science Quarterly* 125, no. 2 (Summer 2010): 281–308.

[27]Malcolm Chalmers, "The Logic of Nuclear Restraint," chap. 3 in *Less is Better: Nuclear Restraint at Low Numbers*, Whitehall Papers 78 (2012).

[28]Austin Long and Brendan Rittenhouse Green, "Stalking the Secure Second Strike: Intelligence, Counterforce, and Nuclear Strategy," *Journal of Strategic Studies* 38, no. 1–2 (2015): 38–73; Keir A. Lieber and Daryl Press, "The End of MAD? The Nuclear Dimension of U.S. Primacy," *International Security* 30, no. 4 (Spring 2006): 7–44; and Keir A. Lieber and Daryl G. Press, "The New Era of Nuclear Weapons, Deterrence, and Conflict," *Strategic Studies Quarterly* 7, no. 1 (Spring 2013): 3–14.

[29]Robert Jervis, *The Meaning of the Nuclear Revolution: Statecraft and the Prospect of Armageddon* (Ithaca, NY: Cornell University Press, 1989); and Kenneth N. Waltz, "Nuclear Myths and Political Realities," *American Political Science Review* 84, no. 3 (September 1990): 730–45.

[30]Keir A. Lieber and Daryl G. Press, "The Nukes We Need: Preserving the American Deterrent," *Foreign Affairs* 88, no. 6 (November/December 2009): 39–51.

[31]Jeffrey W. Knopf, ed., *Security Assurances and Nuclear Nonproliferation* (Stanford, CA: Stanford University Press, 2012); Nicholas L. Miller, "The Secret Success of Nonproliferation Sanctions," *International Organization* 68, no. 4 (Fall 2014): 913–44; Gene Gerzhoy, "Alliance Coercion and Nuclear Restraint: How the United States Thwarted West Germany's Nuclear Ambitions," *International Security* 39, no. 4 (Spring 2015): 91–129. Kurt M. Campbell, Robert J. Einhorn, and Mitchell B. Reiss, *The Nuclear Tipping Point: Why States Reconsider Their Nuclear Choices* (Washington, DC: Brookings Press, 2004). Ariel E. Levite, "Never Say Never Again: Nuclear Reversal Revisited," *International Security* 27, no. 3 (Winter 2002/03): 59–88; and Nicholas L. Miller, "The Secret Success of Nonproliferation Sanctions," *International Organization* 68, no. 4 (Fall 2014): 914–44. However, some scholars question whether nuclear weapons need to be stationed on the weaker ally's territory to get the effects of extended deterrence. See Matthew Fuhrmann and Todd S. Sechser, "Signaling Alliance Commitments: Hand-Tying and Sunk Costs in Extended Nuclear Deterrence," *American Journal of Political Science* 58, no. 4 (October 2014): 919–35.

[32]Vipin Narang, *Nuclear Strategy in the Modern Era: Regional Powers and International Conflict: Regional Powers and International Conflict* (Princeton, NJ: Princeton University Press, 2014).

[33]Matthew Kroenig, *Exporting the Bomb: Technology Transfer and the Spread of Nuclear Weapons* (Ithaca, NY: Cornell University Press, 2010).

[34]Michael C. Horowitz, *The Diffusion of Military Power: Causes and Consequences for International Politics* (Princeton, NJ: Princeton University Press, 2010), 106. See also Francis J. Gavin, "Blasts from the Past: Proliferation Lessons from the 1960s," *International Security* 29, no. 3 (Winter 2004/05): 100–35.

[35] Barry R. Schneider, "Nuclear Proliferation and Counter-Proliferation: Policy Issues and Debates," *Mershon International Studies Review* 38, no. 2 (October1994): 209–34; and Harald Müller and Mitchell Reiss, "Counterproliferation: Putting New Wine in Old Bottles," *The Washington Quarterly* 18, no. 2 (1995): 143–54.

[36]For a global inventory of nuclear weapons, see Hans M. Kristensen and Robert S. Norris, "Worldwide Deployments of Nuclear Weapons, 2014," *Bulletin of the Atomic Scientists* 70 (September/October 2014): 96–108.

[37]The website may be accessed here: http://www.dtra.mil/Missions/Partnering/CooperativeThreatReductionProgram.aspx.

[38]Chaim Braun and Christopher F. Chyba, "Proliferation Rings: New Challenges to the Nuclear Nonproliferation Regime," *International Security* 29, no. 2 (Fall 2004): 5–49; Sheena Chestnut, "Illicit Activity and Proliferation: North Korean Smuggling Networks," *International Security* 32, no. 1 (Summer 2007): 80–111; and Gordon Corera, *Shopping for Bombs: Nuclear Proliferation, Global Insecurity, and the Rise and Fall of the A.Q. Khan Network* (Oxford: Oxford University Press, 2006).

[39]*Combating Illicit Trafficking in Nuclear and Other Radioactive Material*, IAEA Nuclear Security Series No. 6 (Vienna: International Atomic Energy Agency, 2007), 126–7.

[40]Matthew Bunn, "Beyond Crises: The Unending Challenge of Controlling Nuclear Weapons and Materials," in Sokolski, *Nuclear Weapons Security Crises*.

[41]There are no known instances of nuclear terrorism to date or specific reports of attempted radiological attacks since 2000. The first two radiological incidents, in 1995 and 1998, involved Chechen separatists and Cesium-137 materials that targeted Gorky Park in Moscow and a railroad east of Grozny, respectively. The 2000 incident involved a bomb at Russian nuclear facility, but the Russians reported that there was no ongoing nuclear activity at the facility. The Pakistan Taliban has also targeted that country's nuclear facilities. Ibid.

[42]Betts, "The New Threat of Mass Destruction;" Ashton B. Carter, "How to Counter WMD," *Foreign Affairs* 83, no. 5 (September/October 2004): 72–85; and Stephen Flynn, *America the Vulnerable: How Our Government is Failing to Protect Us from Terrorism* (New York: HarperCollins, 2004).

14

The Fukushiman Future

Environmental Catastrophe and the Limits of National Power

HUGH LIEBERT AND AARON SPIKOL

Disasters are moments of discovery. Under the rule of a benevolent God, disasters discover sin and piety, transgression and obedience, pride and humility. In a world ordered by human ingenuity, disasters discover failures in foresight, inept institutions, pride and self-criticism. What a natural disaster means has to do with the human world—the culture—in which it occurs. When a culture contains varied ways of making sense of the natural world and its misfortunes, disasters can discover that, too.

The paradigmatic modern disaster in the West—the earthquake and tsunami that struck Lisbon in 1755—was a disaster of this sort.[1] Some, like the Jesuit priest Gabriel Malagrida, saw the thousands of casualties and ruined monuments as generations before them had done: they were divine retribution for man's sins, sent both to punish the guilty and to sustain and restore the piety of those who had been spared. But others were less sure. Voltaire questioned God's justice: "What crime, what sin, had those young hearts conceived/ That lie, bleeding and torn, on mother's breast?"[2] Rousseau found reason to praise the justice not of God, but of nature, which prized some modes of life over others. "Nature had not assembled two thousand six- or seven-story houses there," Rousseau observed. "If the inhabitants of that great city had been more evenly dispersed and more simply lodged, the damage would have been far less and perhaps nil."[3] Yet others, like the Marquis de Pombal, the Portuguese Secretary of State, were impatient to ponder the justice of God or nature, as they set straightaway to rebuild a city sturdier and stronger than the one that lay in ruins.[4] What, then, did this disaster mean? It was testimony to divine benevolence and indifference, to nature's provision for human happiness and man's ability to provide for his own happiness. The earthquake discovered a culture of contradictions, in which both old and new modes of sense-making held sway.

When an earthquake and tsunami struck Japan on March 11, 2011, it was immediately evident that they constituted a great disaster. Nearly sixteen thousand died; hundreds of thousands were evacuated from homes that would soon be washed out to sea. This was a "tragedy," as we have come to use that word—an occasion for exceptional suffering. There have been a number of such tragedies of late: the 2004 Indian Ocean earthquake and tsunami killed some 230,000; in the following year, Hurricane Katrina killed nearly two thousand and caused more than $100 billion in damage; in 2010, an earthquake in Haiti left between 100,000 and 160,000 dead and a considerably greater number homeless. Each initiated a familiar pattern of remorse and response: global attention via television and Internet, followed by international aid and reconstruction. The Japanese earthquake seemed, at first, a tragedy of this sort, one that discovered today's Pombals ascendant over the Malagridas, Voltaires, and Rousseaus.

But this initial impression changed once the nuclear power plant at Fukushima-Daiichi began to malfunction. Suddenly a new prospect opened: not only vast suffering but an ancient island rendered radioactive and uninhabitable. A nuclear disaster as severe as any the world had seen threatened the only nation to have been targeted by nuclear weapons—a nation which had subsequently risen from rubble by making Western industry and technology its own. Given this poignant history, the Fukushima disaster had a profoundly Japanese meaning. But it also had the potential to instruct the world in what disasters might mean within modern, advanced societies.

The primary purpose of this chapter is not to determine the meaning of Fukushima. Instead, we hope to frame the question of what lessons U.S. policymakers might learn from the Fukushima disaster. We will focus on three main areas: nuclear policy, the challenge of government regulation, and U.S. strategy in Asia. We will then conclude by asking how cultures in tension with themselves might respond to a "Fukushiman Future"—one in which great disasters seem to elude our collective ability to respond adequately to them, in theory as well as in practice.

I. (Almost?) the Worst Case: The Fukushima Nuclear Disaster

Before there was nuclear disaster there was a (mostly) good news story. The six nuclear reactors at Fukushima-Daiichi responded as planned to "the Great East Japan Earthquake." Reactors one through three shut down immediately; reactors four through six had already been shut down for periodic inspection; all seemed to react as hoped, even though the earthquake—measuring 9.0 on the Richter scale—exceeded the "worst case" envisioned in two of the reactors' designs.[5]

As external power to the plants failed, emergency diesel generators sprang to life. For fifty-one minutes after the earthquake, the reactors' cores cooled and radioactive material was contained.[6]

But then the waves hit. Tsunamis, like earthquakes, are not uncommon in Japan; five significant tsunamis have occurred within living memory of Japanese citizens, in 1944, 1946, 1964, 1983, and 1993. But this tsunami far exceeded what planners had anticipated. The seawalls surrounding the nuclear plants stood just short of twenty feet, while the highest waves at Fukushima reached forty-six feet. As water surged over the walls and into the nuclear plant, failures in foresight quickly became apparent. Many of the back-up diesel generators, which now provided the electricity required to cool nuclear material inside the plants, were located in low-lying areas. These were flooded and ruined, as were electrical switchgear rooms. The back-up for the back-up—batteries intended to provide eight hours of power, should all else fail—were also lost in the flood. As the tsunami waves receded, the systems intended to cool nuclear material had failed and meltdown seemed imminent.

This is the moment of crisis. Pressure inside the reactors mounts. Overseers decide to open vents, allowing radioactive steam to escape into the atmosphere. Attempts to cool the reactors with seawater fail to stop the cores from overheating. More pressure mounts. And then, twenty-four hours after waves first breached the plant's seawalls, the first of the six reactors explodes. Days later the third and fourth reactors also explode. The crisis continues. It is not until December of 2011, in fact—nine months after the tsunami—that all reactors enter "cold shutdown."[7] Even then, radioactive material continues to escape the crippled plant. In August of 2014, a Japanese government official acknowledges that three hundred tons of radiation-contaminated water escape Fukushima into the Pacific Ocean each day—a leak, he admits, that has existed since 2012.[8]

Fukushima was immediately recognized as one of the worst nuclear disasters in history. According to the International and Radiological Event Scale, Fukushima was a "category seven"—equivalent to the 1986 Chernobyl catastrophe, and considerably worse than the meltdown of Pennsylvania's Three Mile Island plant in 1979 (a "category five").[9] But these categorizations and accompanying retrospectives erroneously suggest a fait accompli. The Fukushiman disaster is still very much ongoing, as of this writing, for it is as yet unclear just how hard it will be to scrub radiation from the plant's immediate radius (early estimates of a forty-year cleanup suggest it will be hard indeed), and how badly the health of nearby residents will suffer.[10] A 2013 World Health Organization (WHO) report suggested individuals in the worst-affected areas would be at slightly greater risk of most cancers; in some cases, however, the effects were more dramatic.[11] Females exposed as infants to Fukushima's radiation, for instance, were predicted to be at seventy percent greater risk of suffering from thyroid cancer.[12] While the WHO judged health risks outside of the areas adjacent to the plant low, credible scientists have called this judgment optimistic.[13] Others worried—needlessly, it now seems—that the "Fukushima plume," a cloud of radioactive particles released into the Pacific, would devastate the U.S. West Coast.[14]

II. Policy Implications

What does all of this mean for U.S. policymakers? While at present it seems that the Fukushima disaster will have little direct impact on U.S. citizens, Fukushima is nevertheless a powerful cautionary tale.[15] In what follows, we will focus on three (of many) issue areas where the Fukushima case raises important questions.

Nuclear Power

The Fukushima disaster immediately caused countries all over the globe to reexamine the safety and viability of nuclear power as an energy source, an effort which is still in progress today. Japan has kept all of its nuclear reactors in shutdown since the disaster, though its pro-nuclear prime minister is currently attempting to hasten the rate at which they will come back online. In France, the country most reliant on nuclear power, reductions in nuclear power have been small, despite vows by the current president to begin phasing it out as a power source.[16] Germany has reduced its reliance on nuclear power more rapidly, quickly decommissioning several of its oldest plants, although it will continue to generate nuclear power for much of the next decade.[17] Although globally the total number of nuclear power plants has decreased since 2011, continued commitment to nuclear power on the part of many countries, including all of the BRICs (Brazil, Russia, India, and China), suggests that energy production from nuclear power will continue to increase in the future.[18]

No country, however, has failed to utilize the lessons learned from Fukushima to create relevant regulations. In the United States, these initiatives are spearheaded by the U.S. Nuclear Regulatory Commission (NRC), the primary federal agency for overseeing the nuclear industry. The NRC has reacted to Fukushima by issuing a number of new rules and regulations designed to guard against 'beyond design basis events,' the catch-all term for Fukushima-level disasters.

Recent reforms fall into several categories.[19] First, there are requirements for hardened venting for Type I Boiling Water Reactors (the same design as the Fukushima plant); these help to ensure that the mechanisms that manage heat and pressure in the reactor's core are not rendered ineffective in the event of a disaster, thus maintaining the integrity of the containment building and preventing core meltdown. Second, the NRC has instituted stricter standards for monitoring the water levels of pools containing spent fuel rods, while requiring backup strategies to maintain those water levels, to ensure that floods or seismic activities do not lead to radioactive contamination from already-processed nuclear fuel. Because the United States has for some time lacked a long-term strategy for dealing with spent nuclear fuel and a large amount of spent nuclear fuel is therefore stored on-site at many nuclear facilities, alleviating risks associated with processed nuclear fuel is of particular concern to U.S. nuclear regulators.[20] Third, considering the Fukushima plants' inability to maintain electricity for its critical cooling systems, the NRC has issued additional requirements for backup electrical access. While reforms after 9/11 ensured that many nuclear facilities already possess backup electrical capacity, the fact that they were primarily designed to help mitigate the effects of a terrorist attack means that most are not sufficiently hardened to survive a natural disaster.[21] Finally, the NRC has instituted a host of other measures, ranging from increased monitoring of seismic activity to community disaster preparedness.

Few question the wisdom of the NRC's post-Fukushima reforms. Indeed, the International Atomic Energy Agency (IAEA) has commended the NRC for its performance since 2011.[22]

But the *implementation* of the NRC's recent reforms remains a subject of debate. Some have suggested that the NRC's timelines for implementation are insufficiently aggressive and that the Commission has allowed the nuclear industry to avoid critical issues, such as the hardening of surplus electrical output.[23] These criticisms illustrate a broader critique of the NRC, which suggests that it is too deferent to the nuclear industry, given the large amount of transfer between its members and the private sector.[24] Despite these potential shortcomings, it appears that the NRC performs better than most of its international equivalents (with the exception of France). The NRC is also considered far better than its peer domestic agencies, which regulate energy sources such as oil and natural gas.[25]

While increased regulations following Fukushima might endanger the U.S. nuclear industry's international competitiveness, most industry advocates are more concerned by the rapid increase in natural gas production and the rise of renewable sources of energy; these developments, even more than regulatory burdens, may make nuclear power economically unviable.[26] Previous claims of a 'nuclear renaissance' have proved unfounded, as licensing, construction, and maintenance costs remain high.[27] At present, nuclear power plant construction and research on nuclear power are highly subsidized in many developed countries, but there are signs that subsidies for renewable sources of energy may replace them.[28] In light of the increased public risks that nuclear power poses, it is difficult to determine its long-term viability in the United States.

Given this state of affairs, U.S. policymakers face a number of questions with regard to the domestic nuclear industry. Should the United States continue to support nuclear power as a form of energy production, or should other sources of energy be privileged? If nuclear power is to remain a part of the U.S. energy portfolio, how can the need for regulation be balanced with the economic vitality of the industry? How can U.S. nuclear regulators best prepare for the worst-case scenarios?

Regulating the Regulators

In December of 2011 the National Diet of Japan's Fukushima Accident Independent Investigation Commission issued a report (henceforth "the Diet report") remarkable for its probity. "Although triggered by [natural disasters of a magnitude that shocked the entire world]," the Diet report claimed, "the subsequent accident at the Fukushima Daiichi Nuclear Power Plant cannot be regarded as a natural disaster. It was a profoundly manmade disaster—that could and should have been foreseen and prevented."[29] The report criticized both the Tokyo Electric Power Company (TEPCO), the corporation controlling the plant, and its regulators, the Nuclear and Industrial Safety Agency (NISA) and Nuclear Safety Commission (NSC). But the root cause of the disaster, according to the Diet report, was Japan itself:

> What must be admitted—very painfully—is that this was a disaster 'Made in Japan.' Its fundamental causes are to be found in the ingrained conventions of Japanese culture: our reflexive obedience; our reluctance to question authority; our devotion to 'sticking with the program'; our groupism; and our insularity.[30]

This profoundly Japanese "mindset," the report continued, fueled Japan's quest for energy independence in response to the oil shocks of the 1970s, making nuclear power "an unstoppable force, immune to scrutiny by civil society."

This "single-minded determination" was the same resolve that had joined government and business elites in pursuit of "Japan's postwar economic miracle."[31] As a result, the "manmade disaster" of Fukushima indicted not only Japanese character generally, but Japan's postwar reinvention of itself—the very achievement in which Japanese elites might take the most pride.

For all of its emphasis on Japanese identity, however, the story that the Diet report told has broader relevance. On its surface, it was a tale of "regulatory capture" bordering on collusion, as both government and business were eager to bend regulations to industry preferences. By some measure, regulatory capture is a danger endemic in all bureaucratic regulation, but it also a danger that increases in proportion to the level of specialization in a nation's economy and society. In a number of economically advanced states, both the regulators and those being regulated come from the same social background, share the same expertise and the same professional identity, and often have similar professional ambitions. Within highly specialized fields, it is not uncommon for individuals who appear to the outside world as opposite—regulators and regulated, lions and lambs—to change roles during the course of their careers. The sort of insularity the Diet report describes—in which regulators came to place the interests of a corporation with which they interacted everyday and whose members they consider peers, ahead of the interest of a vague and distant "public"—is likely to continue to arise within economically-advanced states. One finds such insularity not only where industry meets applied science, like nuclear power and pharmaceuticals, but in highly-specialized realms of finance. Wherever there is specialization and professional socialization there is the potential for the consensual regulatory "capture" the Diet report discovered at Fukushima.

How should U.S. policymakers combat regulatory capture? What goods come from collusion between government and business, and how do these weigh against the evident evils? Are there alternatives to regulation by government bureaucracy that might do a better job of preventing corporate endangerment of the public interest?

Nuclear Weapons and the Rise of China

Following World War II and the U.S.-led reconstruction of Japan, the U.S.-Japanese alliance has been central to Japanese security and U.S. strategy in the Asia-Pacific. But whereas most alliances involve some degree of military "burden-sharing," the U.S.-Japan alliance has been premised from the start on the demilitarization of Japan. This demilitarization is enshrined in the ninth article of the Japanese Constitution, which paints a pacifist vision in bold strokes:

> Aspiring sincerely to an international peace based on justice and order, the Japanese people forever renounce war as a sovereign right of the nation and the threat or use of force as means of settling international disputes. In order to accomplish the aim of the preceding paragraph, land, sea, and air forces, as well as other war potential, will never be maintained. The right of belligerency of the state will not be recognized.[32]

Having lived under this fundamental law for nearly seventy years, many Japanese view the renunciation of war as an element of not only policy but national identity. Japan, like other states, has security interests, but to an exceptional degree it has trusted in an ally to protect and promote these interests. Japan's emergence from the rubble of the 1940s to the technologically-advanced state of today seems a vindication of this strategy.

And yet concerns have risen of late. On several occasions Japan and China have skirted military conflict over the Senkaku islands, raising worries of a broader war. Trade disputes between the two Asian powers have grown fierce. And over the past decade North Korea has tested missiles capable of hitting most of Japan. Meanwhile, Japan's latent power—as measured in population and economic strength—has declined, gradually in absolute terms but quite starkly relative to China's. Cumulatively these developments have put new stress on the credibility of the United States' commitment to Japan's security, including the U.S. "nuclear umbrella."

Japanese militarism has risen in response, according to several analysts. A Japanese decision to acquire its own nuclear deterrent would coincide with these developments. Recent evidence suggests that Japan's turn to peaceful forms of nuclear power in the 1970s was linked to its security concerns. Richard Samuels quotes a former Japanese defense minister to this effect: "It is important to maintain our commercial reactors because it will allow us to produce a nuclear warhead in a short amount of time… It is a tacit nuclear deterrent."[33] A nuclear deterrent is an especially compelling option if the Diet report is correct to stress the prominence of insularity in the Japanese "mindset." Nuclear weapons represent a high-tech, relatively low-cost means by which an advanced society with few entangling alliances and little appetite for conquest could nevertheless secure its territory, even while managing a precipitous decline in power vis-à-vis its regional rivals.

In light of Japanese security concerns, the U.S. "pivot to Asia," and the present (and potential) roles of nuclear weapons in both, how should U.S. strategists proceed? To what degree is a nuclear Japan a threat to U.S. interests? How are renewed anxieties over civilian nuclear power likely to influence U.S. strategy in the Pacific?

III. Japanese Identity

The largest question raised by the Fukushima disaster, however, has to do with the meaning of mass suffering in a modern society. Perhaps no writer has put this problem as trenchantly as Richard Lloyd Parry, whose "Ghosts of the Tsunami" depicts a modern world discovered by disaster not to have rendered the ancient world of spirits as obsolete as it once seemed.[34] "When opinion polls put the question, 'How religious are you?,' the Japanese rank among the most ungodly people in the world," Parry writes. He continues:

> It took a catastrophe for me to understand how misleading this self-assessment is. It is true that the organized religions, Buddhism and Shinto, have little influence on private or national life. But over the centuries both have been pressed into the service of the true faith of Japan: the cult of the ancestors.[35]

Parry goes on to describe the "contract" at the heart of ancestor worship: "The food, drink, prayers and rituals offered by their descendants gratify the dead, who in turn bestow good fortune on the living." When the living fail to uphold their side of the bargain—even when that failure stems from ancestral shrines having been washed away in a tsunami—the dead haunt the earth like "orphaned children." To right this disaster requires not a planner but an exorcist. Parry follows Reverend Kaneda, the chief priest of a Zen temple in Kurihara, as he ministers both to those possessed by wandering spirits—and to the spirits themselves.

"Ancestor worship" of the sort Parry describes might seem unusual to a Western audience, but his broader story is not. After Hurricane Katrina, divine providence became a prominent explanation of the Hurricane and its aftermath; according to one poll, twenty-three percent of Americans considered Katrina a "deliberate act of God."[36] Divine providence also loomed large for many victims of the 2010 Indian Ocean tsunami; according to a recent study, all "four major religious groups (Buddhists, Christians, Hindus, and Muslims) affected in South and Southeast Asia by the tsunami interpreted the event as 'divine punishment.'"[37] The power of religion in addressing these worst-case scenarios suggests a world of the spirit still vital under a secular, skeptical veneer. Despite widespread modernization, the Malagrida-Voltaire approach to disaster—in which the crucial question is divine involvement—seems not yet to have yielded entirely to the Rousseau-Pombal approach, in which the central question is how man relates to nature.

Why might this broad question—the meaning of a disaster, not as a matter of policy but of man's place in the world—matter to U.S. policymakers? Insofar as the goal of crisis response is to reconstitute a community, responders attend to not only buildings but the culture that surrounds them. This is a project in which traditional and modern modes of sense-making inevitably come into contact and—potentially—cooperation. Just as the effective general is aware of the non-governmental organizations at work in a war zone, so the effective crisis responder is aware of what a crisis can mean to those who trust more in the exorcist than the bureaucrat. The communities discovered by disasters like Fukushima—or Katrina, or the Indian Ocean Tsunami—are often more torn between old and new than the bureaucrat's worldview, even in its worst-case scenarios, allows.

RECOMMENDED READINGS

Holt, Mark, Richard J. Campbell, and Mary Beth Nikitin. 2012. "Fukushima Nuclear Disaster." Congressional Research Service (CRS) Report for Congress (January 18).

Marques, José Oscar de Almeida. 2005. "The Paths of Providence: Voltaire and Rousseau on the Lisbon Earthquake," *Cadernos de História e Filosofia da Ciência*, series 3, vol. 15, no. 1 (January-June): 33–57.

National Diet of Japan. 2012. "The Official Report of the Fukushima Nuclear Accident Independent Investigation Commission." Executive Summary.

Parry, Richard Lloyd. 2014. "Ghosts of the Tsunami." *London Review of Books* 36, no. 3 (February 6).

Samuels, Richard. 2013. *3.11: Disaster and Change in Japan.* Ithaca, NY.

NOTES

[1]On philosophical responses to the Lisbon Earthquake, see in particular Russell R. Dynes, "The Dialogue between Voltaire and Rousseau on the Lisbon Earthquake: The Emergence of a Social Science View," *International Journal of Mass Emergencies and Disasters* 18, no. 1 (March 2000): 97–115; Susan Neiman, *Evil in Modern Thought: An Alternative History of Philosophy* (Princeton, NJ: Princeton University Press, 2004), esp. 240–50; José Oscar de Almeida Marques, "The Paths of Providence: Voltaire and Rousseau on the Lisbon Earthquake," *Cadernos de História e Filosofia da Ciência* series 3, vol. 15, no. 1 (January-June 2005): 33–57.

[2]This translation of Voltaire's *Poème sur le désastre de Lisbonne* (1755) appears in Voltaire, *Toleration and Other Essays*, trans. Joseph McCabe (New York and London: The Knickerbocker Press, 1912), 255.

[3]Rousseau, *The Discourses and Other Early Political Writings*, ed. and trans. Victor Gourevitch

(Cambridge: Cambridge University Press, 1997), 234.

[4]Marques, "The Paths of Providence," 2–3.

[5]Mark Holt, Richard J. Campbell, and Mary Beth Nikitin, "Fukushima Nuclear Disaster," Congressional Research Service (CRS) Report for Congress (January 18, 2012), 4. The report of the Fukushima Nuclear Accident Independent Investigation Commission (aka, "the Diet report"), however, suggests that the earthquake may have damaged equipment at the Fukushima Daiichi plant. See The National Diet of Japan, "The Official Report of the Fukushima Nuclear Accident Independent Investigation Commission," Executive Summary (2012), 17.

[6]For a timeline of the earthquake and tsunami, see "Timeline: Japan Power Plant Crisis," *BBC News* (March 13, 2011), http://www.bbc.co.uk/news/science-environment-12722719.

[7]Holt et al., "Fukushima Nuclear Disaster," 6.

[8]Arata Yamamoto, "Wrecked Fukushima Nuke Plant Leaking 330 Tons of Contaminated Water a Day," *NBC News* (August 7, 2013), http://www.nbcnews.com/news/other/wrecked-fukushima-nuke-plant-leaking-330-tons-contaminated-water-day-f6C10865611.

[9]Mikka Pineda, "Fukushima Vs. Three Mile Island Vs. Chernobyl," *Forbes* (March 17, 2011), http://www.forbes.com/2011/03/16/japan-disaster-nuclear-opinions-roubini-economics.html.

[10]Ian Sample, "Fukushima Two Years On: A Dirty Job With No End In Sight," *The Guardian* (December 3, 2013), http://www.theguardian.com/environment/2013/dec/03/fukushima-daiichi-tsunami-nuclear-cleanup-japan.

[11]World Health Organization, "Health Risk Assessment From the Nuclear Accident After the 2011 Great East Japan Earthquake and Tsunami Based on a Preliminary Dose Estimation" (2013), http://apps.who.int/iris/bitstream/10665/78218/1/9789241505130_eng.pdf.

[12]Ibid., 8.

[13]Charles Perrow, "Nuclear Denial: From Hiroshima to Fukushima," *Bulletin of the Atomic Scientists* 69 (September/October 2013): 56–67.

[14]Nora Caplan-Bricker, "The Fukushima Fearmongers," *The New Republic* (March 10, 2014), http://www.newrepublic.com/article/116969/fukushimas-radioactive-plume-hit-us-2014-should-we-worry.

[15]It should be noted, however, that several U.S. sailors and marines stationed off Japan during the Fukushima disaster claim to have suffered from exposure to radiation. See "Did Fukushima Disaster Make U.S. Sailors and Marines Sick?" *CNN News* (February 19, 2014), http://thelead.blogs.cnn.com/2014/02/19/did-fukushima-disaster-make-u-s-sailors-and-marines-sick/.

[16]Ivana Hughes, "France: A Study of French Nuclear Power After Fukushima," *The sK1 Project* (September 4, 2014), http://k1project.org/france-a-study-of-french-nuclear-policy-after-fukushima/.

[17]Oliver Joy, "After Fukushima: Could Germany's Nuclear Gamble Backfire?" *CNN News* (September 28, 2013), http://edition.cnn.com/2013/09/27/business/german-offshore-wind-farms/.

[18]Ivana Kottasova, "Interactive: How Fukushima Changed World's Attitudes to Nuclear Power," *CNN News* (March 12, 2014), http://edition.cnn.com/2014/03/12/business/nuclear-power-after-fukushima/.

[19]For background on the following reforms, see in particular the United States Nuclear Regulatory Commission, "Japan Lessons Learned" (January 28, 2015), http://www.nrc.gov/reactors/operating/ops-experience/japan-dashboard.html.

[20]Jack Spencer, "U.S. Nuclear Policy After Fukushima: Trust But Modify," *Heritage Foundation Backgrounder* #2557 (May 18, 2011), http://www.heritage.org/research/reports/2011/05/us-nuclear-policy-after-fukushima-trust-but-modify.

[21]Union of Concerned Scientists, "U.S. Nuclear Power Safety One Year After Fukushima" (March 2012), http://www.ucsusa.org/nuclear_power/making-nuclear-power-safer/preventing-nuclear-accidents/fukushima-anniversary-report.html#.VYAsv_kTTIV.

[22]International Atomic Energy Agency, "IAEA Mission Concludes Peer Review of the U.S. Nuclear Regulatory Framework" (February 11, 2014), https://www.iaea.org/newscenter/pressreleases/iaea-mission-concludes-peer-review-us-nuclear-regulatory-framework.

[23]Union of Concerned Scientists, "U.S. Nuclear Power Safety One Year After Fukushima." David Lochbaum et al., *Fukushima: The Story of a Nuclear Disaster* (New York: The New Press, 2013).

[24]Tom Zeller, Jr., "Nuclear Agency is Criticized as Too Close to Its Industry," *New York Times* (May 7, 2011), http://www.nytimes.com/2011/05/08/business/energy-environment/08nrc.html?pagewanted=all&_r=1.

[25]Peter A. Bradford, "How to Close the U.S. Nuclear Industry: Do Nothing," *Bulletin of the Atomic Scientists* 69, no. 2 (March 2013), http://thebulletin.org/2013/march/how-close-us-nuclear-industry-do-nothing.

[26]World Nuclear Association, "The Nuclear Renaissance" (January 2014), http://www.world-nuclear.org/info/Current-and-Future-Generation/The-Nuclear-Renaissance/.

[27]Ibid.

[28]The National Diet of Japan, "The Official Report," 9.

[29]Ibid.

[30]Ibid.

[31]"The Constitution of Japan," http://japan.kantei.go.jp/constitution_and_government_of_japan/constitution_e.html.

[32]Richard Samuels, *3.11: Disaster and Change in Japan* (Ithaca, NY: Cornell University Press, 2013), 124.

[33]Richard Lloyd Parry, "Ghosts of the Tsunami," *London Review of Books* 36, no. 3 (February 6, 2014).

[34]Ibid.

[35]Anne M. Arlinghaus, "Religion, Rhetoric, and Social Change After Hurricane Katrina," *Vanderbilt Undergraduate Research Journal* 2, no. 1 (Spring 2006): 1–12. Dalia Sussman, "Poll: Most Say God Not a Factor in Hurricanes," *ABC News* (October 2, 2005), http://abcnews.go.com/Politics/PollVault/story?id=1174220&page=1.

[36]Bimal Kanti Paul and MD Nadiruzzaman, "Religious Interpretations for the Causes of the 2004 Indian Ocean Tsunami," *Asian Profile* 41, no. 1 (February 2013): 67–77, 74.

15

Coups and Constitutions

Military Power and Civilian Control in the Developing World

CHARLES G. THOMAS

Following September 11, 2001, the United States re-evaluated its partnerships in the developing world with an eye to helping to train local militaries that had the capacity to defeat regional terror threats. Beginning in 2002, the U.S. military identified the countries of the Sahel—Niger, Mali, Chad, Mauritania, Burkina Faso—as potential trouble spots due to their poverty, large ungoverned spaces, and growing Islamist trends. To counter the perceived threat, the United States engaged in a series of joint regional partnerships to bolster the military capacity of these partner states and help them work together to counter regional threats. For over a decade, a rotation of highly qualified teams[1]—first the Pan-Sahel Initiative (PSI) and later the Trans-Saharan Counterterrorism Partnership (TSCTP)—have been dispatched to the region to train the armies of these states and foster cooperation through a series of engagements with threats including Tuareg separatists and radical Islamists.

One of the central partners of these partnerships was the Sahelian country of Mali. Although Mali retained strong ties to its former colonizing power, France, the country was an enthusiastic partner in the initial Pan-Sahel Initiative and the Trans-Saharan Counterterrorism Partnership.[2] Malian soldiers were trained directly by United States officers in Mali for over a decade and a series of Malian officers trained in the United States through the International Military Educational and Training program. Major military exercises for the TSCTP led by the United States (called Operation Flintlock) were hosted by Mali in 2007–2009.[3] In both these simulations and in occasional joint operations the Malian military proved themselves an increasingly valuable regional partner against radical Islamist threats.

Although the Malian government was seen as somewhat corrupt, there was nevertheless a democratic tradition within Mali. The country had held regular elections since 1991 and although there was significant patronage politics and corruption, by 2012 there had been several peaceful and stable regime changes. Given the positive indications for the 2012 elections and the increasing adeptness of the Malian military, Mali was seen as an ideal partner for the United States in the region. Its successful transition to democracy following the Cold

War and its international security partnerships offered all the indications of a stable, liberal, and professional power in a region that was shadowed by many unknowns. Even when Tuareg dissidents rebelled again in January of 2012 it was seen as little more than a sputtering continuance of the earlier political and ethnic struggles in the North of the country.

Unfortunately, this new revolt occurred in the aftermath of the Arab Spring and the fall of Mohammar Qaddafi's regime in Libya. The routes across the Sahara used for centuries for trade in gold, salt, and slaves, were now awash with weapons, money, and Islamist fighters. In short order, the Malian armed forces were fighting an alliance of veteran Salafist combatants and re-supplied and re-armed Tuareg insurgents, a far more aggressive and powerful enemy than before. On March 22, 2012, following a series of reverses in the North, the military mutinied under the nominal leadership of Captain Amadou Sanogo. Within twenty-four hours, the civilian government was driven into hiding. Sanogo and his cohorts proclaimed the "National Committee for the Restoration of Democracy and State" and closed the borders of Mali.[4]

While the military regime released a large degree of their power within weeks and the Islamist threat was eventually beaten back, the Malian coup d'état was a critical failure in the eyes of U.S. policymakers.[5] The United States had invested tens of millions of dollars in training and equipping what it viewed as a model regional partner, all with an eye to creating stability in a region known for its instability. What the policy instead produced was a military that could not defeat its radicalized enemies in the field and instead overthrew its own elected government. If in the case of Mali even millions of dollars and a decade of partnership had not created a professional military that could safeguard a democratic state, how could policymakers begin to tackle the problem across the developing world?

I. The Unprofessional Soldier and the Developing State

When one looks at the militaries of the developing world, one cannot help but notice the universality of praetorian activity.[6] Since the end of the Second World War, every decade has provided numerous examples of unprofessional military behavior ranging from regional protests to the overthrow of the state government. Although these praetorian actions are most associated with the waves of decolonization in the 1950s and 60s, every year has seen actions across the globe, from Iraq to Argentina and Nigeria to Thailand. The issue of ruptures in the civil-military relations of these states has re-emerged as a serious threat in recent years, with states critical to the War on Terror, such as Mali and Egypt, undergoing successful coups in 2012 and 2013 respectively.

To observers in the developed world, the militaries of the developing world appear to be unstable and unworkable, more a constant threat to the state than its guardian. Western-educated theorists take their model of civil and military structures from the idea of the Westphalian nation-state. In this model, the state is a communal structure with broad legitimacy and the capacity to provide services and protection to its people. The militaries of these states are apolitical and professional, and they provide the monopoly on the legitimate use of violence that is necessary for the state to replicate and sustain itself. In the theoretical structure of Samuel Huntington, this modern professional military requires an existing nation-state, a system of democratic structures and ideals, a single and widely accepted authority over the armed forces, and a minimal level of technology and urbanization.[7] These structures allow for the creation of a military that will remain professional, loyal, and apolitical.[8]

Achieving an apolitical and professional military has also consistently been the goal of the majority of the developing world. However, the failure of these states to achieve this relationship for any appreciable length of time is not necessarily an indictment of the militaries alone but also the states that they serve. Whereas the Westphalian nation-state was the product of hundreds of years of modernization and centralization, the developing world has existed in its modern form for perhaps half a century.[9] The developing states themselves had existed as sources of colonial exploitation or as fractions of larger states, denying them full state functions. Their borders were not chosen through a deliberative process but were forced upon them by foreign powers, cleaving related groups apart and placing alien cultures together. The governments they were left with were often hastily granted sovereignty following decolonization, leading to personalist rulers or unrepresentative democracies. The vast majority of their economic and social structures were subverted and underdeveloped. The structures defined by Huntington that allow the creation and sustenance of a professional military are often weakened or absent in the developing world, leading to the consequent weakness in the professionalism and stability of the militaries within those states.

This combination of factors leads to several questions for the observer of the militaries of the developing world: How does the weakened capacity of the state alter civil-military relations? Does the diversity of subnational actors within developing states effect the structure of their militaries? How has the underdevelopment of economic and social structures altered the states' relations with their military and with the wider world? In what way do these factors interact to exacerbate the difficulties of civil-military relations in the developing world? These are but a few of the questions that must be evaluated before a policymaker can begin to respond to the challenges posed by the often fragile relations between the state and the military in the developing world.

II. Weak State Capacity

The developing world hosts a vast plethora of states with different levels of capacity, but on the whole they maintain a lower capacity than those of the developed world. State capacity in this case may be defined as the capability to penetrate society, regulate social relationships, extract resources, and appropriate or use resources in determined ways.[10] It is through these actions that the state creates the framework by which it provides services to its citizens and protects its sovereignty from threats internal and external. When observers note the challenges of the developing world, weak state capacity is often the primary source of their critique, as within the developing world the state remains the primary mode of social organization.

However, the weak state capacity of the developing world is not a historical anomaly nor is it inherent in the societies that find themselves with such a weakened capacity. The states of the developing world are the product of a history of colonialism and decolonization. Throughout Africa, Asia, and Latin America, states have emerged from a colonial past that involved a series of extractive processes intended to benefit the colonizing power. Latin America was colonized in the sixteenth century by the Iberian powers of Spain and Portugal and although these colonies achieved independence in the nineteenth century, they did not achieve fully centralized administrative structures. The majority of the Middle East had been controlled by the Ottoman Empire until that polity's dismemberment after the First World War; the region was then subjected to direct colonial control by Britain and France. South and Southeast Asia were divided amongst the expanding European powers in a process spanning the eighteenth and nineteenth centuries. Finally, Africa, with the sole exceptions of Ethiopia and Liberia, was conquered and colonized in the late-nineteenth century in the tumultuous and violent 'Scramble for Africa.' Each of these occurrences saw the conquest of local political authority and its subordination or replacement in the service of colonial goals.

Colonizing powers used a variety of strategies to control their colonies. In some cases, as in Latin America and the German colonies of Africa, European states imposed direct control. In other cases, colonizing powers attempted to co-opt traditional systems of governance, such as in Northern Nigeria or the Princely States of India.[11] In other regions, large numbers of European colonists established their own state subordinate to that of the colonial power, such as in Southern Rhodesia or the Italian colonies in Africa. In many cases, these various forms of colonial authority existed side by side within territories that eventually would be placed together, with India and Nigeria each having various administrative approaches that would eventually be amalgamated within their borders. However, the central feature of these apparatuses was their function: producing a stable environment from which economic advantages could be extracted for the benefit of the colonial power. As such, what emerged in each case was not a state government per se but a stripped down and limited version of the state. The colonial apparatus was excellent at extracting and appropriating resources, but its functional abilities in the other facets of the state varied wildly. Few if any colonies were able to determine how their resources would be used. While there was some local autonomy, the development that occurred during the period of colonization was almost entirely for the improvement of colonial control and extraction.

The process of decolonization was often perfunctory and chaotic. In the vast majority of cases, decolonization had either not been planned at all or the colonial power had expected the process to take decades. Instead, either through revolution or forceful negotiation, the process took mere years. Due to the unexpected nature of colonial independence, little had been done to foster a balanced modern society; instead, a thin colonial elite governed a vast population of colonial subjects. In Latin America wealthy landowners oversaw large numbers of local peasants.[12] In the Middle East regional notables retained their elite position. In Africa a wave of educated nationalists blended with the local traditional authorities to emerge as the post-colonial elite.[13]While these groups were able to take the reins of the state in the wake of decolonization, the combination of what was essentially an incomplete state apparatus and a small and limited educated class led to extremely weak independent states. While these states retained their ability to extract and appropriate resources, their abilities in other areas were underdeveloped.

Because the political class in these new states was so limited and faced few internal challenges, they felt little need to develop their capacity to provide services to the societies they governed. Resources could be used to sustain and advance the political class while minimally improving the conditions of the remaining citizens. In essence, political actors inherited the colonial order and maintained it for their own benefit, in many cases retaining relationships with their former colonial power. These weak states, no matter how weak they became, retained power due to the simple fact that they were states and thus were considered legitimate by external actors. The perception of their legitimacy endured even as personalist rule emerged throughout the developing world, with dictators ranging from Saddam Hussein of Iraq to Mobutu Sese Seko of the Congo/Zaire managing to retain power and their limited state capacity for decades at a time. With the post-World War II international order based on the social organization of people as states, the developed world retains a preference for sustaining weak states as opposed to allowing states to fail. Even following the collapse of commodity prices in 1973 and the global economic crash of 2008, the sovereign power of these weak states allowed them to survive and reproduce themselves, even while they lacked the resources to effectively maintain the social and economic developments that they had gained in the late colonial and early independence periods.

Of course, the sustenance and perpetuation of these weak states has significant effects on the relations of the state to its military. The military is the appendage of the state that guarantees the state's sovereignty and its monopoly on the legitimate use of violence.[14] As such, the weakness of the state will ultimately have direct effects on the military. In some cases the military can become essentially praetorian when it aligns itself with the politically elite classes and is sustained through their support. When the military is not so aligned, it is difficult for it to win support and difficult for the state to count on its allegiance. Because the military is often a resource-intensive structure, a weak state unable or unwilling to meet the needs or desires of the military class will find rank-and-file soldiers redirecting their allegiance to figures, military or civilian, who promise to provide for the military. Often this redirection of allegiance involves alignment with a group other than the political elite. In any of these scenarios the military of the developing nation hinders the emergence of Huntingtonian professionalism. Either the military serves the unrepresentative group in power, in which case it undermines Huntington's condition of democratic and representative government, or the military serves an individual or group not in power, in which case it undermines Huntington's precondition of the singular loyalty of the military to state authority. The structure of politics in developing states seems almost to force the military to function as an interest group seeking to fulfill its prerogatives, even at the expense of protecting the nation or more fully developing the state's capacities.

This subversion of the military leads into several questions that U.S. policymakers must face if they are attempting to foster a professional military with a stable relationship to its civil government. If the issue is lack of state capacity coupled with that of governmental apathy to capacity building, what tools does an outside actor have? The United States, as a fully industrialized state, has a wide range of diplomatic, military, and economic tools. However, the developing state still has full benefit of its sovereignty, giving it the ability to grant or deny access to any other actor. This leads to the necessity of incentives for development of state capacity, a model embodied by such programs as the Millennium Development Goals, which couple capacity building efforts to incentives such as debt forgiveness to allow these goals to be met. Despite these efforts, much of the developing world is still lagging behind and there has been little guarantee that released aid funds go fully to their intended recipients. Given that a military solution is a suboptimal one for dealing with a potential partner-nation, what efforts can a policymaker undertake to create incentives for capacity building and how can they insure that their partner follows through with their efforts?

III. Diversity of Subnational Actors

Whereas observers often focus on the weakness of states in the developing world, it is as important to account for the relative strength of nations. Whereas the state is the political structure that provides for and protects its citizens, the nation consists of a far more amorphous and ingrained set of associations and behaviors. Nations are often defined by shared traits like languages, appearance, religious creed, or cultural norms; nations often define themselves against those that do not share these traits.[15] Nationalism rose to become a powerful force in nineteenth-century Europe, eventually culminating in the norm of the "nation-state," that is, a state rooted in a shared national character. The German state, for instance, was thought necessary to protect and provide services for the German people. Although these states rarely encompassed members of only one national group, they catered primarily to the needs of that group; they also used the power of the state to efface differences within that group and remove members of other ethnic, linguistic, racial, or confessional groups from their borders. By means of this lengthy process of consolidation and "purification," the nation-state emerged.

While this slow process of negotiation, identity-building, and acceptance of sovereignty occurred over centuries in the developed world, the post-colonial developing states did not have the luxury of time. Colonial boundaries were rarely formed through a process of negotiation, violent or not, between the inhabiting national groups. Instead they were drawn in accordance with the needs and desires of the competing colonial powers. Most famously, the 1885 Berlin Conference effectively imposed borders across Africa based upon competing claims of European actors, such as Leopold II of Belgium's personal claim to the entirety of the Congo basin. A similar process took place in the Middle East, where the Sykes-Picot treaty, negotiated primarily between France and Britain in 1916, divvied up the former territories of the Ottoman Empire. Even the 1947 Partition of India and Pakistan took place along lines largely decided by British functionaries.

The states that emerged upon independence contained a multiplicity of subnational groups that bore little historical relation to one another; they had even less present integration and sometimes intractable cultural differences. Nigeria emerged into independence with three major and dozens of minor ethnic groups, all of whom had varying levels of development under the colonial regime. In Iraq, the minority Kurds found themselves attached to a largely Arab population within completely ahistoric boundaries. These same subnational divisions were often exacerbated by confessional or even administrative differences. Iraq existed along the fault lines of Shia and Sunni Islam, Lebanon held Muslim and Christian populations, and the Sudan was home to Islamic Arabs in the North and Christian or Animist Africans in the South. The Princely states were integrated into a larger administrative India. Nigeria saw the largely indirectly-ruled and traditional North combined with the largely developed and Anglicized South. In all of these cases, the meager national ambition that pushed these groups together in pursuit of independence quickly dissolved into subnational ambitions. While the state is theoretically intended to penetrate society and help regulate social relationships, the competing subnational groups each already offered regulation of social relationships and often showed little inclination to allow the state to do so.[16] Also, the state itself quickly became an object of competition among subnational groups, as it afforded the chance to enforce particular groups' social norms and to offer patronage to other group members. As such, the subordination of the weak state noted above is often accompanied by the competition of subnational groups for access to its capacity to suppress rival groups.

The persistence and power of subnational groups in developing nation-states have significant effects on the professionalization of militaries in the developing world. The first effect is rather self-evident: without a cohesive and relatively unified national identity, there is no nation-state for the professional military to support, undermining one of Huntington's initial foundations for a professional military. Beyond this, the competition between subnational groups continues to undermine two of Huntington's other necessary functions. The first is the system of democratic structures and ideals. As subnational groups compete for access to the organs of the state, the controlling group marginalizes those without representation. There follows a series of escalating attempts by subnational groups to assert or reassert state control, a process that ultimately further subverts the democratic process. Perhaps the prime current example is Kenya, where the electoral struggles between the Kikuyu and Luo groups has erupted into violence on a number of occasions, while the ethnic Somalis within the state have become marginalized and possibly radicalized.

The second major principle undermined by this plethora of subnational actors is the single and widely accepted authority over the armed forces. In raising armed forces for their colonies, the colonizing powers of the eighteenth and nineteenth centuries often relied on the concept of "martial races." This concept, popularized by the Anglo-Indian Army and subsequently adopted throughout many European empires, posited that certain ethnic groups within the colonies were naturally adept at military service; the colonial military was recruited solely from those groups, and in turn the groups received significant privileges. In India these groups included the Sikhs, Dogras, Pathans, and Gurkhas.[17] In the Anglo-Egyptian Army the Sudanese found favor and many of these soldiers were consequently recruited for the German colonial forces in East Africa.[18] In Nigeria the soldiers for the Royal West African Frontier Force were drawn predominantly from the Hausa-Fulani groups of the North.[19] Upon independence these groups rarely had ties to the new nationalist governments; in fact, many had been at odds with the liberation movements. With few political or social connections to the new governments, the military was marginalized in the new subnational competition for state access and resources, and it was torn between competing allegiances to the legitimate state, the military as an identity group, and the original subnational group. This condition has persisted to the present day in many countries, although almost entirely in regimes where the subnational group has previously seized power. For example, the regime of Tito Okello, the Ugandan officer who overthrew the Obote regime in 1985, continued to recruit heavily from his Acholi ethnic group. In more recent times the army of Nouri al-Maliki in Iraq was recruited almost exclusively from his

Shi'ite majority, creating another lever of power with which to maintain power over the Sunni of that state.

Subnational fractures within a state also raise potent questions for policymakers. The subnational identities of groups often are deeply ingrained and extremely resistant to outside influences—in fact they are often defined by their very resistance to these influences. Given this fact and the impossibility of redrawing boundaries to fit these groups, it seems far more possible to influence the participation of these groups in state functions, whether serving in the military or being provided with state-provided medical care. This brings up echoes of the previous questions for policymakers. In the absence of tools to *force* a state to take action, what can a policymaker do to help integrate diverse subnational groups into the state? Given the United States' ostensible dedication to a liberal democracy representing a diverse population, how can we use our diplomatic and economic influence to create incentives for state representation of the nation? Even simply on the military plane, what steps might be taken by advisors to integrate new ethnic or confessional groups into a military? While efforts to integrate militaries in such places as the Democratic Republic of the Congo have often ended badly,[20] there are examples of working integrated militaries. For example, neighboring Tanzania transitioned from an ethnically-recruited military to a representative model using a national service organization that fostered a collective national identity.[21] With the need for resources, educators, and infrastructure for a solution such as this, is it a workable model for policymakers to consider?

IV. Foreign Dependency and Patronage

The colonial history of the majority of the developing world has also left it with a historical pattern of economic and developmental subordination. As noted, European colonies existed primarily for the sake of producing or extracting raw materials, such as the gold and silver of Latin America, the sugar of the Caribbean, the oil of the Middle East, and the spices of Southeast Asia. While these were certainly not the only goods produced in the colonies, they were a large part of the colonial economies. Production was intended for exportation to foreign markets, primarily if not solely for that of their colonial patron. In return, the colonial power sold completed manufactured goods in the colonial market. This pattern accelerated following the Industrial Revolution, with the quantity and diversity of manufactured goods emerging from the industrialized world creating a vast influx of products that simply could not be produced within the colonies. In return, the developing world concentrated on producing the most lucrative cash crops and extracting what mineral wealth they had, often specializing in single products in high demand. Colonies like the Gold Coast (later Ghana) concentrated almost exclusively on producing cocoa while Peru expanded its copper mines as much as possible. However, as the cost of raw materials could not match that of manufactured goods, the trade remained an unequal one—especially as the developed power could produce machines that were both difficult to create and necessary for the continued growth of the developing states' economies.[22] This underdevelopment of productive capacity created a relationship of dependency, where the colony could not produce necessary manufactured goods and relied upon its colonial patron to provide them at a tolerable market price.

This dependency went hand in hand with the underdevelopment of the majority of the colonial world. Those improvements that were made, whether railroads, canals, telephone lines, schools, hospitals, or electrification, were limited in scope and were intended only to sustain and accelerate the extraction of raw goods. By and large, the colonized world had no capacity or ability to produce these improvements themselves. Even as the developing world was gaining its independence, there was little it could do to develop its infrastructure and manufacturing capacity. Efforts were made to create and support the infrastructure of the modern state, such as schools, universities, hospitals, power grids, and the like. Even when the prices of their exported products were high, there was little domestic expertise in constructing these institutions and less interest by foreign partners to aid in creating them. A brief burst of development in the 1960s was crushed following the 1973 oil crisis. Simply to maintain their gains, the developing world concentrated on producing the cash crops and extracting their commodities for export that would allow them to continue to meet their obligations. The Cold War saw significant patronage offered by both poles to the developing world, but little was intended to actually develop the industrial capacity that would end dependency. Even today the developing world is marked largely by its lack of industrial development, with either exportable commodities produced or subsistence marking the states that fit into the developing world. While some nations in the formerly-colonized world have managed to develop industrial capacity, notably India and South Korea, the majority remain dependent upon world markets and foreign partners for any large-scale infrastructure projects.

The underdevelopment and dependency of the developing world has profound effects on the relations of these states with their militaries. On the purely theoretical level, the lack of industrialization for many of these countries puts them in violation of Huntington's framework. Although urbanization is a significant factor in the developing world, with cities such as Lagos, Cairo, Jakarta, and Mexico City, among others, all passing into the category of megacities, the states that these cities are part of still contain little industrialization, especially in comparison with their relative populations. Beyond this issue of urbanization, though, there is the simple factor of the military and its needs. A modern military is a complex organization containing thousands of personnel, multiple bureaucracies, and a strict administrative hierarchy. The very existence of a modern military requires a degree of technical and professional education and a large amount of military hardware. However, due to the underdevelopment of the majority of the post-colonial world, the structures needed to provide advanced technical training and military hardware do not exist within developing countries. During the colonial era, rank-and-file soldiers in Africa and Southeast Asia were issued military hardware from the colonial power, and the officers were loaned from the metropolitan armies of France, Britain, or the Netherlands.

Following independence, formerly-colonized nations continued to need their colonizers' military hardware, and they still required officers to command their militaries. The militaries of developing countries have turned to patronage to meet their needs. Many of the formerly-colonial militaries maintained relationships with the state that had colonized them, as the militaries' transition to independence was often aided by the colonial officers. The eventual training of the native officers of Nigeria, Jordan, and Kenya was accomplished in the United Kingdom, and all retained the use of British military hardware for years after decolonization.[23] Other states in the midst of the Cold War sought out support from the socialist bloc, having rejected the aid of colonial powers; examples include Northern Vietnam, Algeria, and Ethiopia, which maintained Communist patronage until its collapse in 1991.[24] Even in the present day, powers like China, the United States, and France remain significantly involved in training and equipping the militaries of the developing world.[25]

Although this foreign military patronage seems relatively benign, a form of capacity-building because the military is part of the state, the establishment of a firm patron-client relationship with the military causes significant issues for the civil-military relations, as it undermines the host state's single and widely accepted authority over the armed forces. Throughout the wave of coups in the 1960s and 1970s in Africa, there was significant consternation over the central role of British-trained officers in overthrowing many left-leaning governments.

Given that governments such as Kwame Nkrumah's administration in Ghana were in the process of breaking with British policy at the time of their overthrow, nationalist leaders such as Julius Nyerere of Tanzania expressed concern at British influence within their own militaries.[26] Even amongst those not educated in the United Kingdom, the enduring connection to old partners and the power of new ones influenced coups. Mobutu Sese Seko (at the time Colonel Joseph Mobutu) seized power from the Congolese government of Patrice Lumumba only after he had established the patronage and permission of the United States.[27] In Latin America, the U.S. Army's School of the Americas became infamous for its curriculum and the central role many of its graduates played in coups, terror campaigns, and eventual dictatorial regimes.[28] Given the pro-American, anti-leftist slant of the majority of the resulting regimes, even American intellectuals have expressed concern over undue foreign influence over the national militaries of sovereign states and the destabilizing effects this influence had on the democratic foundations of these states.[29] Even in the present day, the recent coup of Captain Amadou Sanogo in Mali led media outlets such as *The New York Times* to make an issue of his training with the United States' military and the increasing U.S. footprint in Africa following the establishment of AFRICOM.[30] Although many of these cases will never be conclusively proven to have involved the direct collusion of foreign powers, the possibility of influence through education or materiel remains troubling with a view to the relations of developing nations with their militaries.

There are few issues in civil-military relations in the developing world that can be more difficult for a policymaker to navigate than the issue of dependency—or, more to the point, the appearance of dependency or undue influence. The provision of military expertise and hardware is and remains one of the strongest tools United States policymakers have in engaging militaries in the developing world. Given this, from the viewpoint of policymakers, a larger engagement is always preferable. This engagement can not only build valuable partnerships but also deny this same influence to economic or political rivals. However, this leaves somewhat of a paradox: outside actors see this influence as desirable for their own ends, but this same influence has the potential to degrade the democratic and representative institutions of the client. As such, how can a policymaker engage with the issue of patronage? Are there possibilities of offering military training and support without implicitly or explicitly undermining the partner state or its relation with its military? Do non-military partnerships offer a better possibility of influence without destabilization? Infrastructure programs like the Tanzania-Zambia Railway (TAZARA)[31] and the more recent hydroelectric dam in Ethiopia have offered China significant influence without apparently damaging the military and the state.[32] Or would attempts to build civilian human capacity through schooling and training within U.S. partner countries have a longer and more beneficial effect? Will these alternate programs create openings for rival influences within the military?

V. The Interaction of Undermining Factors and Conclusion

The issues of civil-military stability and military professionalism in the developing world are legion, and the factors discussed above are certainly not the sole issues involved. However, the issues of weak state capacity, strong subnational actors, and dependency on outside production and education, all can play a central role in disrupting the desired professionalism of a developing military. Perhaps even more distressingly, these factors often express considerable interaction, which both amplifies and complicates the attendant issues further. Weak state capacity makes it extremely difficult to break dependency on foreign patrons. Foreign patrons, especially former colonizers, often have stronger relations with particular subnational groups that were involved with the colonial project than with those that agitated for independence, and this imbalance can exacerbate the cleavages in developing societies. Finally, a strong state is often required to sublimate subnational identities, but various interest groups will often struggle to prevent the conditions that allow for sublimation; after all, weak states facilitate subnational independence and influence.

Given the complexity of the issue and the multitude of difficult policy decisions involved, the issue of creating apolitical professional militaries to safeguard emerging democracies is one that has seen few solutions. However, a final note must be made regarding the general framework of the analysis so far: the discussion of the issues of weak state capacity, subnational actors, and underdevelopment and dependency have all been made with the understanding that the ideal form of the state is one of representative liberal democracy with broad public freedoms and a generally capitalist economy. This is unsurprising since this is and remains the United States' favored model since the end of the Cold War. However, civil-military relations scholars have not always viewed this as the ideal form for developing countries. Huntington, in his work *Political Order in Changing Societies*, argues that broad-based political participation in counties with underdeveloped political institutions (a condition found in much of the developing world) causes continued underdevelopment and instability.[33]

From the Huntingtonian perspective, a military regime in a developing country might be preferable to limit political participation until firm political institutions are in place. Whether this hypothesis is taken seriously by policymakers in the present day or not, the United States, while decrying military regimes and military intervention, maintains close relations with states that feature these phenomena. Currently, critical international partners for United States policymakers include Egypt, Mauritania, and Thailand, all countries that have seen military interventions in politics within the past five years. How do these relationships alter how a policymaker might balance the drive for democratization, the need for development, the creation of professional regional militaries, and the strategic goals of the United States?

In the end, the policymaker who wishes to address civil-military relations in the developing world must first consider the various issues that set the boundaries on state power, state relations, and the political and social identity of the citizens and military. These in turn will define the limitations on the transformation of militaries from possible threats to the state to the preferred model of apolitical and professional guardians of sovereignty. One must remember that these are not insurmountable barriers, but instead interacting pressures and relationships that must be kept in mind as one works toward the professionalization and stabilization of the militaries of the developing world.

RECOMMENDED READINGS

Fitch, J. Samuel. 1989. "Military Professionalism, National Security and Democracy: Lessons from the Latin American Experience." *Pacific Focus* 4, no. 2 (September 1, 1989): 99–147.

Howe, Herbert M. 2004. *Ambiguous Order: Military Forces in African States.* Boulder, CO.

Huntington, Samuel P. 2006. *Political Order in Changing Societies.* New Haven, CT.

Kamrava, Mehran. 2000. "Military Professionalization and Civil-Military Relations in the Middle East." *Political Science Quarterly* 115, no. 1 (March 1, 2000): 67–92.

Luckham, Robin. 1994. "The Military, Militarization and Democratization in Africa: A Survey of Literature and Issues." *African Studies Review* 37, no. 02 (1994): 13–75.

ADDITIONAL READINGS

Alagappa, Muthiah. 2001. *Military Professionalism in Asia: Conceptual and Empirical Perspectives.* Honolulu, HI.

Barany, Zoltan. 2012. *The Soldier and the Changing State: Building Democratic Armies in Africa, Asia, Europe, and the Americas.* Princeton, NJ.

Bienen, Henry. 1981. "Civil-Military Relations in the Third World." *International Political Science Review* 2, no. 3 (July 1): 363–70.

Cawthra, Gavin, and Robin Luckham. 2003. *Governing Insecurity: Democratic Control of Military and Security Establishments in Transitional Democracies.* London.

Emizet, Kisangani N. F. 2000. "Explaining the Rise and Fall of Military Regimes: Civil-Military Relations in the Congo." *Armed Forces & Society* 26, no. 2 (January 1): 203–27.

Huntington, Samuel P. 1981. *The Soldier and the State: The Theory and Politics of Civil-Military Relations.* Cambridge, MA.

Janowitz, Morris. 1988. *Military Institutions and Coercion in the Developing Nations: The Military in the Political Development of New Nations.* Chicago, IL.

------. 1964. *The Professional Soldier: A Social and Political Portrait.* Reissue edition. New York.

Nielsen, Suzanne C. and Don M. Snider. 2009. *American Civil-Military Relations: The Soldier and the State in a New Era.* Baltimore, MD.

Norden, Deborah L. 1990. "Democratic Consolidation and Military Professionalism: Argentina in the 1980s." *Journal of Interamerican Studies and World Affairs* 32, no. 3: 151–76.

Ray, Ayesha. 2013.*The Soldier and the State in India: Nuclear Weapons, Counterinsurgency, and the Transformation of Indian Civil-Military Relations.* New Delhi.

Rouquie, Alain. 1989. *The Military and the State in Latin America.* Berkeley, CA.

Welch, Claude Emerson. 1970. *Soldier and State in Africa: A Comparative Analysis of Military Intervention and Political Change.* Evanston, IL.

NOTES

[1]For an example of these teams and their work in the early years of the PSI, see Robert D. Kaplan, "America's African Rifles," *The Atlantic* (April 2005), http://www.theatlantic.com/magazine/archive/2005/04/americas-african-rifles/303823/.

[2]Simon J. Powelson, "Enduring Engagement Yes, Episodic Engagement No: Lessons for SOF from Mali" (Thesis, Naval Postgraduate School, 2013), 2, https://calhoun.nps.edu/handle/10945/38996.

[3]Walter Pincus, "Mali Insurgency Followed 10 Years of U.S. Counterterrorism Programs," *The Washington Post* (January 16, 2013), http://www.washingtonpost.com/world/national-security/mali-insurgency-followed-10-years-of-us-counterterrorism-programs/2013/01/16/a43f2d32-601e-11e2-a389-ee565c81c565_story.html.

[4]Adam Nossiter, "In Mali, Coup Leaders Seem to Have Uncertain Grasp on Power," *The New York Times* (March 23, 2012), http://www.nytimes.com/2012/03/24/world/africa/in-mali-coup-leaders-seem-to-have-uncertain-grasp-on-power.html.

[5]The Islamists were defeated primarily by French military intervention, with the French Army launching an aggressive offensive that coincided with accurate airstrikes which weakened much of the local resistance.

[6]Praetorian activity, named after the Praetorian Guard of the late Roman Empire, refers to activities by the military that strike against the civil control of the state in direct or indirect means. This would eventually become synonymous with what Huntington would refer to as "unprofessional" activity, with the concept of professionalism being that of a military that is loyal and responsive to the civil government of the state.

[7]Samuel P. Huntington, *The Soldier and the State: The Theory and Politics of Civil-Military Relations* (Cambridge, MA: Belknap Press, 1957), 32–9.

[8]Admittedly the apolitical military is not always desired, but in general the military is supposed to stay out of the political business of the state, especially in the post-Cold War era.

[9]See for example the work of Charles Tilly on state formation. Tilly, *Coercion, Capital, and European States, A.D. 990–1990* (Cambridge, MA, and Oxford: Blackwell, 1992).

[10]Joel S. Migdal, *Strong Societies and Weak States* (Princeton, NJ: Princeton University Press, 1988), 4.

[11]In both of these cases, the traditional leaders or monarchs were left in power and given official sanction by Britain but were bound to obey British will and requests. This let the British have access to the region for economic and cultural penetration without needing to struggle for legitimacy.

[12]Alain Rouquie, *The Military and the State in Latin America* (Berkeley, CA: University of California Press, 1989), 23.

[13]Basil Davidson, *Modern Africa: A Social and Political History*, 3rd edition (London and New York: Routledge, 1994), 74.

[14]In the developed world the monopoly on the legitimate use of violence is generally shared between the military for external purposes and the police for internal ones. In the developing world the military and police were most often synonymous and acted more as a gendarmerie. This is not to say that other actors cannot inflict violence, but that the military specifically has the state's sanction which legitimizes their violence, whereas other actors' violence is illegitimate and thus criminal. This definition is of course taken from Max Weber's "Politics as Vocation."

[15]Benedict Anderson, *Imagined Communities: Reflections on the Origin and Spread of Nationalism* (London and New York: Verso, 2006), 6, although this does not exactly match what Anderson states. Since Anderson admits there is no useful scientific definition of Nationalism, between this description and Anderson's own this will have to do.

[16]And this is assuming the state had either the capacity or willingness to do so in the developing country. As noted in the section on weak state capacity, the state might not even have interest in regulating these social relationships beyond the efforts necessary to maintain their status as a state. The complex and often amplified interactions between weak states, strong nations, and foreign patrons will be covered further along in this chapter.

[17]Byron Farwell, *Armies of the Raj: From the Great Indian Mutiny to Independence, 1858–1947*, Reprint edition (New York: W. W. Norton & Company, 1991), 182–8.

[18]Ernst Nigmann, *German Schutztruppe in East Africa; History of the Imperial Protectorate Force 1889–1911* (Nashville, TN, and Silver City, NM: The Battery Press, 2005), 2.

[19]Anthony Clayton, *Khaki & Blue: Military and Police in British Colonial Africa* (Athens, OH: Ohio University Press, 1989), 175.

[20]For example, the most recent of the armed rebellions in the Congo occurred when the M23 group rebelled against the still-integrating Congolese military over subnational concerns. See "Q&A: Who Are DR Congo's M23 Rebels?," *Al Jazeera* (November 5, 2013), accessed September 29, 2014, http://www.aljazeera.com/news/africa/2013/08/201382411593336904.html.

[21]See Charles G. Thomas, "To Serve the Nation: Jeshi la Kujenga Taifa and the Development of Tanzania," in *The Political Economy of Modern Africa: Wealth, Exploitation, and Development*, ed. Jamaine Abidogun (London: I.B. Tauris, 2015).

[22]This is the classic dependency thesis, as expounded upon regarding Africa in Walter Rodney, *How Europe Underdeveloped Africa* (Baltimore, MD: Black Classic Press, 2011); the Latin American variation of the thesis can be found in Rouquie, *The Military and the State in Latin America,* 25–9.

[23]Kenneth M. Pollack, *Arabs at War: Military Effectiveness, 1948–1991* (Lincoln, NE: Bison Books, 2004), 270.

[24]Gebru Tareke, *The Ethiopian Revolution: War in the Horn of Africa* (New Haven, CT: Yale University Press, 2009), 134.

[25]From 2008–2011 the United States was involved in $113 billion worth of arms transfers to the developing world, although this was slightly inflated by several major agreements that were finalized with the Gulf States. These agreements made 2011 alone account for nearly half of the total for the period ($56.3 billion). France's share of the arms trade during this same period was $14.3. China's share of the arms transfers during this period of time was approximately $8–10 billion dollars, with much of that going to Pakistan. See Richard F. Grimmett and Paul K. Kerr, "Conventional Arms Transfers to Developing Nations, 2004–2011." Congressional Research Service (Library of Congress, 2012), 6–10.

[26]There is some mention of this in the memoirs of General A.A. Afrifa, *The Ghana Coup* (London: Cass, 1967); This was considered compelling enough that it was explored in the work of Li and Thompson on the "Coup Contagion" Hypothesis; Richard P. Y. Li and William R. Thompson, "The 'Coup Contagion' Hypothesis," *Journal of Conflict Resolution* 19, no. 1 (March 1, 1975): 63–84.

[27]Lawrence Devlin, *Chief of Station, Congo: Fighting the Cold War in a Hot Zone* (New York: Public Affairs, 2008), 78.

[28]Lesley Gill, *The School of the Americas: Military Training and Political Violence in the Americas* (Durham, NC: Duke University Press, 2004), 2.

[29]A comprehensive investigation of these issues can be found in Bill Quigley, "The Case for Closing the School of the Americas," *BYU Journal of Public Law* 20 (2005-2006): 1–34, 1.

[30]Craig Whitlock, "Leader of Mali Military Coup Trained in U.S.," *The Washington Post*, (March 24, 2012), http://www.washingtonpost.com/world/national-security/leader-of-mali-military-coup-trained-in-us/2012/03/23/gIQAS7Q6WS_story.html.

[31]For a deeper discussion of the TAZARA project, see Jamie Monson, *Africa's Freedom Railway: How a Chinese Development Project Changed Lives and Livelihoods in Tanzania* (Bloomington, IN: Indiana University Press, 2009).

[32]Joshua Eisenman, Eric Heginbotham, and Derek Mitchell, *China and the Developing World: Beijing's Strategy for the Twenty-First Century* (Amonk, NY: M.E. Sharpe, 2007), 47.

[33]Samuel P. Huntington, *Political Order in Changing Societies* (New Haven, CT: Yale University Press, 2006 [1968]), 78.

16

Imagining the Worst Case

Learning to Live in the Post-Apocalypse

TONY MCGOWAN AND SEAN CASE

Ebola. The Arab Spring. ISIS. Climate change. Crises inundate our era, feeding into anxieties over the future. However, the Cold War period was just as concerned with the prospect of Armageddon. One specter from that time continues to haunt crisis managers: nuclear war. The successful detonation of a nuclear weapon in 1945 ushered the world into the nuclear age; J. Robert Oppenheimer, the supervisor of the American Manhattan Project, paraphrasing the Bhagavad Gita, famously stated, "I am become Death, destroyer of worlds." As nuclear weapons proliferated as a marker of national power, planners became increasingly concerned with life after the bombs had dropped. According to Arundahti Roy, a public intellectual and political activist, Western anxiety stems from a failure of imagination. In her important essay "The End of Imagination," she describes what there is to fear in a nuclear cascade:

> Our cities and forests, our fields and villages will burn for days. Rivers will turn to poison. The air will become fire. The wind will spread the flames. When everything there is to burn has burned and the fires die, smoke will rise and shut out the sun. The earth will be enveloped in darkness. There will be no day. Only interminable night.[1]

Left with the responsibility of imagining this "unimaginable" outcome, crisis planners focused their energies on preserving the old world order through systems of bunkers. They envisioned continuance of government as their main task.[2]

Consider that Cold War measures went beyond efforts to safeguard key politicians, and still protect foundational documents such as the Declaration of Independence, the Constitution, and the Bill of Rights; cultural artifacts such as President Lincoln's autopsy report and an 1804 map of the Lewis and Clark expedition; and timeless artistic works such as Leonardo da Vinci's *Ginevra de'Benci* and Raphael's *Alba Madonna.*[3] "Preserving the nation's knowledge was even more essential than protecting the nation's leadership[and] the ragged survivors of [nuclear] war," reports Bret Spencer, a scholar of the Cold War era. Survivors "could in time rebuild the nation's government systems, work processes, technology, and financial institutions as long as the shadow libraries shielded their agency handbooks, work manuals, patents, and balance sheets."[4] Strategists preserved the present at the expense of preparing for the future. We ask you to think beyond the paradigm of the bunker—to use your imaginations to push toward new and creative protocols.

We believe that when confronting the "unimaginable," imaginative literature sometimes proves more useful to the policymaker than manuals, patents, or spread-sheets. Through its affective punch and complex ambiguities, literature delivers the policymaker cognitive transport capable of focusing the imagination in the struggle to make useful decisions in advance of impending catastrophe. Our carefully selected test-case here is Cormac McCarthy's 2006 Pulitzer Prize-winning novel, *The Road*, which envisions life in a post-apocalyptic wasteland quite differently than did U.S. Cold War planners. In this scenario chapter, we will paint for you a vivid portrait of Cormac McCarthy's "worst case scenario." Along the way we will ask you to consider some of the questions this scenario raises for the policymaker tasked with planning for the apocalypse. Finally, we will consider contemporary challenges this imaginative approach to policy planning might illuminate, now that the Cold War-era threat of nuclear holocaust is (one hopes) more remote. You are not obliged to take up all or any set number of the questions you find here; we only hope they provoke you to think differently and well about planning for the worst.

I. McCarthy's "Worst Case Scenario"

McCarthy is one of the most celebrated living American novelists, and while most of his work is grounded in American geography and history, *The Road* is an exception. The imaginary world in this book largely floats free from history and instead yields a spare, speculative, realist fable of the human condition *in extremis*. Considering the world as portrayed in this novel should help you imagine the "worst," and allow you to engage with this central question: What is the policymaker to do now if the worst that could happen is not human extinction, but, against all odds, our survival into a shattered world stripped bare of the civil supports we rely upon in the present?

In *The Road*, the world exists in a state of collapse. Fire has consumed much of the world; flora and fauna are dead or hidden; sludgy seas reflect steel-gray skies; and roving bands of cannibals and primordial blood cults wander the landscape or hole up in repurposed homes. There are no borders, nations, governments, or external forms of authority beyond brute primal force. Into this ravaged world McCarthy inserts his two nameless central characters, the man (a father) and the boy (his son).

Because *The Road* cannot be fully useful to you without consideration of its affective cast and innovative style, and to give you a taste of McCarthy's spare and yet strangely lyrical language, we interrupt plot summary and give you here, in full, the novel's two opening block paragraphs.[5] As you read, consider McCarthy's form and content; discuss it together:

> When he woke in the woods in the dark and the cold of the night he'd reached out to touch the child sleeping beside him. Nights dark beyond darkness and days more gray each one than what had gone before. Like the onset of some cold glaucoma dimming away the world. His hand rose and fell softly with each precious breath. He pushed away the plastic tarpaulin and raised himself in the stinking robes and blankets and looked toward the east for any light but there was none. In the dream from which he'd wakened he had wandered in a cave where the child led him by the hand. Their light playing over the wet flowstone walls. Like pilgrims in a fable swallowed up and lost among the inward parts of some granitic beast. Deep stone flues where the water dripped and sang. Tolling in the silence the minutes of the earth and the hours and the days of it and the years without cease. Until they stood in a great stone room where lay a black and ancient lake. And on the far shore a creature that raised its dripping mouth from the rimstone pool and stared into the light with eyes dead white and sightless as the eggs of spiders. It swung its head low over the water as if to take the scent of what it could not see. Crouching there pale and naked and translucent, its alabaster bones cast up in shadow on the rocks behind it. Its bowels, its beating heart. The brain that pulsed in a dull glass bell. It swung its head from side to side and then gave out a low moan and turned and lurched away and loped soundlessly into the dark.
>
> With the first gray light he rose and left the boy sleeping and walked out to the road and squatted and studied the country to the south. Barren, silent, godless. He thought the month was October but he wasnt sure. He hadnt kept a calendar for years. They were moving south. There'd be no surviving another winter

here.[6]

McCarthy's language is deceptively easy to read—made of strings of short declarative language. Some of the "sentences" are actually verbless fragments, lists of attributes and descriptors. Some contractions omit an apostrophe. Except for its rich lyricism, this stripped language seems to echo the stripped world. As a reader you start to learn here also that voice in the novel is limited, third person omniscient. That is to say, McCarthy's narrator can venture inside the man's mind (for example to report his dream), but he will not enter the boy's mind in the same way. We give you the opening description of the dream "creature" to entice you, of course, but not to completely unpack its meaning for you. In fact, the passage is so dense as to warn against the practice of instrumentalizing imaginative literature. Simply, and we hope obviously, great fiction's value to the policymaker is that its meanings exceed complete decoding, that it can't be used as would information on a spreadsheet or in a manual. We do, however, want you to notice that the father's vivid and horrible dream pre-conditions our fall into the plot, as if McCarthy needs to evacuate the last refuge of hope before telling us the tale. This is a world where nightmare is arguably better than the waking world, where the boy alone is the last vestige of hope. We give you the opening paragraphs of *The Road* for one more reason, and that is because the novel also closes with a notable turn to metaphorical language, post-modern allegory to be precise, and near the end of this chapter we will ask you to consider these bookend passages together.

After this opening, the story in *The Road* is actually very simple in its general shape. On the road, the pair, father and son, eke out a meager existence, pushing a shopping cart south, where they hope for warmth and, almost beyond hope, succor of some communal human sort. Along their trek, they evade and encounter individuals and small groups. These people are pure threat—alone and dying or bonded to survive through scavenging and cannibalism. But the man and boy are not cannibals; they consider themselves "the good guys." The man tells the boy that they "carry the fire," and the boy takes up and repeats the idea like a mantra.[7] This is McCarthy's way of revealing that the pair preserve, or think they preserve, humanity's precious moral compass. This idea is central, more important than the physical things they carry. The pair preserve and transport what value is left in the world; their journey is a kind of last pilgrimage on earth, one imbued with sacred meaning.

Interspersed in the trek narrative we get the man's flashbacks to the story of a woman's last days; she was the wife of the man, the mother of the boy.

She has given birth to the boy in the immediate aftermath of whatever has destroyed the world, and in painful dialogue with the man has finally decided to kill herself. Before she wanders off, presumably to slit her wrists with a chip of obsidian, she tells him: "We're not survivors. We're the walking dead in a horror film.... I should have done it a long time ago.... Sooner or later they will catch us and they will kill us. They will rape me. They'll rape him. They are going to rape us and kill us and eat us and you won't face it."[8] The man flashes back to such scenes in the present, on the trek, where his lungs are corrupted and he knows he is dying, where he is driven to live only by the desire to deliver the boy to safety, where he holds a pistol, almost out of bullets, and considers the approaching necessity of ending the boy's life swiftly, to save him the torment envisioned by the woman. We are trying to underline here that this is a hard book to read.

II. Post-Apocalyptic Policy or How to Build a New "Civilization"

The world in McCarthy's book is on its last legs and not sustainable. What can a planner do now to prepare for such a place?

Apocalyptic Security

Survival and the concept of the bunker go together. Whether a means to protect personal life and treasure or to preserve food diversity for the future, the bunker would seem an obvious way to prepare for impending catastrophe.[9] But, when dealing with the unimaginable, real bunkers built now may not provide their intended comfort and may instead offer a new host of horrors for survivors.

McCarthy's man and boy encounter both figurative and literal bunkers in their travels, yet none of them offer real shelter. The gun and bullet we spoke of act as a kind of ideational bunker; salvation lies in control of one's own death. But there are actual bunkers too. In the first of two important scenes, the pair enter a vacated farmhouse and find a basement "locked with a large padlock made of stacked steel plates." They speak to each other in chopped language that is a feature of the book—a sort of survivalists' panicked way of communicating:

> Papa, the boy said. We should go. Papa.
>
> There's a reason this is locked.
>
> The boy pulled at his hand. He was almost in tears.

Papa? he said.

We've got to eat.

I'm not hungry, Papa. I'm not.

We need a prybar or something.[10]

The father finally breaks into the basement and the boy descends with him. We won't relate the entire discovery scene here, the repulsive cannibal cache of once and future meals, the still living dead, the whispers of "help us."

Later, McCarthy has us read a second scene through the terror the reader (and the pair of wanderers) still retain from the first. Again the man and boy find an abandoned farmhouse. Again the man hacks at a lock on subterranean space, breaks the hasp, swings open a door: "Don't open it, Papa, [the boy] whisper[s]." Even repetition of the word "whisper" brings the scenes together. But this time the discovery is of a fallout shelter and bunker—a survivalist's cornucopia. "What did you find?" says the boy. "Everything" says the father. "Wait till you see."[11]

We think McCarthy means us to compare these scenes because both—horrible larder and wonderful store—are anxiety-ridden and indefensible positions. Indeed, the spaces are strangely alike. In the first the sufferers are dying, and the man and the boy must run from the cannibals who maintain the larder. But the second space too fails to shelter:

Why is this here? the boy said. Is it real?

It's real . . . It's here because someone thought it might be needed.

But they didn't get to use it?

No. They didn't

They died.

Yes.

Is it ok for us to take it?

Yes. It is.

The man knows they can't stay, realizes that "anyone [can] see the hatch lying in the yard. . . ."[12] He says, "This isn't like hiding in the woods." And so they go on. If "[t]o renew the old world. . . is the collector's desire," the man realizes it to be a nearly useless practice in this blasted landscape, where nomadic circulation is required.[13] All the pair can do is take a few things and push on.

What passes for security in a place where bunkers cease to function as planned? Should a a policymaker try to prepare for, or ameliorate, human struggle in such a world? How?

Some words of warning as you seek to reimagine the concept of security and break free from the old, cold-war bunker mentality. The escalating nuclear arms race between the United States and Soviet Union emphasized the importance of attack and counterattack. In a war of mutually assured destruction, the fantasy of victory entailed striking first. These strategies filtered into the popular imagination. Recent post-apocalyptic television programs such as *Jericho*, *Revolution*, and even *The Walking Dead* measure survival through possession of firearms and ammunition. McCarthy's scenario also suggests it to be futile to weaponize this future, so take that option off the table. There is no way to insure the "good guys" will still be good in such an aftermath, and no way to insure good guys end up with the arms—to name just two arguments for why this way forward cannot be an option. Instead, discuss more broadly the nature of the defensible and of defense. How does planning for the aftermath require inventive redefinition now of such terms? What does politics look like in a place stripped bare? Is there anything that can be done in advance of a world where no meaningful national memory will remain, where there is no "Constitution," no America, no nations at all? For that matter, you might want to discuss whether is it right or why it might be wrong to resurrect current political forms?

Apocalyptic Politics

This borderless world retains no normal concept of citizenship. Further, racial difference, class and educational difference, geographical difference, language difference, as well as memory of shared national struggle—all these things mean either nothing in this particular aftermath, or mean something entirely new.[14] Traditionally, citizenship is defined as "a relation among strangers who learn to feel it as a common identity based on shared historical, legal, or familial connections to a geographical space."[15] Can there be citizenship without a state, law, or this shared connection to geography? According to our Founders, "true freedom and true popular sovereignty could be attained only with full national emancipation… within a nation."[16] But, the apparatuses of state-making and maintenance have all been wiped away. How might these apparatuses have survived, or be made to survive, or be encouraged to start again, and in what form? How might a planner be able to effect the reconstitution of new apparatuses that support social justice in such an aftermath?

Apocalyptic Economics
What happens to the economy? It goes without saying that contemporary economic models will not continue into this future. There are no banks, no Internet, no shopping malls, no grocery stores. Medical supplies would be destroyed, exhausted, or expired. The only clothing available will be those items worn. Food will be scarce. Fresh water may be the most important commodity. The barter system will be the measure of exchange.

Apocalyptic Ethics
What happens to human beings? Can we recognize characteristics of survivors now? Or will we be presented with a different, perhaps older, perception of humanity? In the wake of this calamity, the human race will no longer adhere to the conventions of our present moment. Such an event, a collective trauma upon the remaining human race, would engender a "crisis mode where [survivors would] develop some broad, enduring intuitions about the way [forward]."[17] In the collapse of state institutions, where personal relationships remain, being a "good person" may not necessarily entail doing things that are "good" as we currently understand morality. In *The Road*, for example, the man is prepared to kill his son—arguably an act of love in McCarthy's scenario. If this new, un-built society *in extremis* radically privileges personal action over political process, how might our current state, i.e. the United States, foster or nurture social bonds to renew civil society?

Again, planning for this worst case scenario entails imagining human beings different from ourselves. Language, for example, might return to the figurative modes of our ancient ancestors. In *The Road*, the man and boy "carry the fire." For us, the trope alludes perhaps to the myth of Prometheus, or nods toward an allegorical reading of the boy as Christ-like vessel, containing the future "fire" of humanity through the act of remembering the "Father." Regardless, it is a new metaphor to the boy, who does not know the textual/scriptural world before the catastrophe. The expression highlights that the dying man alone remembers the values of the previous world, and that he can transmit only elemental morality stripped of the old world's complexities. Perhaps this turn to simple or exhausted figuration suggests the possibility that a relationship between man and nature can be somehow reset and purified. *The Road* closes with a jarring shift from the story of the man and boy to a strange and metaphorical final passage concerning the natural landscape:

> Once there were brook trout in the streams in the mountains.

> You could see them standing in the amber current where the white edges of their fins wimpled softly in the flow. They smelled of moss in your hand. Polished and muscular and torsional. On their backs were vermiculate patterns that were maps of the world in its becoming. Maps and mazes. Of the things which could not be put back. Not be made right again. In the deep glens where they lived all things were older than man and they hummed of mystery.[18]

We ask you to consider this passage on its own, but also alongside the opening paragraph about the dream-creature within the "granitic beast" that conditions McCarthy's turn to waking event or plot in *The Road*. Why does McCarthy close *The Road* with this strange, pre-apocalyptic story? What does it mean that these richly metaphorical passages bookend the story? What might be the role of storytelling in this new world? What might McCarthy be trying to tell you, the policymaker, about the richness or limits of human experience and knowledge?

The trout story casts back to a pre-modern past where nature more freely revealed to humanity its mastery. Essayist and eco-journalist Paul Kingsnorth chronicles the decline of the myth of progress in our time. Particularly, he focuses upon the importance of changing humanity's relationship with the natural world. In the face of environmental collapse, and before it is too late, he argues, human beings must renegotiate their contract with nature. In one powerful essay, for example, Kingsnorth finds himself below ground, contemplating prehistoric cave paintings that for him demonstrate how, through imagination, an ancient people might have related to the natural world:

> I imagine that they [Magdalenian hunters and gatherers who lived in southern Europe and made cave paintings between 18,000 and 10,000 years ago] saw something more than meat and sinew in the creatures that moved around them—creatures in which god, or the sacred, or whatever you want to call it this great, nameless thing, was immanent...this sense of other-than-human nature as something thoroughly alive and intimately interwoven with human existence is and was the mainstream perception. A world without electric lights, a world without engines, is a different world entirely. It is a world that is alive. Our world of science and industry, of monocultures and monotheisms, marks a decisive shift in human seeing.[19]

The world we ask you to imagine would be inhabited by survivors with something like a renewed sense of awe, a people returned to a past where what mattered "once," to repeat McCarthy's word, suddenly matters again. For all of its nightmare scenarios, *The Road* remains firmly grounded in the affective life of our own historical present. Needless to say, we are conditioned by the present. Therefore, from where you stand: Can you imagine how to foster principles now that can cross over from the present into this new world?

III. Our World and McCarthy's: Navigating the Anthropocene

McCarthy hints at nuclear holocaust, but he deliberately withholds from us what has wiped away much of the world. If *The Road* presents no clear cause, contemporary analysts suggest why such a scenario might come to pass. Chemist Paul J. Crutzen and journalist Christian Schwargel argue we live in the Anthropocene, an era marked by "human dominance of biological, chemical and geological processes on Earth."[20] Many critics share this view. Climate activist Bill McKibben claims, "Human effects on the atmosphere and climate can actually be read more easily from the South Pole than almost anywhere on earth, and the results are truly horrifying,"[21] while Paul Kingsnorth and Dougald Hine, the co-founders of the Dark Mountain movement, argue, "We are the first generations born into a new and unprecedented age — the age of ecocide…The ground, the sea, the air, the elemental backdrops to our existence — all these our economics has taken for granted, to be used as a bottomless tip, endlessly able to dilute and disperse the tailings of our extraction, production, consumption."[22] Darker still is Iraq War veteran Roy Scranton's simple assertion that "this civilization is already dead….If we want to learn to live in the Anthropocene, we must first learn how to die."[23]

Poet and eco-critic Glyn Hughes carries forward Scranton's idea of learning how to die. He offers that "Death comes after the last act. Dying is the last act—the last thing you know about."[24] Learning how to die is a central issue in McCarthy's *The Road*, but even McCarthy cannot conceive of what comes "after the last act." Like all imaginative fiction—even works not mentioned here that do directly portray the afterlife—McCarthy's novel must still "bear the aspect of lived experience."[25] In short, imaginative fiction possesses limits. However, if human beings are to endure to re-craft the rituals and traditions inherent to civilization: "we might legitimately hope [even] at a time when the sense of purpose and meaning that had been bequeathed to us by our culture has collapsed."[26] Ultimately, the Declaration of Independence, the Constitution, and the Bill of Rights are not essential; physical contact and relationships with "strangers" are required for the human race to endure.

We would like to close by having you consider a hopeful exchange between Paul Kingsnorth and Glyn Hughes:

> [Kingsnorth]: In *Millstone Grit* [Hughes' 1975 memoir/travelogue of Calderdale, a West Yorkshire metropolitan borough in northern England]... you realise that the moors are not untouched by industry, and in many ways are actually ruins — places where forests used to be or extinct farming communities. It's a caution against Romanticism, I suppose, but it also seems to suggest that we are, as humans have always been, somewhere in a great cycle of the rise and fall of civilisations.
>
> [Hughes]: Yes, absolutely. And it's all cleaned up now, of course. Spring is wonderful [in Calderdale] when it comes, and the irony is that this place which has been so desecrated and covered in soot and industry and everything has, in a mere few decades, cleansed itself. Nature has cleaned itself. We've just stopped pouring soot all over it and it's cleaned itself.[27]

This exchange still situates us near the brink of extinction, but also provides what one might call a topography of hope. To borrow a phrase from philosopher Jonathan Lear's influential scholarship, "radical hope" may be as essential to you, the policymaker, at a time of crisis as an honest confrontation with the real possibility of our world's collapse.[28] As future policymakers, you will need to negotiate the radical difference between Hughes' optimism concerning nature's capacity for renewal and McCarthy's strident pessimism. These two thinkers present the poles of the policymaker's dilemma. How will you situate yourselves and what will you do?

RECOMMENDED READINGS

Crutzen, Paul J., and Christian Schwargel. 2011. "Living in the Anthropocene: Toward a New Global Ethos." *Yale Environment* 360 (January 24). http://e360.yale.edu/feature/living_in_the_anthropocene_toward_a_new_global_ethos_/2363.

Gordin, Michael, Helen Tilley, and Gyan Prakash. 2010. "Introduction: Utopia and Dystopia Beyond Space and Time." In *Utopia/Dystopia: Conditions of Historical Possibility*. Eds. Gordin, Tilley, and Prakash. Princeton, NJ.

Kinsgnorth, Paul, and Dougald Hine. 2009. "Uncivilisation: The Dark Mountain Manifesto." *The Dark Mountain Project.* http://dark-mountain.net/about/manifesto/.
Lear, Jonathan. 2006. *Radical Hope: Ethics in the Face of Cultural Devastation.* Cambridge, MA.
McCarthy, Cormac. 2006. *The Road.* New York and Toronto.
Murphet, Julian and Mark Steven, eds. *Styles of Extinction: Cormac McCarthy's* The Road. London.
Roy, Arundhati. 1998. "The End of Imagination." *Outlookindia* (August 3). http://www.outlookindia.com/article/The-End-Of-Imagination/205932.
Scranton, Roy. 2013. "Learning How to Die in the Anthropocene." *The Stone, The New York Times* (November 10). http://opinionator.blogs.nytimes.com/2013/11/10/learning-how-to-die-in-the-anthro-pocene/?_php=true&_type=blogs&_r=0.
Spencer, Bret. 2014. "The Rise of the Shadow Libraries: America's Quest to Save Its Information and Culture from Nuclear Destruction during the Cold War." *Information & Culture: A Journal of History* 49, issue 2 (May/June 2014): 145–76. http://muse.jhu.edu/journals/libraries_and_culture/v049/49.2.spencer.pdf.

NOTES

[1]Arundhati Roy, "The End of Imagination," *Outlookindia* (August 3, 1998), http://www.outlookindia.com/article/The-End-Of-Imagination/205932.

[2]See Mortimer Zuckerman, "America's Doomsday Project," *U.S. News & World Report* (August 7, 1989).

[3]Ted Gup, "The Doomsday Blueprints," *Time* (August 10, 1992).

[4]Bret Spencer, "The Rise of the Shadow Libraries: America's Quest to Save Its Information and Culture from Nuclear Destruction during the Cold War," *Information & Culture: A Journal of History* 49, issue 2 (May/June 2014): 167, accessed May 5, 2014, http://muse.jhu.edu/journals/libraries_and_culture/v049/49.2.spencer.pdf.

[5]For further consideration of *The Road* in the current context, see Julian Murphet and Mark Steven's *Styles of Extinction: Cormac McCarthy's The Road* (London: Continuum, 2012). See especially Sean Pryor's "McCarthy's Rhythm" for a rich discussion of McCarthy's language.

[6]Cormac McCarthy, *The Road* (New York and Toronto: Vintage, 2006), 3–4.

[7]Ibid., 83.

[8]Ibid, 56.

[9]See Morgan Brennan, "Billionaire Bunkers: Beyond the Panic Room, Home Security Goes Sci-Fi," *Forbes* (December 16, 2003), http://www.forbes.com/sites/morganbrennan/2013/11/27/billionaire-bunkers-beyond-the-panic-room-home-security-goes-sci-fi/, and John Seabrook, "Sowing for Apocalypse," *The New Yorker* (August 27, 2007), http://www.newyorker.com/magazine/ 2007/08/27/sowing-for-apocalypse.

[10]McCarthy, *The Road,* 110.

[11]Ibid., 138–9.

[12]Ibid., 144.

[13]Walter Benjamin, "Unpacking My Library: A Talk about Book Collecting," *Illuminations: Essays and Reflections,* ed. Hannah Arendt, (New York: Schocken Books, 1969), 61.

[14]See Ernest Renan, "What is a Nation?" *The Nationalism Project,* http://www.nationalismproject.org/what/renan.htm. There you will find a provocative enumeration of cultural investments that in your scenario have ceased to define the survivors.

[15]Lauren Berlant, "Citizenship," *Keywords for American Cultural Studies,* http://keywords.fordhamitac.org/keyword_entries/citizenship.html.

[16]Linda K. Kerber, "Toward a History of Statelessness in America," *American Quarterly* 57, no. 3 (September 2005): 727-49, 732, accessed September 11, 2014, https://muse.jhu.edu/journals/american_quarterly/v057/57.3kerber.pdf.

[17]Lauren Berlant, quoted in Donovan Schaefer, "The Promise of Affect: Politics of the Event in Ahmed's *The Promise of Happiness* and Berlant's *Cruel Optimism*," *Theory & Event* 16, no. 2 (2013), accessed September 10, 2014, http://muse.jhu.edu/journals/theory_and_event/v016/16.2.schaefer.html.

[18]McCarthy, *The Road*, 286–7.

[19]Paul Kingsnorth, "In the Black Chamber," *Paulkingsnorth.net*, originally published in *Orion Magazine* (March/April 2014), http://www.paulkingsnorth.net/journalism/in-the-black-chamber/.

[20]Paul J. Crutzen and Christian Schwargel, "Living in the Anthropocene: Toward a New Global Ethos," *Yale Environment 360* (January 24, 2011), http://e360.yale.edu/feature/living_in_the_anthropocene_toward_a_new_global_ethos_/2363.

[21]See Bill McKibben, "Climate: Will We Lose the Endgame?" *The New York Review of Books* (July 10, 2014), http://www.nybooks.com/articles/archives/2014/jul/10/climate-will-we-lose-endgame/.

[22]Paul Kinsgnorth and Dougald Hine, "Uncivilisation: The Dark Mountain Manifesto," *The Dark Mountain Project*, http://dark-mountain.net/about/manifesto/.

[23]Roy Scranton, "Learning How to Die in the Anthropocene," *The Stone*, *The New York Times* (November 10, 2013), http://opinionator.blogs.nytimes.com/2013/11/10/learning-how-to-die-in-the-anthropocene/?_php=true&_type=blogs&_r=0.

[24]Paul Kingsnorth, "The Salmon God," *Paulkingsnorth.net*, originally published in *Dark Mountain*, Issue 2, (2011), http://www.paulkingsnorth.net/journalism/the-salmon-god/.

[25]Michael D. Gordin, Helen Tilley, and Gyan Prakash, "Introduction: Utopia and Dystopia Beyond Space and Time," *Utopia/Dystopia: Conditions of Historical Possibility* (Princeton, NJ: Princeton University Press, 2010), 2. This book is an excellent study of why historians must engage with imaginative fiction, particularly utopian and dystopian texts.

[26]Jonathan Lear, *Radical Hope: Ethics in the Face of Cultural Devastation* (Cambridge, MA: Harvard University Press, 2006), 104.

[27]Kingsnorth, "The Salmon God."

[28]See Lear, especially chap. 3's distinction between radical hope and optimism.

17

The Worst "Worst Case"

The Zombie Apocalypse and National Security Strategy

CHARLIE LEWIS

To each age, a fear. If the Cold War was the age of the alien invasion, ours is the era of the zombie apocalypse.[1] Leading international relations theorists, august institutions like the Center for Disease Control and the U.S. military, humanists, novelists, and filmmakers—all have recently imagined how zombies might rise and humanity might respond.[2] U.S. policymakers have never been better prepared for this worst of the worst cases.

Preparing for this (still) fictional catastrophe is less futile than it might seem. Zombies combine a number of elements normally separated among real-world worst-cases: contagion, shocking violence, delusive borders, mad crowds, and, most importantly, novelty. The zombie apocalypse is a kind of mental proving ground, a form of training for clear thinking amidst our fears. Zombies also add an element of fun to the sometimes-dreary task of devising policies appropriate to the end times.

Come the zombie apocalypse, how must U.S. policymakers respond?

I. Introduction

Purpose of the Strategy

The *National Strategy for Combating a Zombie Outbreak* (NSCZO) incorporates current guidelines, plans, and strategies into a coherent and coordinated national effort to reduce the fallout from a zombie apocalypse. The strategy outlines a system of awareness of, response to, and recovery from an outbreak that balances freedom with security. In addition, the strategy creates no new systems and relies only on technologies already developed for other responses.

Scope

A zombie outbreak's scope presents a challenge in determining the total response required to counter the various contingencies presented. The NSCZO intends to direct efforts to limit the potential risks of an outbreak to all elements of American society. While coordinating federal government response plans, this strategy also recognizes that state, local, and national organizations collectively must develop and execute any action to reduce the outbreak, secure the population, and recover from the devastation.

Much of this strategy developed around three types of response plans—pandemics, natural disasters, and border security. As a pandemic, it is imperative that any plan follows past examples of effective disease response, such as H1N1 or influenza. Evacuations and recovery must follow pre-planned natural disaster responses. Because of the transmission method and globalization of trade and travel, border security is required to limit quarantine breaches.

Scale

Because of the size of the affected area, scale presents a challenge. Zombie outbreaks come in four classes. This response plan is for a Class III outbreak with zombies posing a clear danger to Americans living within a few hundred square miles of the original outbreak.[3] The outbreak is anticipated to have a quick onset in urban areas, with the spread resulting from daily activities—work, travel, and school. Resources from multiple jurisdictions will be required to react and emergency responders will become overwhelmed.[4]

Novelty

Novelty distinguishes a zombie outbreak from routine crises: those which the United States can respond to, is equipped for, and understands through experience.[5] Novel crises result from "threats never before encountered" that "pose unique challenges."[6] No emergency response agency has experienced a crisis of this scale and, therefore, no one can rely on past knowledge and understanding to develop a quick response. As a result, this plan seeks to provide a response outline to this new crisis.

Relationship to Other Plans and Strategies

The NSCZO is not a new, nor is it an innovative plan. Instead, it is a conglomeration of portions of the following applicable legislation and strategies:

Homeland Security Act (2002)
HHS Pandemic Influenza Plan (2005)
Stafford Disaster Relief and Emergency Act (2007)
Small Vessel Security Strategy (2008)
National Incident Management System (2009)
Public Response to Community Mitigation Measures for Pandemic Influenza (2008)
National Infrastructure Protection Plan (2009)

National Health Security Strategy (2009)
Quadrennial Homeland Security Review Report (2010)
Container Security Initiative (2011)
Strategy to Combat Transnational Organized Crime (2011)

Methodology
The President commissioned a Working Group to develop the NSCZO and its principles to address four key components of combating a zombie outbreak:

1) Early identification and isolation
2) Protect the population
3) Secure critical infrastructure
4) Recover from an outbreak

The NSCZO is not a new, separate plan, but instead a coordinated effort of existing responses across various government agencies and the private sector. This synchronization of responses allows the government to rehearse and implement without extensive use of government funds.[7]

II. The Threat: Zombie Outbreak

Background
Zombies result from the virus Solanum infecting humans. Solanum, whose origins are unknown, travels through the blood stream to the brain, killing the human but mutating the brain's frontal lobe into a new organ. When the mutation is finalized, the human being is no longer alive and many of the body's normal functions cease. The human body becomes a support structure for the undead and what was once a living being is now a zombie.[8]

Zombies maintain many human senses, with smell and hearing improving (and reliance thereupon increasing) after a dead human reanimates into a zombie. Zombie physical strength remains the same as that of a human, while muscle coordination and the ability to walk and run quickly diminish. Despite the slow movement, zombies are migratory and will move miles in search of food. Nourishment is their only need and zombies travel to eat without prejudice. A zombie's anticipated lifespan is three to five years. The only way to properly "kill" a zombie is to destroy the brain. Disposing of zombie bodies requires extreme caution as the Solanum can live for up to 48 hours in the cells of the dead.[9]

Transmission

Transmission of the disease is 100 percent fatal and occurs through direct fluid contact. There is no known evidence of waterborne or airborne transmission. Bites from zombies infect most human beings, but are not the only means of transmission. Other means include brushing against a zombie by an individual with open sores or wounds is one method, or sustaining contact with zombie remains after an explosion or shooting.[10]

Rates of transmission vary along a spectrum based on the location of the zombie's reanimation. Urban or densely populated areas will see a reproduction rate (R_0) of eight humans infected per zombie.[11] Much of this comes from reanimation within the workplace or common areas in apartment buildings. Suburban zones will see a lower R_0 of four. This rate results from reanimation within the home and zombies infecting their families. Finally, rural zones will see a R_0 of two due to low population density and increased advanced warning against an outbreak. Because of the nearly one-day infection timeline, humans may travel or move while infected. This increases the potential R_0 if an individual reanimates outside of the home or workplace.[12]

Threat Planning Assumptions

The working group first created key assumptions to facilitate planning and guide the response to a potential zombie outbreak:

- *The planned outbreak is a worst-case scenario, Class III outbreak.*[13] Using a Class III outbreak for planning provides a better understanding of the novelty of the crisis, while the other two classes are limited in scale and require a less coordinated response.

- *The zombie outbreak spreads rapidly worldwide.* Zombies do not care about borders. Those infected will travel prior to demonstrating symptoms and will infect when they reach their destination. As a result, any zombie outbreak will be an international crisis.

- *The outbreak places enormous demands on all emergency management systems.* First responders, government agencies, and the military will all face infection, which limits support personnel. Moreover, the sheer size of a Class III outbreak will overwhelm emergency systems.

- A several hundred square mile geographic area is impacted, affecting *multiple states.* Like international borders, infected individuals and zombies easily cross state borders. One infected car driver can cross multiple states, infecting any rest stop, before showing symptoms.

- *Infections among workers disrupt critical infrastructure operations.*[1] Like the emergency management system, an infrastructure operation requires humans to run and quarantined or infected humans cannot maintain equipment.

III. Strategic Plan

Just one plan for a zombie outbreak response is insufficient as "predetermined emergency plans" that operate well in routine emergencies "are frequently grossly inadequate or even counterproductive" in novel crises.[15] Creative responses and the ability to improvise are vital to adapt and successfully respond to any novel emergency. Acquiring equipment and creating plans specific for crises with drastic consequences but low likelihood is not cost effective. However, combining multiple plans previously created and rehearsed and investing in dual-use equipment can turn novelty into something expected.[16]

Early Identification and Isolation

Health and Human Services pandemic response plans rely on surveillance and early identification of outbreaks to provide maximum space and time to respond.[17] A recent example of early identification and isolation limiting potential spread of a deadly virus occurred on April 26, 2012. Expecting a potential monkeypox outbreak, officials quarantined an airplane at Chicago Midway Airport until medical personnel could clear the plane.[18] This quick response demonstrated the ability to screen and limit movement of potential carriers of disease. While early identification does not prevent a Class III outbreak, it will provide response agencies ample opportunity to respond quickly and develop solutions to the crisis. Early identification and isolation of the outbreak requires four steps.

- *"Foster informed, empowered individuals and communities."* According to the National Health Security Strategy for the United States, empowered individuals and communities have plans, provisions, and the information to respond appropriately to any potential health hazard.[19] Any informed community can identify potential zombies, isolate that zombie, and inform local law enforcement. One way to inform communities is through public service announcements and pamphlets similar to those published during emergencies.[20]

- *Let local law enforcement cordon the infected area.* Local law enforcement takes the second step in early identification. Upon confirmation, termination, and collection for investigation of a zombie, local law enforcement must begin basic disaster response procedures and cordon off the affected area to limit exposure. A thorough search of the cordoned area (including personnel) is a requirement, because where one zombie hunts, many more will follow. Upon identification of more zombies or bitten individuals, the local law enforcement agency must begin notifying its local fusion center.

- *Implement the National Response Plan.* Like any pandemic, a zombie outbreak response requires the support of multiple jurisdictions. The fusion center will recognize similar incidents. Once it becomes apparent that multiple federal agencies are required and states are overwhelmed, the National Response Plan (NRP) can go into effect, assigning responsibilities to FEMA regions and federal agencies through the Emergency Support Function (ESF) framework.[21] With so many agencies involved, a unified command under the National Incident Management System (NIMS) will provide the benefit of coordinated objectives and strategies to combat a zombie outbreak, instead of relying on each individual locality to fight them.[22] Establishing Emergency Operations Centers (EOC) near each outbreak zone relieves local authorities of coordinating, maintains national communications, and provides additional equipment while allowing de-centralized operations by local law enforcement and emergency response organizations.[23] The EOC can also implement identification, isolation, and quarantine at transportation hubs, such as airports, ports, and rail stations, to limit the spread of infected individuals nationally and worldwide.

- *Implement an off-scene coordination cell.* If the outbreak spreads, the EOC must transfer to an off-scene multi-agency coordination system (MACS). Early identification creates the space required to establish the various systems, move equipment, and prepare responses. The identification, however, can only isolate a zombie outbreak long enough to install national support structures. The MACS coordinates activities when isolation is no longer effective, including resource prioritization, equipment staging, and evacuation coordination.[24] Upon establishment of the MACS, focus must shift to protecting the people of the United States.

Protecting the People

Isolation of infected areas in a Class III outbreak is effective for a short period. During the initial isolation, states must initiate evacuation plans. Leaving residents in place and securing access during isolation is an impossible task given the multiple avenues of ingress and egress in urban areas.[25] Instead, to save as many lives as possible (and therefore prevent the reanimation of new threats), people must evacuate infected areas. The evacuation of multiple metropolitan areas to regional reception centers requires the majority of local and state law enforcement to maintain order. In addition, unlike most disasters that affect small areas—allowing outflow of evacuees to other states and towns—a nationwide zombie outbreak requires each region or state to possess its own reception center and living area. Protecting the people is more than evacuation; it also means eliminating the threat. The government must do three things:

- *Establish evacuation routes.* Planning for a controlled traffic flow from infected areas is imperative. Each state and region must create coordinated evacuation routes away from urban centers and other infected regions. The best method to create evacuation routes is to either use pre-established plans in hurricane states or create new ones using the National Hurricane Program's (NHP) Hurricane Evacuation Studies decision-making process. This process involves knowing potential effects, predicting the public's response, and identifying shelters. The NHP also evaluates capacities of existing roads and creates maps for the states.[26] By understanding the best routes in each region, law enforcement planners can both inform the public in advance of routes and determine checkpoint locations, choke points, and danger areas.

  Once evacuation routes are established and open, checkpoints must control outflow along the route.[27] While there is risk in allowing the potential movement of an infected individual, those traveling while bitten will follow the incubation timeline and identify themselves through symptoms. Checkpoints help identify those individuals by viewing the infected individual and using cadaver dogs to sniff trunks and compartments for the undead.[28] Moreover, until the imposition of martial law, officials cannot forcibly remove individuals from their homes in infected regions. Those individuals increase the threat as once attacked, they reanimate into zombies.

A final consideration for evacuation is moving citizens without transportation, as well as the hospitalized, and the elderly. As was experienced during Hurricane Katrina, the inability to move those persons creates severe security crises within the infected regions.[29] Moving those individuals requires the National Guard forces under Title 32 to transport the stranded. Those unable to leave their hospital will be secured by small elements of National Guard units on the top floors of any hospital. The National Guard must take all efforts to block stairwells and access to the roof.

- *Create secure reception centers.* Evacuating millions of people also requires housing them in a secure area. Upon initial identification of a zombie outbreak, each FEMA region must set up previously identified reception centers in safe areas. As evidenced by the problems at the Superdome during Katrina, basic necessities will be in short supply, centers will reach capacity quickly, and reception procedures must be fluid.[30] Rehearsals before any outbreak and checkpoint control over the influx of personnel to each specific reception center channels evacuees to the correct hubs for treatment and handling.[31] In addition, in-processing can occur while vehicles wait in traffic either by license plate identification or EZ-pass technology.[32]

  Moreover, with most individuals arriving by vehicle, parking is an issue. The additional vehicles will provide more shelter for short-term evacuee support during in-processing.[33] Given the size of the outbreak, a long-term shelter requirement is likely and must adhere to FEMA P-760A: Evacuee Support Concept of Operations Template. Any reception center must focus on securing those not infected and containing the infected from furthering the spread.[34] Moreover, any reception elements must also apply concepts from the Centers for Disease Control's Biological and Chemical Terrorism: Strategic Preparedness and Response Plan. This plan ensures each center receives a section of trained health response staff available to quarantine and remove any infected personnel. The section can also train medical personnel who evacuated as well, increasing the capacity of health responses.[35] Reception centers must prepare for continued movement of persons away from the threat and secure those individuals until the threat is dispersed and movement back to infected areas can begin.

- *Prevent zombie infiltration of secure areas.* As the uninfected evacuate, zombies will follow to hunt their prey. The noise of horns, yelling, and conversation attracts zombies, emphasizing the need for efficient evacuation. However, another step is required beyond evacuation to secure persons—preventing zombie movement. While zombies do not follow expected routes to reach humans, implementing established methods can prevent their spread.

  The first method is to deprive zombies of "enabling means," aka humans. Just as the Strategy for Transnational Organized Crime (TOC) tries to deny criminals the structures that feed its requirements, DHS, local law enforcement, and other security elements can deprive zombies of their nutritional source through secure containment areas.[36]

  The second method is to "constrain the reach and influence" of zombies. TOC methods, overseen by elements of Customs and Border Patrol (CBP) and Immigration and Customs enforcement, will limit the reach of zombies. With a slow rate of movement and need for nourishment, patrolling buffer zones around reception centers limits the freedom of movement of zombies and protects the people.

  If certain areas become overwhelmed by zombies because of the small size of the CBP and their requirements on the southern border, Northern Command (NORTHCOM) can control Title 10 (Active Duty) forces after the President authorizes their use in domestic emergencies under the 2007 National Defense Authorization Act. Since Katrina, NORTHCOM has prepared dual-status commanders (DSCs) who control federal and National Guard forces operating under Title 32 within a single state, as well as Title 10 joint staff teams to assist the DSC. In multi-state crises—like a zombie outbreak—the DSC will remain in charge of a single state and answer to the lead federal agency. This control allows the movement of forces to the most affected areas, securing the population and preventing zombie infiltration.[37]

By protecting uninfected, "safe" persons and limiting the movement of infected individuals and zombies, the strategy can be effective. Failure to protect people or stop zombie infiltration only creates more victims, leading to more threats and a longer recovery process. After protecting the people, the next step is to secure critical infrastructure.

Secure Critical Infrastructure

As people evacuate, the government must secure critical infrastructure and key resources (CIKR). The National Infrastructure Protection Plan (NIPP) manages risks to CIKR based on consequence, vulnerability, and threat.[38] In the case of a zombie outbreak, risk management processes remain the same as in any disaster or emergency. The impact of the loss of any CIKR is no different than during a natural disaster. The threat, though, is different and comes from both zombies and the inability to maintain the functioning of the CIKR. Therefore, efforts to secure CIKR must follow "national priorities" and "complement other plans."[39] However, with resources stretched due to evacuations, containment, and a variety of other requirements, a CIKR prioritization based on need during the outbreak, threat from zombies, and consequence must occur now.[40] Four key areas must be secured during a zombie outbreak:

- *Nuclear Reactors.* Unprotected and unmanned nuclear power plants present a grave, long-term danger to the United States. The disaster at the Fukushima Nuclear Power Plant resulted in mass evacuations, contamination of entire towns, and the inability to return the evacuees to their homes.[41] The recovery timeline slows into a multi-year process if a reactor melts down.

  To avoid a nuclear disaster, all nuclear facilities must follow the Nuclear Regulatory Council's emergency preparedness steps. First, all residents within a 10-mile radius of a plant must receive information about the hazards of and evacuation routes from a nuclear disaster. Second, alert systems must function during a zombie outbreak in case a meltdown happens.[42] Third, the plant's employees and owners must understand responsibilities during an outbreak and prepare for its long-term security and operation.[43] Finally, if a nuclear disaster does occur, the Office of Nuclear Security and Incident response will oversee the NRC Incident Response Program steps.[44]

- *Transportation Systems.* Protecting the transportation systems sector maintains the open flow of goods and people to reception centers while limiting the spread of Solanum. This sector consists of aviation, highways, the maritime transportation system, mass transit, pipeline systems, and rail. Protecting each subsector requires different skills, technologies, and organizations. Fortunately, plans exist for each one.

Aviation consists of aircraft, air traffic control, and the 450 commercial airports.[45] The priority for protection is the traveling public as the outbreak does not wait for all passengers to arrive at their destination. The Transportation Security Agency (TSA) must allow the flow of passengers, while preventing infected individuals from entering safe zones. TSA, in conjunction with the CDC, must operate as it did during the SARS response—identifying infected passengers, isolating them, and informing others of the threat through handouts.[46]

The maritime transportation system "consists of about 95,000 miles of coastline, 361 ports, over 10,000 miles of navigable waterways" and numerous avenues of approach for infected persons.[47] Through these means, 10.1 million shipments and thousands of travelers enter the United States yearly. Current systems, such as the Container Security Initiative, provide forward presence for the United States to inspect cargo departing 58 foreign seaports.[48] The incubation of all threats, however, requires quarantining and inspecting each ship prior to its arrival in accordance with Area Maritime Security Plans. This incubation creates a short arrival delay, but secures a port from any threat and prevents a complete shutdown of that port. Any port shutdown creates ripple effects felt worldwide and requires public-private cooperation that may not exist during a zombie outbreak.[49] By preparing for a potential outbreak, understanding procedures, and then responding quickly, maritime systems will experience minimal delays while remaining secure.

With ports functioning, railways and pipelines can remain open for the shipment of goods throughout the United States. Zombies are unable to infect a moving cargo train or enter an oil pipeline. Screening of employees, like all other officials, will minimize the spread of Solanum. Finally, securing mass transit and highways helps protect the population.

- *Energy Sector.* The United States economy and response efforts cannot function without the energy infrastructure. Divided into three segments—electricity, petroleum, and natural gas—energy fuels vehicles, provides electricity to distribution centers, and maintains communications.[50] The energy sector is vulnerable due to multiple connections, private sector ownership, and the distances through which energy travels. Securing the energy sector requires private sector cooperation with the Department of Energy through the Electricity Coordinating Council (ESCC) and the Oil and Natural Gas Sector Coordinating Council (ONG SCC). These councils provide liaisons to DHS.[51]

To prepare and respond to a zombie outbreak, DHS must contact the leadership of the ESCC and ONG SCC to ensure maintenance of the sector. At this time, the SCCs must also request additional security assets and find methods to build resiliency. As is demonstrated during most natural disasters, recovering the energy sector requires outside assistance provided over a period of time to keep energy flowing. With multiple regions affected, the outside support will be limited, requiring electric companies to remain proactive in protecting their hubs. Energy companies must focus on safe zones and move crews and security from contaminated regions to those areas to continue economic activity and provide electricity to citizens in reception centers. By remaining proactive, the energy sector can survive the zombie outbreak.

- *Communication.* The final priority during a zombie outbreak is communication, which "underlies the operations of all businesses, public safety organizations, and government."[52] Like the energy sector, much of the communications sector is privately owned, requiring public-private partnerships to identify risks and develop protection plans. The private sector does work with the government in the implementation of the National Communications System (NCS) through the National Infrastructure Protection Plan (NIPP). In a zombie outbreak, the NCS becomes the main method through which various agencies, regions, and leaders communicate and coordinate activities.[53]

  Preparing for a zombie outbreak requires developing national security and emergency preparedness (NS/EP) communications priorities. This includes defining who receives bandwidth and prioritized cellular communications during an outbreak. By creating the framework in advance and understanding the regulation of these communications, conflict and communications breakdowns can be limited in the beginning of an outbreak. Once the NS/EP priorities are established and dialogue plans rehearsed, the National Coordinating Center (NCC) will operate during the actual crises.[54] The NCC's primary mission is "to assist in the initiation, coordination, restoration, and reconstitution of NS/EP communications" and is therefore the perfect response center for maintaining communications resiliency. Working with the private sector, the NCC will ensure that communications continue, just as it does during national emergencies, even if the medium must shift from current systems to radio.

Prioritizing and securing CIKR is imperative to the success of this strategy. Understanding the threats to CIKR from zombies and the requirements of both safe zones and uninfected humans allows for effective preparation and efficient response to a zombie outbreak. Once the people are protected, CIKR secured, and areas clear, recovery can commence.

Recover From an Outbreak

With hope, the zombie outbreak will be contained. Either through isolation from food sources or termination by security elements, a zombie's life span is short. Safe and controlled recovery requires two steps. First, essential services and utilities must return to cleared areas. Second, residents must return home through a controlled inflow.

- *Restore services and clean cleared areas.* No cleared zone can receive its residents without preparation. Residents cannot return home without utilities such as gas, water, and electricity. Businesses cannot re-open unless they have the same utilities and residents to purchase their goods. The continuity of essential services and functions—a key component of the 2010 Quadrennial Homeland Security Review Report—is critical to restoration. Continuity practices and basic services—like firefighting, police, and ambulances—are imperative before any resident returns.[55] Much of the continuity occurs through resilient community preparation, but in heavily hit areas, this may be impossible. For those cities and zones that require more assistance, the Stafford Disaster Relief and Emergency Assistance Act provides guidance on loans, grants, and funding for recovery.[56]

  Staging supplies, including vehicles, repair equipment, and crews before restoring services allows for a thorough, comprehensive restoration of essential services and utilities instead of a piecemeal effort. Piecemeal efforts make movement of residents difficult and limit the total effectiveness of creating a recovered community. Moreover, removing debris like dead zombies, destroyed homes, and infrastructure minimizes hazards faced by returning evacuees.[57]

- *Return residents.* Once restoration of essential services and functions occurs and the area is deemed safe for residential life, local governments can move residents back home. Logistically, however, this is more difficult than evacuating individuals as it must be based on nodes of residency, where only certain areas are re-populated at a time. Preparation is indispensable and must begin upon evacuee arrival at reception centers and safe zones.[58]

  All individuals and families must register by their nine-number zip code. The zip codes control the inflow of residents to neighborhoods. Planning around zip codes allows state and local law enforcement to know in advance where to establish checkpoints and which areas are open to the movement of persons. Distributing pre-planned routes to residents prevents traffic flow confusion and gridlock at various intersections. In addition, the controlled movement prevents another zombie outbreak from spreading beyond re-populated neighborhoods. One difficulty is that most individuals will desire to return as soon as the first residents leave safe zones. By briefing individuals on the zip code plans, maintaining 24-hour movement, and keeping the flow of traffic moving, officials can minimize frustration.

  Implementing this plan is time intensive. Moving millions of people creates millions of potential variables and issues. The pre-planning and information sharing with residents in safe zones will greatly assist, but does not completely alleviate issues. In addition, as the residents move back safely, local law enforcement is required to move to each subsequent zip code. Therefore, the threat of looting unpopulated sectors exists and requires additional support from the National Guard to secure those areas. As neighbors re-populate and businesses re-open, normal life will continue, just as it does after any disaster or emergency.

While its consequences are great and our vulnerabilities overwhelming, a zombie outbreak is not likely to occur. What a zombie outbreak does, however, is provide a crisis framework upon which to demonstrate the importance of understanding all response plans and strategies. Once emergency response leadership understands the various plans, reacting to novel crises becomes easier. Instead of relying solely on one plan, leaders can draft multiple plans for worst-case scenarios and rehearse command and communication before a novel crisis happens.

The NCSZO outlines the unfathomable difficulties of a zombie outbreak. Emergency resources will be tested and legal boundaries questioned. And—some plans *will* fail. As long as the government understands this, follows the NCSZO, and rehearses the unexpected so it becomes routine, the United States will successfully combat and recover from a zombie outbreak. If the United States can handle a zombie outbreak, it can effectively respond to any crisis—no matter how routine or novel.

RECOMMENDED READINGS

Brooks, Max. 2007. *World War Z*. New York.
------. 2003. *The Zombie Survival Guide*. New York.
Drezner, Daniel. 2011. *Theories of International Politics and Zombies*. Princeton, NJ.
Leonard, Herman B., and Arnold M. Howitt. 2006. "Beyond Katrina: Improving Disaster Response Capabilities." *Crisis Response* (June and September).

NOTES

[1]Kailani Koenig-Muenster, "Flashback: Reagan's Vision for a Unifying Alien Invasion," MSNBC (September 24, 2013), accessed May 28, 2015, http://www.msnbc.com/msnbc/flashback-reagans-vision-unifying.

[2]See, for instance: Daniel Drezner, *Theories of International Relations and Zombies* (Princeton, NJ: Princeton University Press, 2011); Centers for Disease Control and Prevention, Office of Public Health Preparedness and Response, "Zombie Preparedness" (April 10, 2015), http://www.cdc.gov/phpr/zombies.htm; Gordon Lubold, "Exclusive: The Pentagon Has a Plan to Stop the Zombie Apocalypse. Seriously," *Foreign Policy* (May 13, 2014), http://foreignpolicy.com/2014/05/13/exclusive-the-pentagon-has-a-plan-to-stop-the-zombie-apocalypse-seriously/; Max Brooks, *World War Z: An Oral History of the Zombie War* (New York: Broadway, 2006).

[3]Max Brooks, *The Zombie Survival Guide* (New York: Three Rivers Press, 2003), 25. There are four total classes. Class I outbreaks are low level, rural outbreaks that create no more than 50 casualties and can be contained within twenty-four hours. Class II outbreaks double the casualties, but are still limited in geographic space. Class IV is a zombie dominated world where more zombies exist than humans, which this plan seeks to prevent.

[4]Herman B. Leonard and Arnold M. Howitt, "Beyond Katrina: Improving Disaster Response Capabilities," *Crisis Response* (June and September 2006): 20.

[5]Richard Johnson (Massachusetts State Police), in discussion with the author, April 2012. Johnson suggested I research novelty and its application to this scenario.

[6]Leonard and Howitt, "Beyond Katrina,"19.

[7]U.S. Department of Homeland Security, *Small Vessel Security Strategy* (SVSS) (Washington DC: DHS, April 2008). The format of this section was based on the Introduction format in the SVSS.

[8]Brooks, *The Zombie Survival Guide*, 2. Brooks is considered the world's foremost expert on Solanum and zombies. While other theories exist, they would only complicate the NSCZO. Therefore, the working group relied on Brooks' description of the threat as it is most consistent and the most likely to be seen.

[9]Brooks, *The Zombie Survival Guide*, 6–19. Brooks outlines many key features of zombies. Only applicable threats were outlined.

[10]Brooks, *The Zombie Survival Guide*, 3–4.

[11]*Contagion*, dir. Stephen Soderbergh (Burbank, CA: Warner Home Video, 2012). Reproduction rate came from CDC planning in this movie for the MEV-1 outbreak.

[12]The NSCZO Working Group developed the planned reproduction rates based on densities. Relying on past pandemics is difficult because of the transmission method of Solanum.

[13]Brooks, *The Zombie Survival Guide*, 25. Class I outbreaks are low level, rural outbreaks that create no more than 50 casualties and can be contained within 24 hours. Class II outbreaks double the casualties, but are still limited in geographic space.

[14]U.S. Department of Health and Human Services (HHS), *HHS Pandemic Influenza Plan* (Washington, DC: HHS, 2005), 5. Planning assumptions were developed from the "Pandemic Planning Assumptions."

[15]Leonard and Howitt, "Beyond Katrina," 19.

[16]Ibid., 19–20.

[17]HHS, *Pandemic Influenza Plan*, 9.

[18]Don Babwin and Gretchen Ehlke, "Son: Bedbug Bites Caused Rash That Stopped Flight," *Associated Press* (April 27, 2012), accessed April 27, 2012, from apne.ws/IVnkoD.

[19]HHS, *Pandemic Influenza Plan*, 6.

[20]Johnson, interview.

[21]White House, "The Federal Response to Hurricane Katrina: Lessons Learned" (Washington, DC: White House 2006), 15.

[22]U.S. Department of Homeland Security, *National Incident Management System* (Washington DC: DHS, 2008), 50.

[23]Ibid., 66.

[24]Ibid., 64.

[25]Gary Schenkel (emergency management professional, Chicago, DHS, Marine Corps), interview with author, April 24, 2012.

[26]FEMA, *National Hurricane Program* (Washington, DC: DHS), accessed April 27, 2012 from http://www.fema.gov/plan/prevent/nhp/index.shtm#2.

[27]Johnson, interview.

[28]The Working Group believes that cadaver dogs will sniff out zombies and those on the verge of reanimation. Decomposition and similar body breakdown smells will be released, triggering cadaver dogs and allowing the removal of that individual from the evacuation route.

[29]White House, "The Federal Response to Hurricane Katrina," 29.

[30]Ibid., 31.

[31]Schenkel, interview.

[32]This allows flow into centers, tracking the movement of vehicles throughout the country. In addition, if each vehicle is assumed to have five individuals and ½ pets inside, planning for beds and supplies can begin as vehicles initiate their evacuation.

[33]FEMA, "Evacuee Support Concept of Operations Template" (Washington DC: DHS, 2009), 4.

[34]Johnson, interview.

[35]Ali S. Khan, Alexandra M. Levitt, and Michael J. Sage, *Biological and Chemical Terrorism: Strategic Plan for Preparedness and Response* (Washington DC: CDC, 2000), accessed April 27, 2012, from http://www.cdc.gov/mmwr/preview/mmwrhtml/rr4904a1.htm.

[36]White House, *Strategy to Combat Transnational Organized Crime* (Washington DC.: White House, 2011), 13.

[37]Ludwig J. Schumacher, "Dual Status Command for No-Notice Events: Integrating the Military Response to Domestic Disasters," *Homeland Security Affairs*, 7, 3, 6, 8.

[38]U.S. Department of Homeland Security, *National Infrastructure Protection Plan* (Washington, DC.: DHS, 2009), 2.

[39]Ibid., 5

[40]Schenkel, interview.

[41]"Fukushima Accident 2011." World Nuclear Association, accessed April 28, 2012 from http://www.world-nuclear.org/info/fukushima_accident_inf129.html.

[42]Nuclear Regulatory Commission, "How Can I Prepare for a Radiological Emergency?" accessed April 28, 2012, http://www.nrc.gov/about-nrc/emerg-preparedness/prepare-for-radiological-emerg.html.

[43]As with other private industry sectors, this is difficult due to the limited ability to control workers' concerns for their families and evacuation. It is likely that only a few employees will remain at each of the following CIKR sites. Those employees, like the ones in Fukushima, will be required to sacrifice a lot.

[44]Nuclear Regulatory Commission: Office of Nuclear Security and Incident Response, NRC Incident Response Plan: Revision 4 to NUREG-0728, (Washington DC: NRC), 10.

[45]U.S. Department of Homeland Security, "Transportation Systems Sector," https://www.dhs.gov/transportation-systems-sector.

[46]Mark Rothstein, "Quarantine and Isolation: Lessons Learned from SARS," Report to Centers for Disease Control and Prevention, November 2003, 41.

[47]DHS, "Transportation Systems Sector."

[48]U.S. Customs and Border Protection, "Container Security Initiative: Fact Sheet," 1.

[49]Timothy Heitsch (U.S. Coast Guard Captain, Boston), interview with author, April 28, 2012. CAPT Heitsch and his Port Security officer emphasized the importance of not shutting down a port.

[50]U.S. Department of Homeland Security, *Energy Sector-Specific Plan: An Annex to the National Infrastructure Protection Plan* (Washington DC: DHS, 2010), 1.

[51]DHS, *Energy Sector-Specific Plan*, 2.

[52]U.S. Department of Homeland Security, *Communications Sector-Specific Plan: An Annex to the National Infrastructure Protection Plan* (Washington DC: DHS, 2010), 1.

[53]DHS, *Communications Sector-Specific Plan*, 1–2.

[54]As with any communications plan, rehearsals must occur. The federal government must run an annual test to make sure that communications work to the lowest level. If new technologies are acquired, a rehearsal must take place upon their installation. Failure to rehearse creates preventable risks.

[55]U.S. Department of Homeland Security, *Quadrennial Homeland Security Review Report* (Washington DC: DHS, 2010), 64.

[56]FEMA, "Robert T. Stafford Disaster Relief and Emergency Assistance Act: FEMA 592" (Washington DC: DHS, 2007).

[57]White House, "The Federal Response to Hurricane Katrina," 62.

[58]Johnson, interview.

Index